ESSAYS ON
MODERNISM, DEMOCRACY AND WELL-BEING

ESSAYS ON
MODERNISM, DEMOCRACY WELL-BEING AND

A GANDHIAN PERSPECTIVE

RAMASHRAY ROY
RAVI RANJAN

⑤SAGE www.sagepublishing.com
Los Angeles I London I New Delhi I Singapore I Washington DC I Melbourne

First published in 2016 by

 SAGE Publications India Pvt Ltd
B1/I-1 Mohan Cooperative Industrial Area
Mathura Road, New Delhi 110 044, India
www.sagepub.in

SAGE Publications Inc
2455 Teller Road
Thousand Oaks, California 91320, USA

SAGE Publications Ltd
1 Oliver's Yard, 55 City Road
London EC1Y 1SP, United Kingdom

SAGE Publications Asia-Pacific Pte Ltd
3 Church Street
#10-04 Samsung Hub
Singapore 049483

Published by Vivek Mehra for SAGE Publications India Pvt Ltd, typeset in 10/13 pts Berkeley by PrePSol Enterprises Pvt Ltd and printed at Saurabh Printers Pvt Ltd, Greater Noida.

Library of Congress Cataloging-in-Publication Data

Names: Roy, Ramashray, author. | Ranjan, Ravi, author.
Title: Essays on modernism, democracy and well-being : a Gandhian perspective
  / Ramashray Roy and Ravi Ranjan.
Description: Thousand Oaks, California : SAGE Publications Inc., 2016. |
  Includes bibliographical references and index.
Identifiers: LCCN 2015041360 (print) | LCCN 2016001162 (ebook) | ISBN
  9789351508113 (hardback) | ISBN 9789351508106 (epub) | ISBN 9789351508120
  (ebook) | ISBN 9789351508120 (eBook) | ISBN 9789351508106 (ePub)
Subjects: LCSH: Democracy–Social aspects. | Democracy–Moral and ethical
  aspects. | Well-being–Social aspects. | Gandhi, Mahatma,
  1869-1948–Political and social views.
Classification: LCC JC423 .R73 2016 (print) | LCC JC423 (ebook) | DDC
  321.8–dc23
LC record available at http://lccn.loc.gov/2015041360

ISBN: 978-93-515-0811-3 (HB)

The SAGE Team: Rudra Narayan, Isha Sachdeva and Ritu Chopra

For family members who bear with us

Thank you for choosing a SAGE product!
If you have any comment, observation or feedback,
I would like to personally hear from you.
Please write to me at **contactceo@sagepub.in**

Vivek Mehra, Managing Director and CEO,
SAGE Publications India Pvt Ltd, New Delhi

Bulk Sales

SAGE India offers special discounts
for purchase of books in bulk.
We also make available special imprints
and excerpts from our books on demand.

For orders and enquiries, write to us at

Marketing Department
SAGE Publications India Pvt Ltd
B1/I-1, Mohan Cooperative Industrial Area
Mathura Road, Post Bag 7
New Delhi 110044, India

E-mail us at **marketing@sagepub.in**

Get to know more about SAGE

Be invited to SAGE events, get on our mailing list.
Write today to **marketing@sagepub.in**

This book is also available as an e-book.

Contents

Acknowledgements

The chapters collected in this volume were written on different occasions in response to different demands, including our own questions about what happens when the cosmic order gives way to earthly order and how modernism, democracy and well-being are interlinked conceptually and theoretically. This volume addresses these questions by exploring Gandhian alternative to modernism and democracy in contemporary times. Since the seventeenth century, when the advent of the earthly order became a reality, human society all over the world has been driven by the psychological impulse of making human destiny secure from want, disease, ignorance and other afflictions the human race has been suffering from since the beginning of the human civilization. Yet the new order that promised to create heaven on earth has proved highly deficient in it. As a matter of fact, what we can clearly discern is just the reverse of it.

In view of the fact that the promise of emancipation of human beings from suffering and misery, which the act of mere living in this world involves, and of their liberation from ignorance, the promise of enlightenment, has turned very sour and has created what we know as "the modern predicament," it is necessary to have a look at some of the aspects of the civilization-related crisis we face today. The present volume does just that and seeks to point a way out. We are aware that in the world divided into a number of ideological camps, the way out suggested in this volume will invite only ridicule and accusation of orthodoxy. However, the truth has to be told, no matter what the reaction. What also needs to be added is that the way suggested out of the civilization-related crisis may be interpreted as a call for going back to the past. What we propose is not to revive the institutions of the past that gave it its particularity, significance and its importance; our intention is rather that we try to seek an insight into the principles that underlay the institutions of the past and make use of them for organizing human society *de novo*.

In preparing this volume, we have incurred too many debts to acknowledge here. We acknowledge various academic institutions like Gandhi Peace Foundation, New Delhi, Department of Political Science, Allahabad University, and few others who have circulated few essays of this volume as printed lectures/papers in their different academic initiatives. We do, however, thank all our friends and well-wishers for their help and encouragement. Our friends and well-wishers must, for various reasons, remain nameless and, therefore, faceless. We owe special gratitude to our family members for affording us the leisure to play with abstract ideas instead of engaging in solving pragmatic problems of living. Our thanks go especially to SAGE Publications, New Delhi, for undertaking the responsibility of bringing this work to delightful birth. However, authors are alone responsible for the errors, if there may be any, of facts or logic.

Delhi, Makar Samkranti   **Ramashray Roy**
14 January 2015   **Ravi Ranjan**

Introduction

Consider that we may be one in Christ, though we think differently; and we may be friends though not brethren, and let us attain to union though not to unity.
—John Saltmarch, "Smoke in the Temple," 1646

Two kinds of philosophy of life have ever contended for articulation, recognition and control. According to Rigveda I.95.1:

> Two philosophies, diametrically opposed in their conception, are current in this world—heading for their respective goals. They inspire and impel their votaries, each in its own way. In the one, the self-sovereign, Blissful Hari, looms large; in the other, the glittering, showy tinsel greets our eye at every turn. (Trans. Gopalacharya 1978: 68)

These two philosophies have entirely different connotations for human existence. In one, man is not autonomous; his life is ruled and regulated by something outside of himself, something that transcends his earthly existence. This something has been identified by the Rigveda as the transcendent, divine entity. This divine entity is considered not only the creator of the world and all the objects in it, but also its regulator and the source of order in the world including the inner world of every individual man. This perspective on man and his world considers man's soul as open to the transcendent; as such, man's life purposes as well as the pattern of his existence are turned away from "the glittering, showy tinsel" that lies all around him inviting him to enjoy his life to the fullest by making use of this tinsel. When his soul is open to the experience of the transcendent, his gaze focuses not on the tinsel of the world but on something else. This something is higher, something nobler and something that elevates man from overpowering animal instincts. A life devoted to the service of Hari (God) is considered desirable because it is thought to be the basis of the "good life."

The glittering, showy tinsel cannot, however, be dismissed out of hand. This is so for the reason that it is this tinsel that provides sustenance to a man's life and thereby enables him to fulfil his ordinary life's needs. Moreover, it is this tinsel that constitutes the infrastructure that supports the pursuit of the "good life" and makes worshipping Hari possible. It does not need to be pointed out that the very importance of "tinsel" in a man's life is also evidence of the irresistible attraction it holds for him. When its attraction becomes overbearing, this "tinsel" is then considered to be the undisputed objective of a man's desires. It becomes the be all and end all of human endeavour. Man's connecting link with the divine is then weakened, even snapped. He then tends to draw divinity in himself. He considers himself autonomous and omnipotent, capable of desirably shaping his existence and managing his worldly affair on his own. Once this happens, human existence and endeavour are inexorably attuned to the demands of bare life. The Veda calls such a life that of *kamachara*, a life driven by the irresistible force of passions.

It is this distinction between the good life and bare life that we encounter in Aristotle. He notes that the end of the city is life according to the good, that is, a life cultivated to pursue higher life goal. As he puts it in *Politics* (1962: 1278, 23–31):

> This (life according to the good) is the greatest end both in common for all men and for each man separately. But men also come together and maintain the political community in view of simple living, because there is some kind of good in the mere fact of living itself. If there is no great difficulty as to the way of life, clearly most men will tolerate much suffering and hold on to life as if it were a kind of serenity and a natural sweetness.

The distinction between the good life and bare life does not by any means posit opposition between them because the good life cannot ever be conceivable without the satisfaction of an ordinary life's needs. And if the meeting of an ordinary life's needs is infrastructural to the pursuit of the good life, one fails to understand why the sphere of the home should be barred, as Aristotle contemplates in *Politics* (1962: 1252a, 26–35), from becoming the arena where the values of the good life can be cultivated. Whatever may be the case, what is important to note here is that the distinction between the good life and bare life has an important bearing on the kind of order that emerges or is created to protect human beings from their unrestrained pursuit of self-interest. Order becomes necessary for providing shelter to man against the depredations of his self-aggrandizement (or to use Aristotle's term, *pleonexia*). The character of order, however, changes depending upon whether it is the principle of the good life or the claim of bare life that provides the basis on which the edifice of order rests. If it is the pursuit of the good life that provides the primary impetus for the emergence or creation of order, its source will lie beyond the phenomenal world, it will lie in some transcendent divine being. If order is inspired by the claims of bare life, its source as well as its sustaining force will be intra-individual but common to all individuals.

Such a common entity is, of course, human passion. It does not need to be demonstrated that that the element of passion is common to both kinds of order, one based on some transcendental source and another rooted in the material aspect of the existence of the individual. Even the idea of the good life does not eliminate or aims at completely suppressing passion. What it does mean, however, is that order inspired by the idea of the good life aims at controlling and regulating passions and harmonizing them with the common good. In contradistinction to this, the order rooted in the demands of bare life celebrates passions and aims at defending, stimulating, protecting and promoting them.

Thus, passions constitute an element that is common to order of all varieties. However, their role is differently perceived in different types of order. Order is an abstract idea and needs to be sustained through its embodiment. This embodiment is, of course, as Voegelin suggests,

> an essay in world creation. Out of a shapeless vastness of conflicting human desires rises a little world of order, a cosmic analogy, a cosmion, leading a precarious life under the pressure of destructive forces from within and without, and maintaining its existence by the ultimate threat and application of violence against its internal violators of law as well as external aggression. (Voegelin 1997: 225, Appendix A)

For Voegelin, then, the basis of order is the cosmic order whose source can be traced back to the transcendent, divine entity. The idea of cosmic order takes its inspiration from the realization that the levels of being discernible within the world are surmounted by a transcendent source of being and its order. Moreover, this insight is rooted in the real movement of the human spiritual soul towards divine being experienced as transcendent

(Voegelin 2000: 259). What is distinctive about cosmic order is that it represents the yearning of the soul to be connected with the infinite. It is this yearning that helps man see that, as Plato notes, the universe is not a lifeless body of stone and water. It has come to be by the providence of the God, in very truth, a living creature with soul and reason (Plato 1971: 34).

Man happens to be an integral part of this fully ordered cosmos. This cosmos, as Jonas points out, "is considered to be the perfect exemplar of order, and at the same time, the cause of all order in particulars, which only in degrees can approximate the whole" (Jonas 1963: 242). While this is true, it is also true that the totality has "no being except through the expression of these particulars. Similarly, individual particulars have no being except by reason of their mutual relation both with the totality and with other parts" (Collum 1995: 59–60). It is this fitting together of different parts of the cosmos with each other as well as with the whole and the cosmos with its creator that characterizes what is called the "Great Chain of Being." It is also this fitting together that constitutes the basis of harmony in both natural and social worlds.

The cosmic order is thus a testimony to the fact that there is order that has its source in God. As such, all orders, inferior in rank but not in worth, are capable of being harmonized within a comprehensive whole. All particulars within the whole have their importance not because of their achievement in organizing the whole, but primarily because there is a whole that must be given expression through the recognition of their participation in the whole. It is by virtue of partaking of the essence of the transcendent and by participating in the whole, that harmony in the universe is maintained. This harmony is symptomatic of the manifestation of the One through the manifold of beings that makes this world. In this harmony,

> [T]he responsible dignity of man's mind and wills was felt to consist not specifically in their differences from one another but in the variety of their characteristic individuality, thrown into relief, precisely, by their mutual relation and their unity as component differentiated parts of one whole. (Ibid.: 60)

The universe as a cosmos is well ordered and likewise well regulated. The fact that it manifests order and regularity testifies to its divine origin, an origin that human beings also share. It is this understanding of the cosmos that helps in maintaining or restoring, if it somehow has been lost, the original unity between human beings and their creator. It is also this understanding, again, that ever reminds man that he is not self-complete, autonomous and self-sufficient. He is, instead, a part of a larger order symbolized by the idea of cosmos, by virtue of which, he is a part of the divine. The original unity can be recovered, if lost or activated, if dormant or passive, only when, as Cicero points out, "man contemplates the cosmos and imitates it" (quoted in Jonas 1963: 245). It is only through the processes of contemplation and imitation that man can hope to become perfect. Thus, for Cicero, the purpose of human existence is to discern, understand and imitate the cosmos with a view to instilling order and regularity in man's orientation and, through it, sustain man in his endeavour to realize order and regularity in his own life. Thus, the message the idea of the cosmos has for man is that he, as a part of the universe, must conform to the pattern it displays. It also conveys the message that man must mould his existence in accordance with the principles or *Rita*, as the Veda calls them, which braces order and regularity in the universe. Thus, order in the universe constitutes the paradigm of human existence and establishes the necessary "connection between the apotheosis of the universe and the idea of human perfection" (Ibid.: 246).

Submission to the requirements of conforming to the constitutive principles of the universe by no means signifies denial of freedom to man or the imposition on him of a preconceived and prearranged freedom. The fact that man is related with others in the cosmos and with the whole means that man cannot do whatever he pleases. It also means that the creative power of each individual person resides ultimately in his natural relation with others and with the whole of which every person is a reflective facet. This relationship prevents man's freedom from degenerating into license and reaffirms his freedom to forge meaningful connection between the good of one individual and the good of all individuals. The establishment of this connection is possible only when man realizes that he is

> not just a part like other parts making up the universe, but through the possession of a mind, a part that enjoys *identity* with the ruling principle of the whole. Thus the other aspect of man's proper relation with the universe is that of *adequating* his own existence, confined as it is as a part, to the essence of the whole, of reproducing the latter in his own being through understanding and action. (Ibid.: 247)

The real significance of the cosmos, the universe reflecting order and regularity, is not only that it is a structure that incorporates a diversity of beings surmounted by a transcendent divine entity. It is also that certain intelligible principles, when realized in the life of the individual, become instrumental not only in the installation of order in man's interior but also in safeguarding harmony in the world. What also needs to be pointed out in this connection is that two factors have an important bearing upon the question of harmony in the world. First, the capacity to internalizing the principles integral to cosmic order and making them the guide for human motivation and action differing from person to person. This makes for differential achievement in putting man's interior in order. Second, the claim of the "tinsel" does not dim even when the light of the cosmic order burns very bright. The process of satisfying ordinary life's needs, associated with the acquisition of wealth, power and prestige, may make the attraction of external objects irresistible. There is always, then, the possibility that desires for earthly pleasure or, as Gandhi says, "bodily comfort," may drown the call of the beyond in the clamour of the hunger for possession.

The clamour of the hunger for bodily pleasure (see Plato 2010) can be silenced, largely, if society reflects *eunomia*, right-mindedness. However, right-mindedness falters before the advance of self-concern of the egotistic individual. The continued existence in history of a social order marked by right-mindedness is possible if social institutional arrangement reflects the cosmic principles of order and a pervasive sense of commonality based on these principles. But the problem of conflict between the demands of man's pragmatic life and the pull of the need of keeping man's connection with the divine intact, alive and effective is real. Moreover, the heat of this conflict may disrupt the connection with the divine. As a result, man's thought-ways and work-ways may deviate from God's ways. This is most likely to introduce elements of disorder. To prevent order from sliding into disorder and to sustain order against heavy odds is the special responsibility of political order or the state or the *regnum,* as the Indian classical thinking calls it.

Regnum represents an organized system of power. However, its functioning has a double reference. If, on the one hand, it is a system of coercive power, it is also a system of moral authority. Its commands are not only backed by force but also by right. It is in this sense that *regnum* spans over and joins two distinct orders of being, the order of positive reality and that of moral necessity. In order to be able to successfully join these two distinct orders of being, *regnum* needs to be grounded in and ruled by an externally existing body of knowledge, which lies beyond the ken of humanity immersed in materiality. It is only by being grounded in this knowledge that the *regnum* becomes capable of creating and sustaining a commonly shared world of meaning. The creation and sustenance of a commonly shared world of meaning is, of course, dependent upon participation in what Heraclitus calls *xynon*, a shareable commonality. It is this shareable commonality that becomes instrumental in reconciling and harmonizing diverse human emotions, aspirations, appetites and desires.

However, this world of meaning would lack force and effectiveness as long as it is incapable of evoking an appropriate response on the part of man whose emotions, aspirations, affection and desires would run into different, even incompatible directions. In such a case, it is neither the fear of the state nor the long reaching arm of the law that can produce harmony and safeguard the world of commonly shared values. It is only the transformational act of self-realization in the traditional sense of meaning that is capable of ordering, regulating and harnessing human emotions, appetites and desires in promoting individual well-being and social good. This creative act can be facilitated if *regnum* represents a unit sufficiently ordered to transform the amorphous field of human force into a well-integrated unity. And the most essential and convenient object to be transformed into a symbol of unity is always the man himself. One of the important functions of *regnum* is to create and sustain a political order that prevents the unity from being disrupted or to restore it if the aberrations of human desires break it.

Thus, the essential function of *regnum* within this framework of cosmic order is to resolve the conflict between the givens of society and nature, on the one hand, and certain transcendental values associated with and grounded in the realm of the unseen, on the other. In seeking to resolve this conflict, political has to be grounded in ontology. Once the politics is so grounded, the emergent political order functions as what Voegelin calls a "shelter." It is with the help of this shelter that man attempts to give his life a semblance of meaning (Voegelin 1997, Appendix A: 225.) Such a political order is capable of reaching the emotional and spiritual centre of man's existence. By virtue of this, it becomes possible for individuals to outlive their fragmentary personal lives by projecting into the life of a larger community. As such, the political order provides a structure of meaning into which the single human being can fit the results of the biological and spiritual (productive/procreative) energies of his personal life, thereby (relieving) his life from the (disordering) aspects of existence that always spring up when the possibility of life ending in annihilation is envisaged (Ibid.: 226).

The shelter function of political order is to impregnate man's world with meaning so that one can transcend his limitations on tone hand and acquire, by attuning himself to higher realities, sufficient strength to resist and overcome temptations that threaten to disturb order in his interior and make him a *kamachara* (a person who follows the dictates of desires) on the other (*Chhandogya Upanishad*, 8.12.1).[1] This, however, does not mean that desires have to be completely suppressed or annihilated. What it does mean is that desires must be controlled and regulated by a superior faculty in man's being so that their depredations may be checked and prevented from dragging the soul into the mire of corruption. What this perspective on man and his world aims at is the sublimation of human desires.

For various reasons, however, this shelter function loses its effectiveness in course of time. The tension between the demands of the pragmatic aspects of man's life and the need to be spiritually awake grows apace. When the appetite of the body becomes too strong to resist, cosmic order develops fractures. It is enfeebled and finally collapses. It does need to be stressed that the validity of the cosmic order rests on a very thin thread of faith in the existence of the unseen transcendent entity. There is no tangible, rational proof that gods exist. The tenuous bond of faith itself constitutes both the substance of things unseen and the proof of things hoped for. Durability of faith depends upon the strength of the soul, which, in turn, depends on the strength of faith itself. However, not all men are capable of such spiritual stamina that can give them courage and fortitude for facing the uncertainties of life. When these uncertainties accumulate into despair and helplessness, the faith in the unseen erodes. What adds to these uncertainties is the element of doubt raised and reinforced by two important factors. One of these factors is, of course, the rise of Gnosticism that relies on knowledge for understanding and shaping man's world and giving it a desired direction. In short, Gnosticism aims at manipulating and controlling history.

The rise of Gnosticism also means the subjection of the insight that men gain into the structure of order. In the perspective of cosmic order, this insight is made cognizable with logic using a particular analytical strategy. Thus, the insight into the structure of order is made accessible through knowledge. So, at the root of the faith in the unseen is this insight which "must always be really present—not only so that the first steps of the analysis can be taken, but so that the very idea of the analysis can be conceived and developed at all" (Voegelin 2000: 258–59). It is this process of knowledge construction that in India is characterized as *Darshan Shastra*.

When the insight itself is submitted to the scrutiny of reason, it signals the evisceration of faith and symbolizes the victory of reason over faith. Two factors have contributed to the faltering and subsequent obsolescence of faith. First, in the pre-enlightenment view of the world, man was not considered a self-defining subject. The source of his norms and values was the larger conceptual order or form or Divine Kingdom. This trans-human entity was the bedrock of man's knowledge and understanding of himself and the world he inhabited. Central to this perception of the world was the notion of intelligible essence, which is the form that by becoming embodied in matter, lends its distinctive identity.

The rejection of intelligible essence wrought a radical change in man's interior as well as in his relationship with the external world. This was made possible by what Rosen calls "the transformation of actuality into possibility." If objects lack intelligible essence, that is, if their development is not governed by their own nature, it is, then shaped by their surrounding conditions. When actuality is transformed into possibility, form, as Rosen argues, is submitted to the agency of two closely related powers, temporality or history and human will (Rosen 1981: 619–20). Value then consists of the satisfaction of desires. This becomes possible through the transformation/manipulation of nature with the help of ever-evolving science and technology.

Another development that took place was in the field of knowledge construction. Earlier, the basis of knowledge construction was the intelligible essence, which was rejected in favour of the scientific method. The denial of a chain of intelligible essences or essential qualities that could be either inferred from particular objects or perceived face to face in abstract forms meant that objects and events in the world could now be classified in innumerable ways. If there are no intelligible essences, there is no pre-determined classification of objects in the world. The standard for testing the validity of any classification can only be the purpose it is expected to serve, such as prediction and control, and not its fidelity to a true world of essences. In this process of knowledge construction, the representation of the phenomenal world, not insight into the structure of order, assumes crucial importance.

This means, to use Heidegger's apt phrase, transforming the world into a picture by projecting concepts on to the world of objects and events. It is through representation that man can have some understanding of his environment. It is this understanding that enables him to plan and execute his purposes and determine costs and benefits of realizing his chosen purpose through the transformation/manipulation of nature with the help of science and technology. This necessarily involves the demolition of "palaces arrogantly magnificent" built by ancient philosophers and moralists "with no better foundation than sand and soft shifting ground" (Helvetius 1880: 207). When the philosopher's insight into the structure of order is subjected to "scientific method" of knowledge construction, it is found to be lacking in reliability and reasonableness. With the insight losing its validity, "the feeling of security in a world full of gods is lost with the gods themselves" (Voegelin 2000: 187). Then the temptation to fall from uncertain truth to certain truth and to visible truth of existence sans the unseen gods becomes irresistible.

The process of this fall was quickened when, the bickering of competing religious sects that appeared after the breakup of the Catholic Church, as an aftermath of the Reformation movement, failed to produce agreement about the truth related to the most serious thing in life. It evoked only controversy and gave birth to libido dominandi (will to dominate). As a result, sixteenth century Europe saw the prevalence of what Voegelin calls "dogmatomachies," that is, fights among dogmas. Each of these sects claimed to have monopoly on religious virtue and fought for ascendancy and control over minds of men with a view to making the world more amenable to God's ways of its own conception. The conflicts among dogmas shook further the roots of faith and contributed to the erosion of the spiritual substance of Christianity.

As a consequence, the self-rooted in the divine, which formerly constituted the centre of the individual being, came to be located in the self in the naive sense of the term. The transcendent spirit came to be fully absorbed into existence and, as a result, now it no longer attracts man with the pull of its ineffable mystery. The absorption of divine reality within human experience has become indistinguishable from the secular assertion of human independence from all divine connection (Walsh 1998: 17). Thus at the core of the earthly order is the attempt to create an image of reality that sustains the possibility that mankind itself is the source of meaning and order.

In the process of making this possibility real, man has cut off his connection with the divine. This has completely eroded shareable commonality. As a consequence, without the underlying substratum of common order, common responsibility and common stake in social harmony, the mere institutional forms of representation and consent prove inadequate. It is this shareable commonality that Plato identifies as the basis of *philia politike,* that is, friendship among members of a community. This friendship eviscerates when man breaks off his connection with the divine and claims to have the autonomy and the power to give a particular shape, direction and meaning to his earthly existence. Man then proceeds on to venture to establish heaven on the earth and turn God into man and man into God. Commenting upon Henry Niclaes' Family of Love movement in Munster in the sixteenth century, the Puritan divine John Knewstub said: "H. N. turns religion upside down. He buildeth heaven here upon earth; he maketh God man and man God" (Hill 1978: 27).

The making of God into man is clearly indicated by Feuerbach's enunciation of "the psychology of projection." All religious ideas, especially the idea of God, were conceived by Feuerbach as a projection of the content of the human mind into the beyond. If Feuerbach was content with making God only a projection of the human mind, Marx went a step further and insisted on pulling divinity back into man and making him a god or if not god, then at least into a superman as Nietzsche did. Nietzsche turned God into the function of man. "Alas, my brother, that God, whom I created, was human work and human madness" (Nietzsche 1957: 271).

The assumption by man of the power of God is only possible when man treats knowledge as power, not as wisdom as made very clear by Bacon. And to achieve this, he has first to displace God. When God has successfully been displaced, only then man can engage in the laborious task of giving a concrete shape to the final realm that he envisages bringing about. The principle instrument in this effort is, of course, reason devoid of the moderating impact of faith. What is distinctive about reason now is that it is bifurcated from faith. It is "severed from the substantive goal that directed it and disconnected from the source of its confidence in the order that assures its efficacy. In its place we recognize the emerging instrumental reason that no longer knows either itself or its purpose in existence" (Walsh 1998: 8–9).

It is knowledge incarnated as power that assists man in his endeavour of giving a concrete shape to the final realm. The final realm, however, lies in the future and the claim of giving a concrete shape to the future amounts to a Utopian exercise representing an apocalyptic project of what Voegelin calls "the creation of dream world" (2000: 224). It is interesting to note that the term "future" came into use only after 1750 (Voegelin 2000: 309; 2004: 181). The coming into currency of the term "future" means that the past is meaningful in one of the two senses: as either the womb of the future or the necessary condition for the coming of the future. In either case, the past has lost its pristine value in the sense of determining man's life patterns. Again, the future represents only a hope, that of creating a dream world.

The creation of a dream world is based on the belief that the present world is not at all satisfactory and that another world is possible. This "another world" is supposed to be qualitatively different from the present. This belief is, however, "always unpredictable and fraught with risk that dwells in all open-ended possibilities." Such a belief is impregnated with apocalyptic overtones that proclaim the end of the world and the advent of the next, final world. This belief, it does not need to be pointed out, is based on the shaky foundation that "the present can be reduced to a *tabula rasa* (empty state) upon which the infinitely malleable future will be erected" (Marder and Vieira 2010: 37). The idea that another comparatively far better world is possible conceals the idea of the final realm.

By doing so, contemporary liberal democratic societies close themselves off to the future since they believe that the end-point in history has been reached. The long fight waged against tyranny, ignorance, hunger, human indignity, etc., is supposed to be now over. They have, it is believed, progressively conquered freedom, autonomy and emancipation. There is, it is supposed, no further fights to win and frontiers to conquer. Man's journey in this phenomenal world for material well-being has come to a happy and salubrious end. For this reason,

[T]he long fight to overcome natural obstacle that stand in the way of human desires is considered as being at its end. The end point is represented, above all, by the reconciliation between humanity and nature, or by what Kojeve... has described as the animalization of man. (De Sa 2010: 29)

Paradoxically, the very idea that the future is malleable renders it unable to be made. To think that the past and the present can be erased and the future moulded in accordance with man's will and reason is to manipulate history. The manipulation of history, as Arendt observes, leads to the loss of the ability to anticipate the future and "to begin something new." As Arendt puts it:

If the past and present are treated as parts of the future—that is changed back into their former state of potentiality—the political realm is deprived not only of its main stabilizing force but of the starting point from which to change, to begin something new. What then begins is the constant shifting and shuffling in utter sterility which are characteristic of many new nations that had the bad luck to be born in an age of propaganda. (Arendt 1993: 258)

The anxiety to bring the final realm into being promotes the acceleration of time in which social and economic changes occur at such a rapid pace that the process of anticipating them and of thinking in terms of the future becomes impossible. Political structures charged with the responsibility of deliberating and thinking prospectively lose their ability to anticipate the future. The principle of the separation of power, the core characteristic of democratic political systems, fades away in the rush of capturing the future and crystallizing it in the end of history. As Scheuerman notes:

What classical writers failed to foresee is that social acceleration potentially undermines core features of the temporal separation of powers, disfiguring liberal democracy as initially conceived. In particular, social acceleration presents a direct threat to the notion of prospective or future-oriented legislation leading to undermine the paramount position of legislative rule-making in the traditional liberal democratic temporal division of labour. (Scheuerman 2004: 45)

The fading away of the principle of the separation of power has made the executive branch of the government the locus of collective decision. This has, as Rossiter puts it, paved the way for "constitutional dictatorship" and the relegation of the parliament to the mere status of auxiliary agent of the government. As a result, real thinking, argumentation and persuasion have become more and more rare. This makes it impossible for the political organization of society to open up to the future. Thus, liberal democratic political systems today are post-modern in the sense that their defining characteristic is the absence of the future.

The underlying promise of giving a particular shape to the final realm is to overcome and remove all obstacles that stand in the way of human desire. This promise has sprung from the belief that the fulfilment of human desires holds the key to human well-being that is reflected in a very important sense in self-determination, equality and dignity. This involves, on the one hand, development of material resources and on the other, realization of equality among men located in a highly differentiated social universe. Thus, one of the substantive aspects of this twofold objective is the removal of differences. In removing differences—social, cultural, economic, etc.—man has played havoc with the present in his endeavour to build a desirable future. In this endeavour, his life goals are determined not by the need of becoming or by the effort to develop in the traditional sense of the term, but by the simple desire of vindicating an immediate "authenticity," pursuing his desire to be here and now. What it does is to transform man into a child whose desires must be satisfied whenever they raise their head. It is in this context that Bruckner describes the contemporary man's experiences as that of an infantile being:

> I do not "become" anymore, I am all that I must be at every moment, I can stand my emotions, desires and fantasies, without second thought. Whereas freedom is the faculty of breaking free from determinisms, I, on the contrary, intend to wed them. I will not erect any barriers to my appetites, I do not have to introduce any distance between me and me; I have to follow my inclinations to become one with myself. (Bruckner 2000: 112–13)

The endeavour of erasing differences is thus to free man from a representation of substantial identities and prejudices by placing him in a sort of selfless existence. It does not necessarily entail openness towards others or to what is different. It is this kind of erasure of differences that

Plato described in the *Republic* as the essential meaning of democracy (526d–62e.)

All this combines to create a situation where there is in the air the perpetual hope of what Derrida calls "democracy to come." As he puts it:

> For democracy remains to come, this is its essence insofar as it remains; not only will it remain indefinitely perfectible, hence always insufficient and future, but, belonging to the time of the promise, it will always remain, in each of its future times, to come; even when there is democracy, it never exists, it is never present, it remains the theme of a non-presentable concept. (Derrida 1997: 306)

And the main reason behind this is the utter failure of democracy to give effect to its promise of establishing heaven on earth, a promise that represents human hubris today. It is not, therefore, surprising that the final realm ever eludes mankind because it violates what Plato calls *sophrosyne*, that is, recognition of the limits on human capacity.

This failure is clearly reflected in the fact that even today the slogan of the French Revolution, "Liberty, Equality and Fraternity," remains just a slogan. As Albritton observes, "Capitalism's main achievement with regard to the slogan of the French Revolution has been to advance, to some degree, forms of individual freedom and shallow degrees of equality for a minority of the world's population" (Albritton 2010: 60). In the light of this fact, freedom essentially means freedom to compete against one another in an economic game, a game, the outcome of which is, as Raventas argues, to continually expand the huge number of losers. For billions of people freedom simply means freedom to feel continual hunger and to be free to desperately scrounge for food.

The failure to create the much hoped for heaven on earth has played havoc with the much-vaunted promise to achieve human emancipation and enlightenment. It is no wonder that liberal democratic political systems depend now more on propaganda as a means of determining opinions, wishes and feelings of the people (Bernays 2005: 37). What propaganda does is to transform factual historical truths into imaginary constructions. This further adds to the strangeness of the dream world that the idea of the final realm signifies. In view of all this, it is not surprising that what we face today is the state of exception in which the rule of law gets lost in the maze of bewildering unrealized promises and unfounded propaganda. Thus in transforming the future in the name of securing human emancipation and welfare, man has created a mess. A few examples of this are presented in this volume. It is in view of this mess that the question "what is the way out," assumes importance. It is this question that this volume seeks to answer.

The Rationale

There are many answers available; one of the answers may be from the Gandhian perspective to explore the connection between well-being, modernism and democracy. As days go by, the relevance of Mahatma Gandhi's thinking about man and his world becomes more and more relevant and appropriate for relieving, if not totally, then at least to a large extent, the troubles of mankind afflicted with economy-driven developmental malaise. The advancing footprints of this malaise can be seen not only in the spiritual vacuum that characterizes man today and generates discontent leading to anomie, alienation, withdrawal, etc., but also in the growing frustration of a large number of people around the world caused by their inability to satisfy, on the one hand, their basic needs and on the other, the ever-escalating hunger of privileged people to possess more and more material goods and services.

This twofold malaise has, no doubt, been engendered by the widespread belief prevalent in Victorian English society that material advancement is the seed-bed of spiritual and moral upliftment. As Charles Kingsley insisted, "The moral state of the city depends on the physical state of that city; on the food, water, air, and lodging of its inhabitants." To put it differently, it was believed that progress in physical conditions led inevitably to the eradication of social evils. This would pave the ground for social concord and world peace. This belief persists even today as exemplified by Lord Keynes' dictum: "Economic development is the possibility of development." It is this belief that lies at the root of today's development policies and programmes. It is believed that pursuit of the economy-driven development is the key to human well-being.

The reality is, however, entirely different. This reality demonstrates the vacuity of this belief. It also points to the perniciousness of the translation of this belief into reality. This is because the very process of translating the modern paradigm development has engendered several paradoxes, such as the paradox of determining the well-being of the psyche through the measurement of that which affects the comfort of the body, the paradox of celebrating separation as the ground of unity, the paradox of promoting particularism for attuning universalism, the paradox of the pursuit of self-interest as the vehicle of serving collective good, etc. These paradoxes are characteristics of modern-day living that, pursuing the material goal of satisfying the ordinary life's needs involved with production and reproduction, strives to attain spiritual and moral fulfilment. And the trouble is that these paradoxes are insoluble within the framework of the modern world view.

Interestingly enough, legitimacy of political systems depends on the extent to which they succeed in resolving these paradoxes and pave the way for ensuring and promoting human well-being. While the concern with the well-being of the people is undisputed, the substantive meaning of the term "well-being" is variable. That is, its meaning and referents are malleable and one can put any meaning to it as one likes. Two diametrically opposed versions of its meaning can be identified here. While one version of its meaning focuses on the good care of the soul as the fulcrum of human well-being, the other version relies on what Gandhi calls "bodily comfort" as the sole denominator of well-being (Rigveda I.95.1).

Modern democracy is associated with the latter view. This association is by no means accidental. Certain developments in history, particularly the passage of Christianity in time since its inception, tied democracy up with this understanding of well-being. The historical developments impinging on the immanentization of Christianity prepared the ground for a radical transformation of the idea of order. The traditional concept of order posited the idea that there was only one order with its source in God; as a consequence all inferior orders must be capable of being harmonized within a comprehensive whole. Integral to this concept was the expression at the deepest level of the consciousness of living within one common overarching order and the impossibility of severing the parts from it. These parts were said to occupy their position not because of their achievement in organizing the whole, but primarily because there was the whole that must be given expression through the recognition of their cooperative endeavour.

Opposed to this is the understanding of order that treats the parts as autonomous entities, whether individuals or groups, and posits the idea that order flows out of the interaction among individual beings who are driven by their passion to act. On this view, public order is fashioned out of private passions; it does not have its source in anything outside or beyond either in any divine entity or something else. It is the struggle between traditional idea of cosmic order and the modern idea of order based on individual psychology and the final triumph of the latter over the former that not only ushers in but also defines modernism. Two instances of the triumph of the new idea of order (Chapter 1) illustrate how this transformation of order from the cosmic to the psychological occurred in fifth century B C Athens and seventeenth century AD England. Chapter 2 traces, through the example of Christianity, the birth of modernism pointing out how a primarily otherworldly religion came under the pressure of emergent historical forces to embrace worldly concerns as being of prime importance. This proved instrumental in jettisoning the idea of *homo religiosus* and replacing it with the idea of *homo laborans,* the autonomous, secular individual. It is developments associated with this transmutation that paved the way for the birth of democracy in modern times. As a political institutional arrangement, it is of prime importance for facilitating the making of public decisions.

It is true that democracy as a political institutional arrangement has swept clean other varieties of political institutional arrangements; however, this victory represents not the victory of democracy but of democratic ideology. This is evidenced by three of its distinctive characteristics, as Burzio identifies: (a) the reality of the rapid circulation of elites, (b) the desire for equality that is hard to satisfy and (c) the illusion that the people rule. As a result of these characteristics, a mismatch has been introduced between democratic theory and democratic practice. It is this mismatch that overlays a deeper mistrust of the people as is evident from the writings of such thinkers as Fortescu, Marsilius of Padua, Machiavelli, Madison, etc. (Chapter 3). The result is that the sovereignty of the people has been constricted to their sovereignty for a day and that too for choosing who is to rule over them.

Apart from this, another transmutation has been associated with democracy. This transmutation, as Michel Foucault points out, concerns the jettisoning of the idea of the good life and the inclusion of natural life in the mechanism and calculations of state power and the consequent turning of politics into bio-politics. This means the almost total eclipse of all ideas of the good life; only the fulfilment of ordinary life's needs, being involved with production and reproduction, are recognized as essential. It is not necessary to emphasize that this defines the principal characteristics of the bare life. As a result, there has occurred politicization of the bare life, which constitutes a decisive moment in modernity and signals a radical transformation of the philosophical categories of classical political discourse. Also important in this connection is the rise of the autonomous self, by which the processes of subjectivity bring the individual to bind himself to his own identity and consciousness and, at the same time, to an external power. This brings into play the Hobbesian "war of each against all" or as MacIntyre puts it, "civil war carried on by other means."

Along with all this is set into motion a dual process that signifies, on the one hand, that the state power makes man as a living being into its own specific object and on the other, the birth of democracy, in which man as a living being presents no longer as an object but as a subject of political power. These processes—which in many ways conflict with each other, ways that oppose each other bitterly—nevertheless converge insofar as both concern the bare life of man. The concern with bare life has far-reaching ramifications. In the first place, democracy is simply an instrument of public decision making that facilitates the making of public decisions in a situation, where subjectivity rules supreme. As an instrument, it sheds off all moral pretensions (Chapter 4). Thus, an ideal political institutional arrangement that we know of as democracy has been willy-nilly turned into nothing more than an instrument projecting a utilitarian perspective on democratic political life and relations.

Second, biological needs of the people (it was Rousseau who equated the fulfilment of biological needs with moral fulfilment), and needs concerned with the quest for wealth, power and prestige have stood out as being of central importance for ensuring human well-being. The inevitable consequence is intense competition for access to and control over scarce societal resources. This competition has become an integral part of democratic politics and has induced what Hobbes calls "war of each against all" or what MacIntyre characterizes as "civil war carried on by other means." When this phenomenon constitutes the backdrop of the functioning of democratic politics, groups form to lend isolated individuals with the capacity to act politically. This further increases the gap between the individual citizen and the state. In a situation where the governmental apparatus controls enormous power resources and turns out to be very assertive and self-aggrandizing, the individual citizens who at times could stand up to trample over kingdoms and empires kowtow, as Tocqueville reminds us, to seek the indulgence/assistance of the lowliest clerk. On yet another plane, he is reduced to the stature of a child most of whose needs are taken care of by the powerful state.

All these anomalies that characterize modern democratic theory also sharply reflect in the practice of democratic politics. This is evident in several policy and programmatic domains of the state, two of which are taken up for analysis here. The first domain concerns the programmes of reverse discrimination (i.e., protection of socio-economically depressed social segments). These programmes aim at pulling up the socially and economically deprived and depressed social groups with a view to remove various inabilities so that they can contribute meaningfully to the national political life and relations. However, the fact remains that these groups are still not free of handicaps and inequality among social groupings. It remains a great problem to be successfully handled (Chapter 5).

The question of reverse discrimination is inexorably linked up with the question of social justice. And democratic politics encounters a profound dilemma. This dilemma flows out of the tension between two antagonistic principles of social justice. One principle asserts that just acquisition and entitlement sets limits to distributive justice. If this results in inequality, it has to be tolerated. The other principle underlines that the principle of distributive justice sets limits to legitimate acquisition and entitlements. If this principle leads to policies of redistribution by the state, then it is justified in order to promote social justice. The programmes of social justice are, however, severely affected by the conflict between these two principles of social justice (Chapter 6).

Chapter 7, titled "The Elusive Search for Community," dwells at length upon the very acute problem that has been thrown up by modernity.

The problem concerns the quest of the lonely separate individuals for the warmth of an intimate community, the warmth woefully lacking in the situation prevailing today. This warmth cannot be provided by the groups that form seeking political action and the prominent tendencies brought into operation by the advent of modernism make this search quite elusive. Given the anomalies associated with modern democracy in terms of both its theoretical articulation and pragmatic functioning, human well-being suffers in two important senses. If there is a definitional restriction in the sense that well-being now underscores the central importance of meeting the material needs of human beings, there is also the pragmatic aspect of life which signifies a situation that induces and buttresses socio-economic inequality with adverse consequences for the weaker sections of the population. Taking note of these facts, we should ask the question whether modern democracy is the apt instrument for ensuring and promoting well-being. If not, what is the alternative? Persuaded by the inadequacy of modern democracy in securing human well-being, the thrust of the present work discusses a viable alternative that is available in Gandhi's thinking. However, before the Gandhian alternative is discussed, the need to go back and the principles that should be the desideratum of an alternative are elaborated in Chapter 8.

Following the cues contained in Chapter 9, Gandhi's thinking on an alternative design of the political institutional arrangement seems to be eminently appropriate for securing human well-being. As such, it becomes necessary to closely examine the philosophical background of Gandhi's thinking. Chapter 10 details the Gandhian critique of modern democracy. Insofar as Gandhi made local democracy or village republic the cornerstone of true democracy, Chapter 11 examines, in a comparative perspective, two models of local democracy: one put forth by Jefferson and the other that of Gandhi. On closer examination, the Gandhian model proves to be far superior. The crust of Gandhi's thinking concerns the urgent need of restoring man's wholeness (*sarvata*) by attuning the soul to the divine ground of being. It is interesting to note that the very idea of wholeness (*sarvata*) is not original to Gandhi; it finds its fullest expression in the Vedas, particularly the Rigveda. Chapter 12, therefore, discusses the Vedic idea of *sarvata*.

Note

1. For the 12 oldest *Upanishads*, with an up-to-date bibliography see Olivelle 1998. The two oldest of these 12 *Upanishads* are the *Brhadaranyaka Upanishad* (BU) and the *Chandogya Upanishad* (CU), representing almost two-thirds of the whole *Upanishads*.

References

Albritton, Robert. 2010. "Neither Utopian, nor Scientific Socialism: A Practical Utopia for Twenty-first Century," *Journal of Contemporary Thought, 31* (Summer), 57–78.

Arendt, Hannah. 1993. "Truth and Politics." In *Between Past and Present: Eight Exercises in Political Thought*. New York: Penguin Books.

Aristotle. 1962. *Politics*. Trans. T. A. Sinclair. London: Penguin Books.

Bernays, Edward. 2005. *Propaganda*. New York: Ig Publishing.

Bruckner, Pascal. 2000. *The Temptation of Ignorance*. New York: Algora.

Collum. 1995. *Manifold Unity: The Ancient World's Perception of the Divine Pattern of Harmony*. Calcutta: Rupa.

Derrida, Jacques. 1997. *The Politics of Friendship*. Trans. George Collins. London: Verso.

De Sa, Alexandre Francis. 2010. "From Modern Utopias to Contemporary Uchronia," *Journal of Contemporary Thought, 31* (Summer), 21–35.

Gopalacharya, Mahuli (Trans.). 1978. *The Heart of the Rigveda*. Bombay: Somaiya Publications.

Helvetius, Claude. 1880. *A Treatise on Man*, Vol. 1. Trans. W. Hooper. New York: Burt Frankling.

Hill, Christopher. 1978. *The World Turned Upside Down: Radical Ideas during English Revolution*. Harmondsworth: The Penguin Books.

Jonas, Hans. 1963. *The Gnostic Religion: The Message of the Alien God and the Beginning of Christianity*. Boston: Beacon Press. First published in 1957.

Marder, Michael and Patricia Vieira. 2010. "Existential Utopia: Of the World, the Possible, the Finite," *Journal of Contemporary Thought, 31* (Summer), 37–56.

Nietzsche, Friedrich. 1957. *The Use and Abuse of History,* 2nd Revised Edition. New York: Macmillan.

Olivelle, P. 1998. *The Early Upanishads: Annotated Text and Translation*. Oxford: Oxford University Press.

Plato. 1971. *Republic*. Ed., Ernest Barker. Oxford: Oxford University Press.

———. 2010. *Plato's Apology of Socrates and Crito, and a Part of the Phaedro*. Ed. Cornelius Ladd Kitchel. Carolina: Nabu Press.

Rosen, Stanley. 1981. "Man's Hope," *Social Research* 18, 3 (Autumn), 614–37.

Scheuerman, William. 2004. *Liberal Democracy and the Social Acceleration of Time*. Baltimore: John Hopkins University Press.

Voegelin, E. 1997. *Collected Works of Eric Voegelin*. Vol. 19, *History of Political Ideas, Vol. I: Hellenism, Rome, and Early Christianity*. Ed. Athanasios Moulakis. Columbia: University of Missouri Press.

————. 2000. *Collected Works of Eric Voegelin*. Vol. 5, *Modernity without Restraint: Political Religions, the New Science of Politics and Science, Politics and Gnosticism*. Ed. and Trans., Manfred Heningsen. Columbia: University of Missouri Press.

————. 2004. *Collected Works of Eric Vogelin*. Vol. 33, *The Drama of Humanity and Other Miscelleneous Papers (1939–1985)*. Ed. William Petropulos and Gilbert Weiss. Columbia: University Missouri Press.

Walsh, David. 1998. *The Growth of Liberal Soul*. Columbia: University of Missouri.

1

Transformation of Order: Two Examples

Without order there is no living in public society because the want thereof is the matter of confusion, whereupon division of necessity followeth, and out of division inevitable destruction.
—Richard Hooker, *The Laws of the Ecclesiastical Polity*, Book VIII, p. 168

Once again, history has produced a type specially adapted to endure his own period: the trained egoist, the private man, who turns away from the arenas of public failure to re-examine himself and his own emotions.
—Philip Rieff, *Freud: The Mind of the Moralist*, p. 2

I

History can, in one sense, be considered an unbroken series of political orders; in this series, one kind of order rises only to give way to another after it has lost its meaning, relevance and utility for men. History, so understood, is more than a document of the rise and fall of political orders; it is also a reflection of the primal need of man to protect himself as well as his possession from encroachment from his fellow men. This is especially true of a society where natural liberty has a free play. As Hobbes notes, "the estate of men in...natural liberty is the estate of war" (Hobbes 1969, 14.4, part 1). It is to escape this estate of war that man creates political order with the hope that it will prevent disorder from unravelling and messing up the fragile fabric of man's existence.

The danger of disorder is real not because man is irrational but because he is fully rational in the sense that he is wholly committed to promoting and safeguarding his own interest. This pits the good of one individual against the good of all. It also tends to encourage as well as confirm man's tendency towards self-aggrandizement paving the way for what Hobbes calls "war of each against all."

This eventuality can be escaped if some mechanism for containing disorder engendered by the untrammelled pursuit of self-interest can be installed. Such an institutional device is the state/government. The state can prevent disorder from messing up people's lives and can mobilize individual energies for enriching and ennobling collective life. As Voegelin puts it, "to set up a government is an essay in world creation" (1997, Appendix A: 225). To set a government is to offset the consequences of the shapeless vastness of conflicting desires. This vastness of conflicting desires is a harsh reality that confronts human beings everywhere. It is a reality that nurtures and nourishes in its womb the demons of disorder, chaos and anarchy.

It is for controlling these demons of disorder and chaos that the government, symbolizing a little world of order, is created and maintained in time. This little world of order, signifying a cosmic analogy, a cosmion, "leads a precarious life under the pressure of destructive forces from within and without" and maintains "its existence by the ultimate threat and application of violence against the internal breaker of its laws as well as the external aggressor" (Ibid.: 225). That the government may have to use violence in order to preserve itself against the danger of disorder and chaos is, however, not its ultimate reason; "the function proper of order is the creation of a shelter in which man may give to his life a semblance of meaning" (Ibid.).

Broadly speaking, two polar conceptions of order, one grounded in the idea of divine cosmos and the other rooted in the psychological attributes of the individual, can be identified. The former, modelled as it is on the idea of cosmic order reflects divine presence and is considered the natural order of things. This is akin to what Lovejoy (1960) calls "the Great Chain of Being". There is order in the heavens, in nature, in society, in man. In this "Chain of Being," everybody is linked with one another and all are linked to the whole. Such an order reflects proportion, balance and harmony. Order that reflects divine *telos* can be maintained by following the principles definitive of it. Such an order prevents man from slipping into disorder by requiring him strictly obey the principles underlying it.

In contradistinction to this, there is another conception of order that treats the individual as the centre of experience. What distinguishes it is the psychological conception of the self of the individual defined by forces associated with his psychosomatic being. Such an individual lives for himself and forever looks for ways and means of realizing his self-defined purposes in a situation where other individuals are similarly occupied. Given the autonomy of the individual and the inexorability of the realization of individual purposes, the shelter function of order can then be interpreted from a utilitarian point of view.

Viewed from the utilitarian perspective, the primary concern of the shelter function is with the fulfilment of man's material needs that arise from his psychological make-up. It is further concerned with institutions that are created and maintained as instruments of mobilizing material resources needed to realize man's purposes. However, the utilitarian perspective, while not being without sense in justifying a political order, does not prove successful in satisfying man's emotional needs. True, such a perspective is justified on the ground that man's autonomy, signifying his freedom from dependence on authorities external to him, is more fundamental for his well-being. It is also claimed that since man's material needs are primary, rationality in linking means to ends is more appropriate than satisfying emotions because they pollute rational thinking.

These two conceptions of order are based upon two different perceptions of man's existence and his relationship with the external world, both society and nature. Given this difference, however, they are both concerned with the status and the role of passions in man's life. The transcendental perspective considers passions as destructive of common life and seeks to sublimate them so that they may prove helpful in preserving what Plato calls *philia politike* (friendship among men in a political community). For this, man needs to link his fragmentary existence to a larger entity. This enables him to develop a sense of self-transcendence. Self-transcendence enables the individual to go beyond the pursuit of self-interest and develop a sense of concern for the good of others; it constitutes the basis for the emergence of the sense of commonality. Man's motivation for acting to realize his purposes is not, as Collins argues, totally "other-oriented" (Collins 1989). Man cannot, it is true, fully sacrifice his self-interest. As such, his purposes are determined by what he thinks is good for him; however, his actions must also be influenced by the consideration of what ensures his good while not harming the good of others.

In contradistinction to this, another perspective focuses on the autonomous individual and his needs rooted in his psychological being. It is argued that only by listening to the call of his passions that man can promote and protect his own well-being. And if everybody promotes his own good, the good of all would be served. It is admitted that some passions are indeed destructive. However, it is claimed, as does Adam Smith, that these passions can be controlled by yoking them to a master passion, for example, avarice. When so yoked, they lose their destructive potentiality. The consequence of this thinking is, of course, the concept of interest in merely the material sense. Originally, interest signified the totality of human aspirations; however, it came later to be narrowed down to "augmentation of fortune." The desire to better one's material condition became the overriding motive of man and, therefore, it was placed at the highest pedestal for taming wild passions. The idea of promoting collective good by harnessing each man's passions in isolation from each other and aggregating them to workout general welfare is well illustrated by Mandeville's notion of "private vice and public benefit."

Man's passions constitute the focus of both of these conceptions of order. However, both of them treat passions differently. If the transcendental conception of order emphasizes disciplining them for ensuring the good of all, the psychological perspective on order believes in harnessing them to a master passion for ensuring individual good as the basis of collective good. Traditionally, almost all societies were said to be modelled upon the cosmic order. However, for various reasons, the disciplining elements that were instrumental in sublimating passions got eroded. As a result, order rooted in the psychological needs of the individual replaced order based on cosmic analogy. It is of interest to explore how this displacement occurs and what factors govern the process of displacement. What follows is a discussion of the process of displacement focusing on the examples of ancient Athens and seventeenth-century England.

The process of transformation of cosmic order into the earthly order is governed by a particular kind of dynamic relationship between the conceptual world and the social world. As Pocock puts it:

> People think by communicating language systems, these systems help constitute both their conceptual world, and the authority structures, or social worlds related to these; the conceptual and the social worlds may now be viewed as a social event, a moment in the transformation of that

system and of the interacting worlds which both systems help constitute and are constituted by. (Pocock 1971: 15)

The interaction between the two worlds—the conceptual and the social—is the driving force behind the transformation. When changes in the factual order render the order based on cosmic analogy less and less satisfying it begins to decline till it is displaced by order based on man's subjectivity. The operation of this process in the Hellenic world as well as in seventeenth-century England exemplifies the process of the transformation.

II

The transformation of order in Athens that was based on cosmic analogy into one grounded in man's subjectivity spans a long period ranging from the Homeric beginning to the post-Peloponnesian Athens. Homer's epics, *Iliad and Odyssey*, portray a powerful reflection of aristocratic, violent culture that celebrated chivalry. The style of existence evolved by aristocratic genes in the Aegean-wide Mycenaenean civilization remained the dominant pattern of Hellenic civic culture. "Political power of the aristocracy might be broken but its culture permeated the people; democratization of Hellas meant an extension of aristocratic culture to the people—even though in the process of diffusion, the quality was diluted" (Voegelin 1986: II, 117).

Thus, as Xenophanes observes (Lesher 2001: 10), "from the beginning (*ex arche*) all have learnt from Homer."[1] And what Homer focuses on is "the position of man in the universe, a universe that displays order of being which permeates man and transcends him" (Jaeger 1973: I, 429, fn. 34). The universe that Homer portrays is inhabited both by men and gods in Olympia, both living in harmony. However, this harmony signifies divine guidance to human action.

> There is no clearly circumscribed order of man, over-arched by a transcendent order of the gods; the forces that operate and interact in the comprehensive order of being rather reach into man himself in such a manner that border-line between human and trans-human is blurred. (Voegelon 1986: 88–89)

This interpenetration of man's world and that of the gods indicates that man has yet to develop self-consciousness in the sense of a full-blown subjectivity. Man's action does not flow from his interior psychological being; it is not a phenomenon of human consciousness. Nothing happens without the aid of a divine power (Jaeger 1973: I, 51). Despite all this, the Hellenic society Homer portrays is a cosmos in the sense that it is considered to be "the perfect exemplar of order, and, at the same time, the cause of all order in particulars, which only in degrees can approximate the whole" (Jonas 1963: 242). Central to this cosmos is the concept of *dike,* a legal terminology signifying the giving back or restoring what has been unlawfully taken away. The idea of *dike* presupposes a particular pattern of the distribution of social resources both physical and non-physical, a distribution that has been sanctified by custom and law. This acknowledges certain rights that are to be restored when infringed. When such a restoration takes place, the cause of *dike* is served.

Thus, *dike* is used in the sense of compensating the injured party by a person guilty of the act of infringement. In this sense, *dike* implies "due share" (Jaeger 1973: 103). Later, Anaximander of Miletus (about mid sixth century B C) transferred the concept of *dike* from the social life of the city-state to the realm of nature. He forged a causal connection between coming-to-be and passing away as equivalent to the lawsuit in which things are compensated by the decision of time to compensate each other for their immorality (Ibid.). Thus the substantive meaning of the term "cosmos" is right order first in nature and then in the state or a community as an analogue of the former. However, this order is disrupted when man's pride propels him to encroach upon the right or honour of others. What drives men to cross the limits of propriety is his *thumos.*[2]

It is true that customs and social conventions are meant to bridle anger. However, often passion swells *thumos.* Occasions may, then, arise when customs and conventions fail to restrain a person in the grip of anger, propelling him to overstep the correct path of action. This is symptomatic of a person being gripped by *Ate,* a divine force and the eldest daughter of Zeus. A person gripped by *Ate* tends to ignore all restraints and to commit an improper act. This, in turn, invites *cholos*, mighty wrath, that propels man to seek formal compensation. *Cholos* generates *Andreia,* courage, which is the habit of the soul. It is moved to counteract an unjust action. *Sophia,* wisdom, is required to guide and restrain courage, since emotion, however justly aroused, may overstep the measure (Voegelin 1986: 90). Undoubtedly, then, *cholos,* when properly exercised, becomes instrumental in preserving order. To be gripped by *cholos* and to ignore the counsel of reason in dealing with *cholos* is the symptom of disorder in man's interior. This disorder then gets externalized and appears as the disease of society. Homer's epics, particularly, *Iliad,* demonstrate how unbridled passion of the noble heroes brought the Mycenaean civilization to an end. As such, Homer's epics are concerned with disorder and tell the story of a disordered society.

The Homeric portrayal of the heroic *arête* in the Mycenaean culture and the worldview that guided its pursuit left several issues unresolved. In unravelling these issues, later poets and philosophers gradually moved away from mythic way of thinking to rational and logical way. However, mythical elements were not fully eliminated. Love and hate, the two natural forces of binding and separation in the philosophy of Empidocle, which later assume a central theme in Anaximander's philosophical thinking, are prime examples of mythological thought in "scientific" philosophy.[3] The foci of this "scientific" philosophy were mainly two. First, it was the issue of the relationship between numerous Olympian gods and man who lacked self-consciousness. The world of gods and that of man interpenetrated in such a way that rift among men brought about disturbances in the Olympian order of the world and division among the gods resulted in a disturbance of human order. Thus the thrust of "scientific" philosophy was to separate these two worlds but within the parameters of one integrated cosmic order.

The second set of issues concerned the status of man in society and his relationship with the polis. The latter concerned not only the place and role of the polis in man's life but also the question of *arête* (excellence, virtue) that the polis must commit itself to. To resolve this issue, the philosophers had to turn away from the study of nature to the study of man. Ionian philosophers, such as Thales and Anaxagoras (610/112–547 BC) were committed totally to pure and disinterested research without any reference to the pragmatic world.[4] The principal concern of these philosophers was to identify the substance that underlay the perceptible, changing phenomena. Thales (630–546/5) identified water as the substance out of which things were made. He conceived the world of nature as an organism. The world, that is, earth and heaven, which together came to be known as cosmos, that is, a community of things under law, was for him "en-souled," within which resided lesser organisms with souls of their own. The world was, however, not born; it was made by the only maker that dares its fearful symmetry—God (Jaeger 1973: 165).

Rejecting Thales' idea, Anaximander (mid sixth century B C) posited the notion of *to apeiron,* the Boundless, the Infinite, which he identified with God, characterized by infinity and eternity. In contrast, any given world was finite in extent as well as in its duration of life. Anaximander thus posited the two senses of *physis* or nature: on the one hand, in its original sense, *physis* means something within or intimately belonging to a thing, which is the source of its behaviour. The secondary meaning of *physis* is the sum total or aggregate of natural things. Thus there are, for Anaximander, two different but organically linked worlds, one an unchanging, infinite and eternal world of being and the other world of being which is an ever-changing, finite and impermanent world. Thus, inherent in Anaximander's thinking is the distinction made later between *natura naturata* and *natura naturans* with the former being finite, while the latter was supposed to be the creative nature of the boundless (Collingwood 1976: 32). Therefore, it is to the credit of Anaximander that he took a decisive step in originating something of all qualities that were given infinite experience and to posit an infinite something as the origin of the world (Ibid.: 35).

Change in the world of "becoming" is, as already indicated, caused by the interplay of opposite principles, for example, love and hate as Euripides identified them. "War is the father of all," declare Heraclitus. But this war is prevented from letting *hybris* have its own by the element of *dike*. As Anaximander puts it, "It is necessary that things should pass away into that from which they are born. For things must pay one another the penalty and compensation for their injustice to the ordinance of time" (Jaeger 1973: 159).

What Anaximander means is that when things are produced by *Apeiron,* they leave the original unity "in which all the warring contraries of this world are brought together in peace." However, since they belong to this finite world, they are likely to be gripped by *pleonexia* or aggrandizement; as such, they might cause damage to other's status or honour. When this happens, the aggrieved person is sure to get compensation in time. This signifies, as Solon confirmed later, that justice is a part of divine world order. Sooner or later, punishment comes and the aggressor's *hybris* must pay the penalty for overstepping the bounds set by justice (Solon, *Fragments,* cited in Jaeger 1965: I, 17–32). Thus, the power of justice is immanent in the process by which all inequalities compensate themselves in time. The compensatory process also operates in human life as well as in nature. Thus, earthly justice is seen to be rooted in the justice of heaven. For Anaximander, then, nature is the sum total of all that is divine. In it rules the same law and the same justice that men revere as the highest moral standard. In effect, Anaximander propounds a moral law, not a scientific explanation.

This moral law assumes importance, as Hesiod (900 BC) had pointed out, in a situation where corruption becomes so pervasive that injustice becomes rampant. Thus, the present tends to degenerate. These points to "the tension between a hard-won civilizational order, precariously in balance, and a rumbling underworld of demonic forces, which, at any time, may break loose and destroy it" (Voegelin 1986: 132).[5] True, ultimately justice and order triumph; however, men must cultivate *dikaiosyne* (righteousness) or justice. The need for justice in the pragmatic affairs of man finds a powerful expression in Anaximander's philosophical thinking.

Thus the old conception of *arêteg* courage in the old aristocratic culture, that Tyrtaeus celebrated and Sparta embraced, was given a new content, justice. *Dike* also received, as did the concept of justice, another attribute—equality. This was unavoidable because of class struggles that marked post-Homeric centuries. What was needed in these struggles was a correct norm to measure legal rights and that norm was found in the concept of equality, an idea implicit in the concept of *dike.* This ultimately gave birth to the concept of *isonomia,* equality before law. Thus, equality before law and the maintenance of just order acquired a palpable content in written law, which, in turn, was considered a reliable criterion for right or wrong. In contradistinction to Sparta, Ionia and Athens spurned the authority of tradition and myth and endeavoured to distribute constitutional privileges in conformity with a more or less universal, social and legal ideal, *isonomia* and justice in the sense of safeguarding due share, which a man can rightly claim.

It was the polis that disposed justice and maintained order. It occupied a strategic place in personal lives and communal relations of the people. From this was derived the ideal of citizenship. This meant that citizens must do their duty that membership in a political community entailed.

And it entailed that citizens must not only obey the law but also must mould their conduct by its patterns. With the polis assuming a central place in man's life, the law became the objective expression of the state and therefore, it became the king,

> an invisible ruler who does not only prevent the strong from transgressing and bring the wrongdoer to justice, but issues positive commands in all the spheres of life, which had once been governed by individual will and preference. Even the most intimate acts of the private life and moral conduct of its citizens are law prescribed and limited and defined. (Jaeger 1973: 109)

The role of the city-state in shaping the citizen's character and the texture of social life became crucially significant in as much as it required the individual to live for the well-being of the polis. Thus, as Jaeger points out:

> [The polis emerges as] the sum of all its citizens and of all the aspects of their lives. It gives each citizen much but it can demand all in return. Relentless and powerful, it imposes its way of life on each individual, and marks him for its own. From it are derived all the norms which govern the life of its citizens. (Ibid.)

It is, therefore, not surprising that Xenophanes (515–470) attacked the Homeric conception of the universe when he abandoned the old, polytheistic world of gods. Instead, he posited the idea of one God. Moreover, he also rejected the ideal of chivalry celebrated in the old aristocratic culture and replaced it with the new ideal of humanity. Xenophanes exposed the irrelevance of the deeds of the heroes of Olympic games by pointing out that victory at Olympic games gives little joy to the city, for it does not fill its storerooms.[6] The meaning is very clear: the well-being of the individual person depends on that of the polis. And it is the polis that imposes, as Cochrane puts it, "effective check upon the passions, especially those of avarice and ambition, and to achieve something of moderation..." (Cochrane 1957: 84).

For Solon, the lawgiver of Athens, too, avarice constituted the greatest threat to the polis because it leads to conflict of interests, which, in turn, paves the way for the doom of the polis. "Driven by avarice," Solon notes, "the leaders of the people enrich themselves unrighteously; they spare neither the goods of the state nor the temple treasures, and they do not preserve the venerable foundation of *Dike*..." (Solon, *Fragments,* cited in Jaeger 1965: I, 3, 6). When avarice gets hold of citizens, they, in their folly, risk the ruin of the city. True, *dike* comes to punish the wrongdoer in time. However, the inner rule of law is *sine qua non* for a harmonious social order. Of course, the permanent law of nature underlies the process of eternal coming-to-be and passing away. But it must be reinforced by the law of the polis and its internalization by citizens. There is thus the need for harmonizing law and divine justice. And law of the polis would become effective if men recognize the invisible mean of judgement, "which alone contains the limits of all things" (Jaeger 1973: 137). In other words, what Solon insists upon is *sophrosyne,* which is the source of the balance or proportion.[7]

Solon, who, according to Jaeger, is the first embodiment of truly Attic spirit, and at the same time the greatest of its creators (Ibid.), struck a balance between the outward striving energy of the individual and the unifying power of the state. However, Solon failed to curb the power of the landed nobility who still governed Athens. Earlier, the Draconian Law aimed at curtailing the power of the landed aristocracy but it only strengthened it. Solon, did put an end to the enslavement of indebted farmers; however, he could not clip the wings of the landed aristocracy, who, with its selfish estate pride and its arrogant disregard of the landless commoners, was unwilling to surrender its power. As a result, the conflict of interest between the landed nobility and farmers was transformed into unrest and revolution and counterrevolution. And since Solon's steward-ship of the Athenian polis did not do much to remove its cause, a revolt was successfully led by Pisistratus who ruled for 20 years as a tyrant.[8]

It was only after the fall of Pisistratid tyranny that the reform carried out by Cleisthenes swept away the power of the landed aristocracy. He installed a democratic government and reinforced it by dividing Athens roughly into three divisions and 10 brand new demes, each of which contained a cross-section of the population and mixed economic interests. Pisistratus had, however, raised Athens from a small country town to a city of international importance and solidified the base of cultural richness of Athens. The tyrant Pisistratus and aristocratic democrat Cleisthenes contributed mightily to the rise of Athens as a power in its own right. Their rule transformed Athens in less than a century, from a second rate polis, torn with economic and political strife, into a flourishing city with a unity, a new purpose and a new confidence.

Consolidation of Athenian democracy as an important power unit constitutes an important stage in Athenian political development. It is parallelled by a cultural development in the form of the Orphic movement. This movement had the effect of pitting the claim of the soul against that of the body. It laid stress on the need of taking care of the soul by protecting it from bodily corruption. The Orphic conception of the soul marks an important advance in the development of man's self-consciousness, which treats the soul as the sensorium of the divine. However, when earthly difficulties make life hellish, the character of the self changes—from man's transcendental orientation to a material one. Thus, the notion of self-consciousness becomes schizophrenic in the sense that it now signifies, on the one hand, the spiritual orientation of man and on the other, the spiritual tends to merge with and find its anchor in the psychological make-up of the individual.

The rise of Athens as a powerful polis and its victory in Persian wars— Marathon (490 BC) and Salamis (480 BC)—were causes enough for Athens to feel exalted since victory in these wars was won not by good fortune but by good sense. As such, it gave spur to further consolidation of Athenian power. Politically, Athens saw the possibility of becoming the leader of Greece. To counter the Peloponnesian League under the leadership of Sparta, its traditional rival, Athens organized a naval confederacy, the Dorian League, ostensibly with a view to meeting any threat coming from Persia. Even after this threat was removed, Athens treated the members of the confederacy with harshness and brutality, if any member wanted to disaffiliate (Thucydides 2000: I, 98). As Voegelin comments:

> The Athenian rise to power was physically and emotionally an outburst of forces, an aggrandizement of the hegemonic city at the expense of the weaker allies and neighbours, which morally it was a ruthless indulgence in violations of justice and satisfaction of greed, a breakdown of ethos, a great fall containing the seeds of the subsequent political disaster. (1986: 301)

The swift rise of Athens, still more the transformation of the Dorian League into a hardly disguised empire aroused both fear and resentment and led to the Peloponnesian wars. Interestingly, Thucydides considered Athens to be responsible for the war with Sparta insofar as three vital issues of national interest—security, honour and self-interest—were involved. As Athenians argued in Sparta:

> We have done nothing extraordinary, nothing contrary to human nature in accepting an empire when it was offered to us and then refusing to give it up. Three very powerful motives prevent us from doing so—security, honour and self-interest. And we were not the first to act in this way. Far from it. It has always been a rule that the weak should be subject to the strong; and besides, we consider that we are worthy of our power. (Thucydides 2000: I, 76.1)

The Peloponnesian war lasted for a long duration and, throughout its course, brought unprecedented sufferings for Hellas. Apart from the huge cost in human suffering, it also led to a permanent change in the temper of the people and led to the emergence of a different attitude towards life. Thucydides' confirmation of this underlines the reality of "a general deterioration of character throughout the Greek world." His reference to corruption that overtook Corcyra is proof enough. As he notes:

> [T]here were the wicked resolutions taken by those who particularly under the pressure of misfortune, wished to escape from their usual poverty and coveted the property of their neighbours, there were savage and pitiless actions into which men were carried not so much for the sake of gain as because they were swept away into an internecine struggle by their ungovernable passions. (Ibid.: III, 84.1)

This was enough to exalt "vengeance above innocence and profit above justice" (Ibid.). It also signalled the rise of individualism. Several factors account for this. First, Athenians pursued, in their own sober and practical ways, the Athenian ideal of "a particular kind of inspiration in which patriotic self-sacrifice and cold practical calculations of means and ends were united and enhanced each other's power" (Jaeger 1973: 334). This inspiration combined two incompatible principles: the search for pleasure that reinforced individualistic tendency and the promotion of collective good requiring self-transcendence to some degree on the part of the individual. All societies have, at one time or the other, faced the problem caused by the depredation of aggressive individualism. They have sought to regulate and control it by installing order on the erratic movement of individual appetites and passions. The solution that Athens embraced consisted in forging an artificial unity between individualistic pursuits and allegiance to collective good. "The Athenian state had convinced each of its citizens that he could prosper only if his city were growing in power and wealth and thereby converted natural egoism into one of the strongest motives for communal action" (Ibid.).

Uninterrupted flow of satisfaction—material, emotional and spiritual—from the state to the individual is a necessary condition for making sacrifices for promoting collective good. Allegiance to common good cannot be assured if the gains that the individual gets or expects from the state do not outweigh the losses. The Peloponnesian war seriously disturbed this balance between individual satisfaction and collective good. During the Peloponnesian war, this principle proved to be a more serious problem growing increasingly serious as the war continued and material benefits that individuals derived from contributing to the national effort became smaller and smaller. The war had exhausted Greece materially and spiritually. And the city-state was no longer able to provide a tolerable way of life. As a consequence, the focus of philosophical thinking turned away from the polis and concentrated on the psychological needs of the individual. Thus fourth century BC Athens exemplifies a permanent change of temper underlining a different attitude to life. This signalled the rise of individualism in all spheres of life (Thucydides 2000: III, 83).

The change of temper is best reflected in the writings of Euripides, who, while a part of the old world, was set upon destroying it (Jaeger 1973: Book 2, Chapter 4). The Peloponnesian war had put paid to the Athenian worldview with the result that, as Voegelin puts it, "the island of *Dike* was swallowed by the sea of disorder" (1986: 264). Consequently, man's subjectivity came to the fore. Jaeger refers to Euripides as the first psychologist, who discovered the soul, in a new sense—and revealed, in his dramas, the troubled world of man's emotions and passions (Jaeger 1973: 335). It was in the swirling sea of emotions and passions, that man was to find a fixed point that would serve for him as a lighthouse to direct the ship of his life to some safe shore. The heroes of Euripides indulge in passionate self-vindication underlining the collapse of individual character depicted so well by Thucydides (Ibid.). The change of temper is best illustrated by the fact that "man is now no longer able and willing to abandon himself to any new view of life which does not make *himself*...

the ultimate standard" (Thucydides 2000: III, 833), in the Protagorean sense. Protagoras expresses this change when he asserts that "Man is the measure of all things."

Thucydides reflects the change of temper through his approach to history. When his approach to history is contrasted to that of Herodotus, it becomes clear that the world of spirit had descended from the God to the nature of man insofar as Thucydides considered actions of man to be the cause (*aitia*) of the movement of history. "In Herodotus' view of the world, political events are always a part of the theological conception of life, which comprises the totality of things human and divine. In Thucydides the political element predominates and nothing is left of Herodotus' theological framework" (Jaeger 1973: 354). Thucydides considers human nature to be constant defined by the principle of the strong ruling the weak (Ibid.: 484, fn. 6) as is reflected in the justification of the Athenian position by an Athenian in Sparta. He justified the right of a strong power to rule to be in accord with the law of nature, rejected God as the guardian of justice and submitted it to a pattern of earthly authority and force. Thucydides made power the driver of human affairs. In short, the ethical power of divine descent was replaced by a general conception of human nature with all its individual accidents and ambiguities.

The shift from the heavenly to the earthly basis of order was no doubt fashioned by several factors. But it was mainly the Peloponnesian war, which shattered Athenian democracy and, with it, its cultural ethos. The Athenian rise to power was physically and emotionally, no doubt, an outburst of forces, an aggrandizement of a hegemonic city at the expense of the weaker allies and neighbours; morally it was a ruthless indulgence in violations of justice and satisfaction of greed, a break-down of ethos, a great fall containing the seeds of the subsequent political disaster (Thucydides 2000: I, 76.2). Even Pericles justified this aggrandizement on two very dubious grounds: the stronger must rule over the weaker, and Athens represented a superior and progressive culture and the dependent peoples had no objection to being ruled by the stronger power.

No doubt, it is in the logic of a growing power to go on seeking ever-new avenues of power and looking for ways and means of safeguarding its power. Moreover, expansion implies dynamism in every aspect of civil life. It means expanding economy, a rising standard of living, development of skills and individuals' growing confidence. As such, it is very difficult to stop the process of expansion, much less to revert it. Thus, the irreversibility of the empire was symptomatic of the brilliance of expansion, but this proved destructive of moral personality. "The process, spreading from the public to the private sphere, begins from the habituation to unjust actions in affairs of state and ends with the dissolution of honesty, loyalty, and shame in personal relations" (Voegelin 1986: 358). In addition, the state lost in this process its predominant position not only as an embodiment of law but also as an educative institution.

The weakening of the state was symptomatic of the fateful shift from the spiritual to the psychological. "The ethical power of the divine descent was now replaced by general consciousness of *human nature* with all its individual accidents and ambiguities..." (Ibid.: 362). This brought to the fore three difficult problems that plagued Athenian democracy. The Athenian state demanded a lot of sacrifice from its citizens, which they willingly made. However, with the weakening of the state, the quantum of satisfaction the citizens derived from their sacrifice also dwindled. This raised the question of the relationship between individual welfare and that of the community. Earlier, the welfare of the community and its parts were measurable by an objective standard, that is, *dike*. However, with the rise of individualism, two things happened. In the first place, democratic mode of governance demolished, to a large extent, the hold of the feudal elements. However, the struggle for power never ceased. And as it became virulent, the promotion of sectional interest became progressively important. The question "who gets what, when and how" became the desideratum of politics.

In the second place, as purely physical explanations of human conduct became more and more pronounced, the question of the status of man-made law became central. Law was considered to be externally imposed; and as laws multiplied, they were seen to be hostile to nature. Aristophon was to underline this; he called law "the chain of nature." This view posed a serious threat to the conception of justice as it was conceptualized in the old constitutional state. The positing of opposition between law and nature pointed to the growing importance of private life as against a life dedicated to the service of the state. And if private life has its own separate existence, then the question of the opposition between individual morality and political morality becomes crucial. Earlier, the state was the sole source of political morality; public and private morality coincided. However, when man becomes the measure of all things and since now man claimed to have his private life,

> the standards of the state conflicted with those established by nature or God, so that man could not accept them, in which case, he ceased to be a member of the political community; and the very foundation of his life dissolved, unless he could find some certainty in the eternal order of nature. (Jaeger 1973: 306)

Since the city-state was no longer in a position to provide a tolerable way of life, philosophical thinking turned away from the polis and focused either on cosmopolis, as advocated by Diogenes, or on the search for utility as Aristoppus advocated. Aristoppus, for example, taught his students that a good life consists of the enjoyment of pleasure and avoidance of all pain, worry and anxieties. He also called for withdrawal from the useless cares of public life. He asserted that the state was the result of contract among selfish men who enter into it out of fear of each other. Thus, if Aristoppus emphasized self-sufficiency in purely naturalistic manner, Diogenes treated the individual as a member of the cosmopolis and argued that neither the city nor the law is required to make man virtuous and happy; one's own virtue alone can make a man virtuous and happy.

III

More than 2000 years separate seventeenth-century England from the Athens of 400 BC. The passage of time does not, however, erase the similarity in the experience of the transformation of the cosmic order into an earthly one. This fateful change involves what Collins calls "the relationship between consciousness and order." This relationship was defined in the late sixteenth and early seventeenth centuries by a shift in the locus of order from the divine cosmos to secular sovereign state. As a result of this shift, social order began to incorporate rational utilitarian authority which could no longer be "a matter of acquisition or definition," it is only "a matter of exercise." Secular order, then, observes Collins, "redefines the social good. Society is no longer a transcendentally articulated reflection of something predefined, external and beyond itself which orders existence hierarchically. It is now a nominal entity ordered by the sovereign state, which is its own articulated representative" (Collins 1989: 7).

How did this shift in the locus of order take place? Francis Ferguson asks: "At what point in history, by what process, was the clue to the vast system of medieval analogies lost, the threads broken, and the way cleared for centreless proliferation of modern culture?" (Ferguson 1953: 153). True, the identification of the exact point in history when modern consciousness burst out of the fallen pieces of the medieval civilization in Western Europe inspired and braced up by the ethos of Christianity is impossible; however, the process of the shift can certainly be identified and described. At the core of the centreless proliferation of modern culture is the transmutation of the givens of a particular pragmatic situation into psychological orientation. It is true that perceived anomalies in the social order impels "re-conceptualization of the relationship between consciousness and order; this happens when traditional redemptive institutions begin to function less adequately. As a result, social reality appears less cohesive and more coercive" (Collins 1989: 4).

This situation clears the way for the eruption of conflicts; this, in turn, facilitates the formulation of alternative modes of relationship between consciousness and order. Minor breakdowns in the pre-existing paradigm and the very first blurring of its rules induce a new way of looking at things, giving birth to a new paradigm (Kuhn 1970: 86). Minor breakdowns cumulate; relationship between individual self and the collectivity called society changes, and the need to evolve a new conception of identity becomes pressing. All this reflects what Collins calls "the evermore conspicuous reality of political and, as it were psychological, truth that moulds consciousness and shapes man's understanding of order not as natural but artificial created by man" (Collins 1989: 28). Collins' discussion of transformation of order in the seventeenth-century England rests on this theoretical perspective. As he says:

> Since order can be conceptualized as the perceived historical interpretation of self-coconsciousness and social reality, a careful discussion of relation between the idea of order and the redefinition of meanings requires, both as complement and as supplement, an analysis of the changing consciousness and the conception of self during the period. (Ibid.: 22)

Collins focuses on the intellectual history of "consciousness-in-general" and highlights the gradual process of meaning production and redefinition in the medieval England and elsewhere in Europe. What is missing from his analysis are those religious, sociopolitical and economic changes that prepared the ground for this shift, in the first place. These anomalies cleared the way for change in consciousness. This change necessitated a radical reinterpretation of self-hood and of the nature of relationship between self and society. Medieval England saw in the seventeenth century the displacement of the cosmic order by the earthly order grounded in the material needs of the newly emergent self-conscious individual. This individual was committed fully to the fulfilment of ordinary life-needs. Thomas Hobbes enunciates best the philosophical or, rather, psychological foundation of the new, emergent secular social order. The one factor that stands out as vastly important is, of course, the radical change in the cultural ethos brought about by progressive decline in the spiritual aspect of human existence. This helped the individual to free himself from traditional constraints associated with the primacy of religion that endowed legitimacy to the feudal social order. Once this happened, economic forces emerged to give direction to man's life. We briefly touch upon the factors that led to the process of secularization as the regnant mode of looking at man and his world. Economic factors increasingly shaped thought-ways and work-ways.

Medieval civilization in Western Europe happened to be the playground of two opposing forces. The integrative force, the Roman Empire, which as *sacrum imperium* (Eusebius 1975: 120), was to bring the entire human race with all its bewildering and troubling diversity into unity and concord under the banner of Christianity. Opposed to it was the force that insisted on making diversity itself the basis, both within and among nations, of organizing social and political life. The struggle was finally decided in favour of those forces that wrecked disintegration. The victory of disintegrative forces was, however, not achieved without struggle. This struggle expressed itself first in indifference, then condemnation, followed by attempts to establish a balance and, finally, an abject surrender to disintegrative forces. What made the aspiration of realizing a single order symbolizing the transformation of Christianity into a single universal civilization impossible was, as Tawney notes, the Reformation which undermined spiritual forces as it modified not the facts but the minds. This was instrumental in rubbing off the spiritual substance from Christianity and in loosening the bonds of traditional constraints on thought-ways and work-ways. Reason triumphed over faith and, as a result, the quest of happiness, it was believed, could be successful only thorough Mammon worship.

The victory of reason over faith stimulated the growth of individualism and sustained against attacks from the crumbling bastions of traditionalism. Reformation succeeded not only in splintering Christianity and promoting the forces that not only saw the growth of religious sects but also succeeded in dismantling the institutionalized control, as symbolized by the Catholic Church, over religious life and relations. It recognized the priesthood of every individual and asserted that the inner light implanted in everyman's breast would show him the path of God. The inner light was supposed not only to be the source of religious knowledge but also an instrument of freeing the individual from inherited traditions, customs and laws, leaving the individual to work out his salvation alone in the sight of God only. The doctrine of the inner light can very well be linked to later developments such as Locke's *tabula rasa,* J. S. Mill's Religion of Humanity and Tocqueville's proposal (de Tocqueville 1959: I, 225) on combining right with private interest for cultivating the sense of concern for others. It also stimulated the growth of radical individualism.

Each of the diverse protestant sects insisted on the authenticity of its own perceived truth and claimed monopoly over it. This was indicative of a situation in which cultural consensus was irrevocably lost. As a result, philosophical discussion of what is good came to be suspected as a cloak for manipulation. Mysteries of the being were lost and Bible readers in the sixteenth and seventeenth centuries "wanted to democratize these mysteries and abolish mumbo-jumbo men, whether priests, lawyers or scholars" (Hill 1978: 66). Shorn of its mystery, the Bible became the source of finding some message of direct contemporary relevance. Paradoxically though the glimmer of the inner light did not succeed in preventing the dazzling but harsh explosion of religious zeal translating itself into apocalyptic vision reflecting a millenarian ecstasy. It held out the prospect of the Kingdom of God around the corner. Milton declared the arrival on earth of "Christ the shortly expected King." And interestingly enough, "to many men, the execution of Charles I in 1649 seemed to make sense only as the clearing of the way for King Jesus, as the prelude to greater international events" (Ibid.: 96).

All these developments created a situation of ambiguity and confusion. True, the inner light was expected to guide man in his journey in the phenomenal world. However, agreement on what that inner light really meant was completely lacking. What it meant in practice was that each of the warring sects held on to its own version of truth, which it wanted to prevail over all others. It was also willing to shed blood for upholding the superiority of its own perceived truth with a view to ensuring uniformity of religious belief and practice. As a result, the question of ensuring the practice of government in a situation where no cultural consensus existed assumed critical importance. Thus, the zealous struggle for installing a partisan version of religious truth gradually rubbed off the substance of spirit from Christian religion. What helped in it was the long tradition of popular materialist scepticism and anti-clericalism that had prevailed in England (Ibid.: 28–29). With the erosion of the substance of spirit from Christianity, it was possible to begin the task of building heaven on earth and making God man and man God (Ibid.: 68). If this task failed at Munster in the sixteenth century, it certainly succeeded later by enveloping the whole world. As a result, the quest for happiness through Mammon worship became the preferred mode. Medieval England was no exception to this.

Medieval England, as Tawney (1958: 22) reminds us was primarily a pastoral society with a heavy reliance on agriculture and export of food and wool. It stood "on the outer edge of economic civilization, remote from the great highways of commerce and the bustling financial centres of Italy and Germany" (Tawney 1982: 16–17). It basked in economic innocence since it was primarily a pastoral society, exporting raw materials and little food till it experienced the excitement of expanding commerce promoted, in a large part, by the newly emergent joint-stock companies and the growing strength of financial organizations. Manufacture of woollen cloth, which caused the enclosure movement that produced certain adverse consequences for the social order, was the principal English industry and the most valuable source of export. Though small factories were beginning to spring up, industry lay scattered and towns were still the chief sites of markets.

Economic inequality was ingrained in medieval England; so was the class division of society, although its rigidity was in the process of melting inasmuch as social mobility was quite in evidence. For example, the yeomen class, the backbone of the economy of medieval England, was a disappearing class, not because they were becoming paupers but because they were becoming gentlemen. Also the gentry, immediately below the peers, had begun, in the late sixteenth century, to be powerfully reinforced by the influx from the professional and merchant classes. Lawyers, government officials and successful merchants were buying land not only to better their social standing but also for augmenting their income. Their entry into agriculture changed radically the traditional pattern of relationship between those who owned land and those who tilled it. All this indicates the ongoing slow but certain change in the temper of the people insofar as their economic behaviour is concerned. The driving force was, of course, the growing economic distress of the common man and his aspiration to seek freedom from it or build sanctuaries against it. What fed this aspiration and reinforced the money motive was, on the one hand, the gradual fading away of religious faith and the growing irrelevance of religion for human existence and, on the other, the economic power of Italy, which was leaking through a thousand creeks and inlets into Western Europe. The leaking currents of money motive were prompting men to opt for moneymaking economic activities by acquiring mastery over nature. The potent weapon chosen for this was commerce, which fuelled the expanding energy of the people bitten by the bug of cupidity. The enclosure movement is a testimony to this. "Cottage industry was spreading by the second half of the fifteenth century, and a century later, it began to be the feature of the countryside" (Tawney 1958: 58). "The enclosure movement signified the conversion of arable land to sheep run for producing woollen cloth for export" (Polanyi 2001: 36).

True, the wool produced on the sheep farm gave employment to small tenants and landless cottagers forced out of tillage and the new centres of the woollen industry secured an income to a large number of people whose economic fortune had been adversely affected by the enclosure movement. However, Polanyi calls enclosures "a revolution of the rich against the poor." As he puts it, "The lords and nobles were upsetting the social order, breaking down ancient law and custom, sometimes by means of violence, often by pressure and intimidation. They were literally robbing the poor of their share" (Ibid.). But most important of all, enclosures disrupted what Polanyi calls "embeddedness of economy," which expresses the idea that economy is not an autonomous, self-regulated system; it is, on the contrary, subordinate to politics, religion and social relations. The disruption of the embeddedness of the economy made it auto-telic.

The enclosure movement is, however, not an isolated example of the stirrings of the moneymaking motive. Undoubtedly, economic necessity was the driving force behind the endeavour to liberate economic activities from its thralldom to traditional moral standards. These moral standards were an integral part of the traditional conception of social order, which treated society as analogous to body, a derivation from medieval worldview in general. It projected a "conception of man as united to each other and of all mankind as united to God by mutual obligations arising from their relation to a common good..." (Tawney 1982: 18).

Society as an organism is viewed as comprising different members, each of whom has its own function and is endowed with means suited to its station. Given different functions and stations in society, all of them are united in the service of one common end, that is, salvation. The main thrust of this conception of the social order was to underline the fact that society is not an expression of economic self-interest; it is held together by a system of mutual though varying obligations. These varying obligations also signify graded social locations underlining equality within the classes and inequality among the classes. Despite differences of social location and functions, human activities form a hierarchy of functions, which differ in kind and in significance, but all of them have value on their own plane, provided they are governed, however remotely, by the end which is common to all (Tawney 1958: 26).

The commonly shared end was, as John of Salisbury puts it, "to know the truth about God and to live in communities." Earlier, Saint Thomas Aquinas had already declared that "the perfect happiness of man cannot be other than the vision of the divine essence" (St. Aquinas 2012: Div. I Q iii. Art iii). For Aquinas, all activities fall within a single system that embraces the whole of life. Such a system is supposed to be geared to serve a common end, that is, salvation. However, it is differentiated on the basis of status and role. Insofar as the economic doctrine enunciated in *Summa Theologica* is concerned, it rests on two fundamental assumptions: one, the pursuit of economic interest must be subordinated to the real business of life, that is, salvation and two, economic conduct is one aspect of personal conduct, upon which, as on other parts of it, the rules of morality are binding.

Aquinas admitted that material riches are absolutely necessary for man's well-being; however, they have only a secondary influence since their lack would mean deprivation, even starvation. Moreover, material riches can be used to help those in need and thus lessen their pain of destitution. Add to it also the fact that economic activity and other such activities form the outer aspect of man's existence, while his inner aspect is meant to acquire the vision of the essence of the divine, the transcendent entity. The outer is ordained for the sake of the inner; economic goods are instrumental to the pursuit of the higher goal of life, that is, salvation. "It is lawful to desire temporal blessings, not putting them in the first place, as though setting up our rest in them, but regarding them as aids to blessedness, inasmuch as they support our corporal life and serve as instruments of acts of virtue." Thus, for Aquinas, it is right for a man to seek such wealth as is sufficient for a livelihood commensurate to his station. However, to seek more than that constitutes avarice, therefore, a sin that must be condemned. Thus, trade is legitimate but a dangerous business; it must be carried out for public benefit and the profit that is earned must be treated as wage for the labour of the trader.

Thus, while economic activity was considered legitimate, the idea of getting more profit than what is proper was condemned as a deadly sin. Yet it was a compromise necessitated, as Tawney points out, by the growth of trade, of town life and of a commercial economy in a world whose social categories were those of the self-sufficing villages and the feudal hierarchy (1958: 34). This was a compromise between medieval worldview and the new burgeoning economy raising its head in rebellion but seeking legitimacy from those who were determined to preserve the status quo; it is symptomatic of the growing weakness of the traditional worldview.

The prevalent traditional worldview that prevailed unchanged from the twelfth to sixteenth centuries in England aimed at giving a spiritual tone to the material by incorporating it in a divine universe, which was expected to absorb and transform it. However, the religious teaching prescribing a moral standard that condemned moneymaking motive was out of tune with the prevalent reality. The traditional worldview did underline the organic unity of the social order, a unity that saw the complementarity of social divisions as a basis of realizing the common purpose entailed by the quest of salvation. However, its stress on solidarity was parallelled by the forces that gradually transformed social divisions into a system of reciprocal resistance graduating into opposition and open conflict.

The structures that gave birth to this unchristian behaviour were, however, considered not alien to religion because religion is all-comprehensive. They had some ethical meaning because they were, it was argued, the expressions of a higher design, some larger plan. It was expected that the power of religion would sublimate them so that they could serve the cause of salvation. It is not, therefore, surprising that the Church tolerated them and blessed them and, as a result, "privilege and power became office and duty." The Church condemned extortion of poor peasants and small traders who were charged interest on the money lent to them by the moneylender. However, it was helpless in checking the serried abuse of the medieval land system. Pressing economic needs forced small traders, businessmen and peasants to borrow money, but the Church did nothing more than condemning usury. The alternative that the borrower faced was, as G. G. Coulton, a medieval cynic, to point out: "He who takes it, goes to hell and he who does not, goes to the workhouse."

What is most hypocritical about it is the conduct of the Church itself. Undoubtedly, the teaching of the Church was violated by the people and violated grossly. But the Church itself violated its own teaching. As such, religion-supported moral standards lost their validity and usefulness. The Church was not only the most important financial institution at that time, it was also the great source of inequity. Right from the middle of the thirteenth century, a continuous wail arose against the inequity of the Church and its burden might be summed up in one word, "avarice." At Rome, everything was for sale (Tawney 1958: 32). The splendour of the Church led St. Bernard (circa 1125), as he gazed at the glory of Gothic architecture of the Church building in Paris, to exclaim:

> Thus wealth is drawn up by ropes of wealth, thus money bringeth money.... Vanity of vanities, yet no more vain than insane. The Church is resplendent in her walls, beggarly in her poor. She clothes her stones in gold and leaves her sons *naked*. (Ibid.)

Hypocrisy, so strongly condemned by St. Bernard, is what characterized the teachings of the Church. In addition, the fragmentation of the Catholic Church into several theological and ideological segments broke irreparably the unity of the Church teaching as well. If Martin Luther condemned money motive and usury, Calvin favoured them. The fragmentation of the Church dealt a death blow to the laboriously crafted conciliation between the inner and the outer dimensions of man's existence and gave a fillip to transition from status to contract as the basis of social organization. What accelerated the process of transition was not only "avarice," but also the pressure of economic need in a situation where opportunities of relieving them and for indulging in avarice were gradually expanding.

As Tawney reminds us, among the peasants and small masters, who composed the mass of the population in medieval England, borrowing and lending were common (Ibid.: 62–63). These classes were hit hard even by a slight change in their economic condition. Commercial establishments, even when small, were watched closely because they tended to create shortages for larger profits. The tendency to create shortages with a view to making money was quite rampant. What broke the back of resistance to new emergent forces of disintegration were not the leaking currents of moneymaking motive from Italy. They did weaken the resistance, to be sure; however, what swept away resistance were "Discoveries." With the climax of great "Discoveries," the flood came to breast high. It is not surprising that scattered, decentralized commercial establishments began to come together to form big joint-stock companies to exploit the riches of the countries outside Europe. No wonder, the reign of Queen Elizabeth I saw the burgeoning of such companies in the sixteenth century.

The big push, which released moneymaking motive from the traditional moral restraints, came from "Discovery." It afforded European powers the great opportunity of growing enormously rich in a short time at the expense of those peoples who still cherished their tradition, culture and simple ways of life. The phenomenon which dazzled the contemporaries was the swift start into apparent opulence, first of Portugal and then of Spain. The spirit of gain subsequently encouraged other powers too and the rat-race for establishing colonies and creating empires started to rob countries of other continents of their wealth, their culture, their simplicity and their identity. The great East India Company is just one example of this.

The competition for finding new colonies for the expanding economic energy unleashed by greed caused wars and tore Europe to pieces, each of these pieces clamoured for more colonies, more money and more spheres of influence. Writing in 1517, Erasmus likened the European state with the eagle:

> Of all birds the eagle alone has seemed to the wise men the type of royalty— not beautiful, not musical, not fit for food, but carnivorous, greedy, hateful to all, the curse of all, and, with its great power of doing harm surpassing them all in its desire of doing it. (Ibid.: 73)

And the greatest harm it did was to the cosmic vision of order on earth, the cosmion, as Voegelin calls it.

The expanding economic energy was very difficult to contain within the narrow confines of either medieval economy or traditional morality. It pushed men to achieve mastery over their environment. It is this determination to conquer the environment and transform/manipulate it that heralded the birth of a new age bristling with ideas of man-made order and of recreating the material conditions of man's preferred mode of existence. The fire of the expanding economic energy was stoked not by the industrial revolution but by commerce and finance. The expansion of commerce and finance offered opportunities of speculative gain on a scale unknown before. And individualistic competition swept the foundations of the old order away.

The new economic realities in England, as elsewhere in Europe, collided with the inherited traditional conception of order. There was, of course, resistance, opposition and reassertion of traditional doctrines of morality. However, as economic forces gathered strength, a gradual retreat from the old, entrenched position before the advance of new conceptions, both of economic organization and of the province of religion, led finally to the decline from a militant creed into a kind of antiquarianism. "They lingered venerable ghosts, on the lips of churchmen down to the Civil War. Then the storm blew, and they flickered away" (Ibid.: 116). And the growing complexity of economic life and relations coupled with the division within the Church ensured that religion had now to make large concessions to individualism if it wished to prosper. After the Civil War, a return to traditional mores and economic practices was impossible not only because of the lay opposition but also because of divisions within religion. Thus, private passions triumphed to provide a new conception of order as well as of secular state. And the prophet of the new ways of looking at and doing things is, of course, Thomas Hobbes, who gave voice in *Leviathan* to the new perspective on individual—society relationship and on the individual's responsibility for defining order and purpose for himself and for society as a whole.

IV

The two examples of transformation of order discussed above amply testify to the process through which one type of order is replaced by another. When accretions of slow and small doses of deviance of behaviour cumulate and become difficult to contain within the parameters of traditionally regnant worldview, it encourages new ways of looking at things. A process of redefinition begins and when changes become too deviant to sustain the habitual context of thinking and doing, the prevalent order is experienced as coercive. New thought-ways and work-ways then force the traditional perspective on life to recede and finally fade away. This happened in the case of both Athenian democracy and the seventeenth-century England. It is now happening in India when the sun of the British Empire set after initiating the process of change from cosmic to earthly order (see Roy 2006, Chapter 3).

Notes

1. As Jaeger notes, "What Homer's epics have in common with Greek philosophy is the fact that they both present the structure of reality in its entirety, though philosophy presents it in rational form where the epos shows it in mythical form" (1973: I, 429, fn. 34).
2. There was no conception of the soul in Homeric epics; the word "psyche" is mentioned but it does not refer to "a living body." This signifies that there was no idea of an animating principle that endowed body with form. In the absence of the soul, emotions, passions, etc., aced as energy or force (*thumos*.) (Voegelin 1986: II, 90).

3. Anaxagoras, for example, is accused of caring nothing for his kinsfolk and his country. He points to heaven and says, "There is my country" (Jaeger 1973: I, 151). See also Lindberg (2007, Chapter 2).
4. A story is told about Thales that while he was watching some celestial phenomenon, he fell down in a well and his Thracian house cleaner jeered at him for wanting to look at things in heaven when he could not see what was at his feet (Jaeger 1973: 153–54).
5. Voegelin 1986: II, 132. Voegelin refers here to Hesiod's *Theogony* where he deals with the cardinal problem of order. Hesiod's characterization of the present as degenerate is derived from his own experience inasmuch as he lost his lawsuit involving illegal acquisition of his property by his brother who has been claimed to have bribed the judges.
6. This is clearly articulated in the last stanza of his poem:

    > And little joy will accrue to the Polis
    > If a man through his efforts conquers at the bank of Pisa,
    > For that will not fatten the store-rooms of Polis.
    > —(Voegelin 1986: II, 184)

7. Sophocles too underlines the importance of *sophrosyne* in the fifth century. See Jaeger (1973: 277).
8. As Voegelin puts it:

    > The aftermath of the reform, the tyranny of Pisistratus (561–527) reminds us that the solemn effort was probably no more than a partial solution of the type of crisis which engulfed the whole polis world from Ionia to Sicily and manifested itself in the rise of tyrants, in the period from 650–500 BC. (1986: vol. III, 128)

References

Aquinas, Thomas. 2012. *The Summa Theologica of St. Thomas Aquinas*. Toronto: University of Toronto Libraries.

Cochrane, Charles Norris. 1957. *Christianity and Classical Culture: A Study of Thought and Action from Augustus to Augustine*. Oxford: Oxford University Press.

Collingwood, R. G. 1976. *The Idea of Nature*. London: Oxford University Press.

Collins, Stephen. 1989. *From Divine Cosmos to Sovereign State*. New York: Oxford University Press.

de Tocqueville. 1959. *Democracy in America*, 2 vols. New York: Vintage Books.

Eusebius, Bishop. 1975. *In Praise of Constantine: A Historical Study and a New Translation of Eusebius Tricennial Orations*. Trans. Harold Drake. Berkeley: University of California.

Ferguson, Francis.1953. *The Idea of the Theatre: A Study of Ten Plays, the Art of Drama in Changing Perspective*. Garden City, New York: Doubleay.

Hill, Christopher. 1978. *The World Turned Upside Down: Radical Ideas during English Revolution*. Harmondsworth: The Penguin Books.

Hobbes, Thomas. 1969. *Elements of Law: Natural and Politic,* 2nd edition. Ed. Ferdinand Tonnies with a new Introduction by. M. Goldsmith. London: Frank Cass.

Jaeger, Werner. 1973. *Paideia: The Ideals of Greek Culture*, Vol. 1. Trans. Gilbert Highet. New York: Oxford University Press.

Jonas, Hans. 1963. *The Gnostic Religion: The Message of the Alien God and the Beginning of Christianity.* Boston: The Beacon Press.

Kuhn, Thomas. 1970. *The Structure of Scientific Revolution.* Chicago: University of Chicago Press.

Lesher, J. H. (Ed.). 2001. *Xenophanes of Colophon: Fragments: A Text and Translation with a Commentary by J.H. Lesher,* Kindle Edition. Toronto, Buffalo, London: University of Toronto Press.

Lindberg, David C. 2007. *The Beginning of Western Science: The European Scientific Tradition in Philosophical, Religious, Institutional Context, Pre-history to AD 1450.* Chicago: University of Chicago Press.

Lovejoy, Arthur. 1960. *The Great Chain of Being.* New York: Harper and Row.

Pocock, J. G. A. 1971. "Languages and their Implications," in *Political Thought and History.* New York: Athenium.

Polanyi, Karl. 2001. *The Great Transformation: The Political and Economic Origin of Our Time.* Boston: Beacon Press.

Roy, Ramashray. 2006. *Democracy in India: forms and Substance.* New Delhi: Shipra.

Tawney, R. H. 1958. *Religion and the Rise of Capitalism.* New York: Mentor Books, Harcourt, Brace and Co.

———. 1982. *The Acquisitive Society.* Sussex: Wheatsheaf Books.

Thucydides. 2000. *The History of the Peloponnesian War.* London: Penguin Books.

Voegelin, E. 1986. *The World of Polis,* vol. II of *Order and History,* 5 vols. Baton Rouge: Louisiana University Press.

———. 1997. *Collected Works of Eric Voegelin.* Vol. 19, *History of Political Ideas, Vol. I: Hellenism, Rome, and Early Christianity.* Ed. Athanasios Moulakis. Columbia: University of Missouri Press.

2

Modernism and Democracy: Twin Props of the Autonomous Self

The shift in the basis of order from its mooring in a transcendental entity to that of human psychology permitted the emergence of detached subjectivity that made possible the prominence of the autonomous self. As an autonomous self, it needed certain props to buttress its autonomy. These props are, in the main, modernism and democracy. Both of these props are organically linked. How they came to be linked has an intellectual background. In order to make this background vivid, an intellectual journey is necessary. This journey must begin at a point in the world history when transforming the world of here and now into the Kingdom of Christ as a symbol of the celebration of the spiritual quest for salvation was underway.

Two important considerations impinge upon this exploration. First, modern democracy is substantively different form the Athenian democracy in two vital respects, despite the fact that it shares some common traits with it. In the first place, modern democracy marks a decisive shift from the organic conception of society to the idea of society as a mechanical aggregation of separate, autonomous individuals. The second difference involves a shift from direct democracy to representative democracy. These two differences acquired in time thick layers of new meanings that point to different empirical situations that we associate with modern democracy. It is in this context that Dahl notes: "What we understand by democracy is not what an Athenian in the time of Pericles would have understood. Greek, Roman, medieval and Renaissance notions intermingle with those of later centuries to produce a jumble of theory and practices that are often deeply inconsistent" (1991: 3).

Second, modern democracy owes much to the fateful changes that Christianity had to undergo since its inception in attaining its goal. The gradual abandonment of its eschatological fervour and several concessions to and compromises with the world led to the rise of intra-mundane forces that define modernism. This resulted not only in the differentiation of faith and reason and religion with politics, but also in the emergence of the autonomous individual as the arbiter of his social, economic and political destiny. Beginning with Pauline compromise with the world, the process of making concessions went through several stages. One of the most important stages was the alliance with the Roman Empire, which was guilty of causing the death of Jesus. It was, however, made the vehicle of spreading Christianity all over the world.

The Christian community did acquire two swords for not only defending the community from persecution and harassment, but also for uniting the whole of mankind, as Bishop Eusebius (ca 264–340) expected, in the bond of love and harmony. However, it also engendered the fear of being reduced to the status of a state religion as well as of dimming the eschatological zeal and fervour that kept the Christian community attuned to the world beyond this world. If Christianity retained its unique status, it failed in keeping the eschatological fire burning. Consequently, it had to incorporate the temporal power in general and the Roman Empire in particular, in divine economy. It signalled, at the same time, the gradual dissipation of apocalyptic fervour and excitement inasmuch as it meant the willingness to give ever more concessions to intra-mundane forces. This is confirmed by Pauline compromises.

The tension of the believers engendered by their mission of struggling for the new while entrapped in the old was heightened by another factor. They feared that if the Roman Empire was to fall, their spiritual pursuit would be endangered because the possibility of chaotic social conditions would make life hazardous if political state of nature prevailed. It was this fear, as Wolin argues, that inclined them to seek some *modus vivendi* of conciliation with the world of magistrates, tax collectors and law courts (1960: 98). This *modus vivendi* was the recognition of temporal power, as St. Paul did, not as an instrument of salvation, but as a divine instrument of not only creating and maintaining social conditions conducive to spiritual pursuit but also of preventing the political state of nature to return. The operation of these psychological factors made it easier for Christian leaders to embrace the Roman Empire without any qualm not only as an ally in the cause of Christianity but also as *restitutor orbis,* the restorer of a dying system.

The inclusion of the temporal power in the divine economy consolidated the foundation of the worldview that underlay the medieval civilization. Its organizing principle was the idea of *sacrum imperium*. It underlined the notion of order equipped with two swords—secular and temporal, the church and the state—dedicated to the realization of *regnum Christi* (the Kingdom of Christ). Its driving force was the conviction that these centres of authority could be held together within one overarching order which has its source in God. All other inferior orders must be capable of being harmonized within it. In this order, "the papal and imperial authorities occupy their position not because of their achievement in organising the whole but precisely because there is a whole that must be given expression through the recognition of their cooperative authority" (Walsh in Voegelin 1998: 7).

The main thrust of medieval civilization was the realization of *sacrum imperium* as a pure aspiration. The degree of its efficacy determined the unfolding of medieval civilization. However, it had to function in a situation where intra-mundane forces were not only recognized as unconditionally viable but also had become sufficiently strong to counter the spiritual movement quite forcefully. It is this contest between two forces opposed to each other that lent a particular quality to medieval civilization. This quality underlines the struggle that medieval civilization had to experience because of its effort to realize a single order of temporal and spiritual authorities and to adjust to the movements and forces that rendered that aspiration finally impossible to attain. The irony of medieval civilization is that the very effort to spiritualize the world ended finally in enfeebling spiritual orientation to such a degree that had to seek shelter in private spaces.

One of the most significant factors in the retreat of spiritual orientation was, of course, the gaining of independence of secular forces ironically by the efforts to renew spirituality itself. Once the claim of the world of here and now was recognized not only as valid but as desirable, the world no longer stood in need of perfection beyond itself. With the rise of secular forces, the eschatological impulse of spiritualizing the world found a new goal, the goal of remaking the world in a way that guaranteed material progress of mankind with the twin convictions of the participation of all—socially, economically and politically—in making the world safe for self-indulgence and the freedom of mature individuals.

It is this ethos of a new, secular order that took a definite shape after the collapse of medieval civilization. It is, again, this new ethos that forges the link between modernism and democracy. What follows is the exploration of the manner in which this came to be about. It presents a brief survey of the intellectual reconstruction of the process of interaction between the forces of integration and disintegration that paved the way for the fateful shift to the older to the new dispensation facilitating the birth of modernism and the introduction of a new political institutional form that we know as democracy. The emphasis here is on the intellectual apprehension of reality by men as they perceived the reality they confronted.

I

Christianity represented a community of believers that, at least in the early years of its history, had the apocalyptic expectations of establishing a heavenly city, the Kingdom of God, of virtuous souls on this earth. This was possible only when the believers wrought twofold transformations: transformation in their personality and then transformation of the world of here and now to make it reflect the values integral to the Kingdom of God. This double transformation depended upon the epochal consciousness that the old order must give way to the new. The appearance of Christ signalled the creation of a new world. "He taketh away the first that he may establish the second" (Acts 10:9). The establishment of the second realm was possible only through the nurturing element of faith. Once the epochal consciousness combined with faith, the change could be brought about by the renovation of personality through the alchemy of faith in Christ.

It is in this sense that Christianity constituted a revolutionary spiritual movement. It was, however, bedevilled by several difficulties in realizing its revolutionary objectives in a world which was, if not completely hostile, at least, inhospitable. Three such difficulties need to be mentioned here. The making of peace by the community of believers with the world and its subjection to the spiritual concern constituted the first difficulty. However, this objective was given up because the need to make compromises with the world became pressing. The process of reconciliation was, however, slow, but once it started, rise of intra-mundane forces could not be checked. It is true that some significant changes in the characteristics of the social world, such as the spreading urbanization, education and growing intellectual controversies, heavily impinged on the process. All these changes made for significant perceptual change in terms of how some of the key thinking people perceived the world. Thus, the role of the perception of the social world was crucial in bringing about social change, even if only slowly.

The process of reconciliation with the world of here and now was slow and painful. During the first two centuries, the apocalyptic fervour was high and the excitement of the coming of the promised Kingdom of Christ was at a fever pitch. Christianity professed a resolute indifference to the world, especially the political order. The rampant belief that the promised second coming of Christ was near at hand, made the Christians think of social and political affairs as quite irrelevant for the realization of their expectations of the heavenly city. Their alienation with the world was not only due to their continued persecution by the political order; it was reinforced by their apprehension of the imminent fall of the Roman Empire. This confirmed them in their conviction of the impermanence of the world (Luke 3:32–33).

Indifference to and alienation from the world, however, were not sufficient to allow them to completely withdraw from or to create the heavenly city in some isolated corner of this world. They had to live and work in this world. The community of believers, however, thought of itself as located outside of the political order. It also thought of itself as a body of "chosen generation, a peculiar people" (I Peter 2:9), the bearer of a special responsibility of cleansing this world. They regarded their community to be of far greater purity and higher purpose. It was, therefore, not surprising that there would be conflicts of values that would colour their attitude towards this world, especially the political order.

Attuned as the community of believers was to the need of social transformation, it was natural for them to think of themselves as journeying selves as indicated by Romans 12:2: "And be not conformed to this world, but be ye transformed by the renewing of your mind...." And it was the renewal of mind through faith and devotion that set them not only apart from but also opposed to the world, especially the political order. Tertulian's comment confirms this: "the fact that Christ rejected an earthly kingdom should be enough to convince you that all secular powers and dignities are not merely alien from, but hostile to a citizen of the city of Jerusalem that is above" (Wolin 1960: 99–100).

The feeling of alienation from and indifference to the world did, however, give way to its acceptance. They could have withdrawn from this world and lived an isolated existence and then, hope for the transformation of the world, participate in social relations and discharge myriad social responsibilities along with others not of their own kind. They had then to dismiss the idea of retirement or escape from the world and work for salvation of their own and of others while living in this world. The need not to leave the world could not have been ignored by them for long.

The fear of the return of nature did impel them to make compromises with the world. Undoubtedly, the greatest barrier to the return of nature was, of course, the Roman Empire. It was widely believed that the existence of the Roman Empire was all that stood between order and anarchy, since it maintained peace and helped civilization to flourish. Any danger to the continuance of the Roman Empire was, therefore, looked upon with apprehension not only of the breakdown of peace and order but also to man's existence itself.

This apprehension was reinforced by two very potent factors. Not only bitter rivalries among political factions of the late republic but also the danger of the annihilation of the Roman Empire by "barbarian" invasions lent pungency to the apprehension of anarchy. Thus, the continued existence of the Roman Empire was considered to be essential for civilization to survive and to permit art and culture to flourish. It was this apprehension that led Tertulian to pray for the continued power of Rome despite his antipathy and hostility towards the political order. "We pray for Emperors, their ministers, for the continuous existence of the world, for peace everywhere, and for delaying the end" (Ibid.: 103).

The phrase "delaying the end" is revealing since it illustrates a paradox that lay at the heart of the Christian attitude towards the world. If, on the one hand, there was the awareness that Christianity needed the protection of the political order for ensuring its survival and for the success of its mission, chiliasm, shared by Tertulian, too, encouraged Christians to believe that the end of the world was imminent and that the cataclysm preceding Christ's return was happening before their eyes in the form of the disintegration of the Roman Empire (Ibid.: 104). However, when the uncertainty about the second coming of Christ persisted, the apocalyptic fervour dimmed and the willingness to make peace with the world as it is gathered strength.

The fear of the end of civilized existence pushed Christians to reconcile themselves with the political order. This fear induced the universal recognition of the Roman Empire as the *restitutor orbis,* the restorer of the dying system, whose providential existence guaranteed the salvation of the tottering world. It is this recognition that forms the background of Pauline compromise with the political order.

> In exhorting Christians to render to Caesar the things that were due to him, Paul did not mean to imply that civic loyalties as a whole were separate from religious loyalties and that, consequently, the political order existed in tarnished isolation from the rest of God's creation. (Ibid.: 98)

For him, everything, whether in heaven or on earth, was created by God. As such, the political order, too, was a divine creation. It was, therefore, the duty of Christians to obey the command of the ruler: "The powers that be are ordained by God...whosoever, therefore resisteth the power resisteth the ordinance of God...wherefore ye must needs be subject, not only for wrath, but also for conscience sake" (Romans 13:1–5).

And yet their allegiance was still given primarily to their own community. The value discrepancy between the Christian vision of the world and the end that the political order pursued still affected the attitude of Christians towards the world of here and now. They were firm in their conviction that their society was superior to the political order since the basis of the former was love while the latter gave preference to power. The experience of the gulf between the law of love and the harshness and the compulsory character of the social and political world prompted Christians to treat the world as inferior. It is true that the Pauline prescription made it necessary for the Christians to obey the worldly authorities as they were ordained by God; however, he also enjoined them to obey God more than men. If Christianity consisted in the burning desire for deliverance from this world, then society and political order were not at all helpful in it.

The *summum bonum* of salvation that Christians celebrated produced tension between the picture of the world they had and the world as it was, and it persisted although in a subdued form. There was a greater appreciation of the relevance of society since it enabled them to pursue their quest of salvation without molestation or persecution. What helped in this was the shift from the idea of natural law to that of what Voegelin (1997a: 203) calls "relative natural law." This meant a shift from the Golden Age, that is, the age before the Fall of Man, to a civilized state caused by the viciousness and acquisitiveness of man. As such, society of the civilized state could never be helpful to the believer in realizing his ultimate goal, that is, salvation, since it was sunk in the mire of worldly concerns and considerations.

The shift from natural law to relative natural law helped the Christians to overcome their antipathy to the social world and accept it as a necessary condition for the quest of virtue. The change in perspective meant that they now came to view society as something that created and maintained social conditions conducive to their mission. Earlier, Seneca had argued that coercive institutions of the government are no doubt bad; however, they are necessary for supplying the remedy for the evils of human nature. The church fathers, too, taking cue from this, treated governmental authority as a divine instrument of punishing and repressing worldly evils. It is this shift from the natural law to relative natural law that constituted the source of Pauline thesis that political authority was divine creation. What this thesis did was to

> transpose the community of the perfect saints with Christ into an idea that took into account the practical problems of a community that did not at all consist of perfect saints.... It led to the momentous step from radical perfectionism to the compromise with the realities of the Christian community in its environment. (Voegelin 1997a: 169)

St. Augustine, too, was prepared to concede that society was natural to man even while it was racked by greed and bitter contestations. He maintained that far from being an unmitigated evil, it was "better than all other human good" and that even a society alienated from the true God possessed a degree of value.

Yet the tension continued to agitate the Christian community which oscillated between the extremes of eschatological expectations of the coming end of the world and its acceptance as inevitably the necessary condition of peaceful orderly life as a precondition of the spiritual quest. The easing of the tension was the second factor; it was made possible when the conversion of Constantine (ca 306–337) into Christianity led to the sanctification of the Roman Empire. This helped Christianity to acquire a secular arm capable of making it truly a universal religion. It was Bishop Eusebius (1975: ca 264–340) who expanded the Christian meaning by including the vision of converting the whole worlds to Christianity:

> The Roman Empire…in order to merge the entire race into one unity (*enosis*) and concord, has already most of the various peoples, and it is further destined to obtain all those not yet united right up to the very limits of the inhabited world (ecumene). (1975: 120)

With the conversion of Constantine,

> a new and fresh era of existence has begun to appear and a light heretofore unknown suddenly dawned from the midst of darkness of the human race and all must confess that these things were entirely the work of God, who raised up the pious emperor to withstand the multitude of the ungodly. (Ibid.)

With the "Christianization" of the Roman Empire, the former enemies became alliance partners working together for establishing the Kingdom of Christ. However, this alliance, supposed to lessen the distance between the Kingdom of God and the society of man, raised certain questions that filled the community of believers with unease. And answers to these questions were not easy to come by since upgrading the status of the temporal power from a hostile entity to a divine instrument for giving Christianity a universal spread meant the toning down of the apocalyptic fervour. It also put a question mark on the status of the church when the state was to undertake to advance faith and police the behaviour of the believers. Questions surrounding these two issues divided the community. As a result, conflicting responses to the emergent situation made it difficult for the community leaders to cope it effectively. Donatus' protestation, "What has the Emperor to do with the Church?" was responded to by Optatus with the reassurance that "the republic is not in the ecclesia but the ecclesia is in the republic." As the conflict defied solution, the answers to the range of questions were left for history to give. And the answers that history gave were not kind to the Christian spirituality.

With the alliance in place, it was necessary, once again, to assert the supremacy of spiritual values in a world badly afflicted with cupidity. This task was performed by Augustine (ca 354–430), who etched out in sharpest relief the religious identity of Christianity, its way of life and mission and its complex nature as an existential society as well as an intimation of a celestial society, its involvement in history and its aim of ultimate triumph over time (Wolin 1960: 121). While Augustine established the superiority and primacy of the spiritual quest of man, he had no hesitation in recognizing the claim of the *civitas terrena*.

> Christians will not refuse the discipline of the temporal life, in which they are schooled for life eternal; nor will they lament their experience of it, for the good things of the earth they will use as pilgrims who are not detained by them, and its ills either prove or improve them. (1924: I, 109)

For Augustine, then, the Christian is nothing more than a pilgrim, a journeying self, whose gaze is focused on the heavenly city above. "Incomparably more glorious than Rome is that heavenly city in which for victory you have truth; for dignity, holiness; for peace, felicity; for life eternity" (Ibid.: I, 109).

In raising the central issue of whether society served the end of eternal life or man would be satisfied with transient goods that existed in time, Augustine firmly asserted the pursuit of salvation as the primary and the most valued goal of the Christian. The question of the relevance of the social boiled down, for him, to its ability to create conditions conducive to the pursuit of eternal life and safeguard justice. For Augustine, then, the highest aspiration of political society was satisfied if it permitted those of its citizens enrolled in the *civitas dei* to pursue salvation unhindered by political distractions. The highest and, therefore, the most fundamental needs of man were those which no human society could ever hope to satisfy. However, if it could keep peace and maintain order so that the believer can pursue undisturbed the quest for eternal life, then society contains a measure of worth. This constituted the third factor.

The hope of the *saeculum senescens,* waiting for the end, that Augustine confidently affirmed was soon overtaken and left behind by certain worldly forces that gave fillip to *saeculum renascens.* One of the forces of considerable importance involved the migration of Germanic and Asiatic tribes and peoples and their interactions, especially after the fourth century AD. This determined the general framework of the medieval institutions and ideas.

Along with the rise of feudalism that defined the institutional format of societies in Europe, three other important factors contributed, to a great extent, especially after the eleventh century, to the formation of Western mind, character of the social world and the ideas that shaped history.

These three factors concern (a) the recovery of the Roman-Greek tradition of thinking and institutional principles, (b) the assimilation of Greek thought through Islamic transmissions and (c) the growth of cities and towns, in addition to Italian Renaissance. Add to these factors the disintegration of the empire into national political units by the twelfth century. All these factors combined to upset the smooth working out of the interaction between the Holy Roman Empire (*sacrum imperium*) the mystical body (*corpus mysicum*) of the church and the Kingdom of Christ (*regnum Christi*) the balancing force that constituted the prop that sustained the hope of realizing the idea of *sacrum imperium*.

II

We can add to this list also the collapse of the idea of the *sacrum imperium* signifying the transformation of Christian Church as a loose association of believers into a formidable power unit. This transformation holds the key to the understanding of the phenomenon of retreat of Christianity as a transformative spiritual movement to a religion comprising of a dogmatic belief system, a set of doctrines and certain rituals. This transformation was the outcome of the growing tension between two different but hard to reconcile aspects of the constitution of the Christian community, a community that is, at one and the same time, a divine and historically active substance. The sanctification of the Roman Empire did make for a radical change in the status of the temporal power. It also meant something more; the Roman Empire incarnated as a powerful instrument for the universal expansion of Christianity.

The sanctification of the Roman Empire reinforced the medieval conception of order and heavily underlined the need for cooperation between the spiritual authority, that is, the church, and the temporal power, that is, the political ruler. The Christian community now represented one unified order presided over by Jesus, the Priest–King, having two heads, the spiritual and the temporal. In this perspective, there is no question of rivalry and contention between them for status and power. However, Germanic invasions, beginning with the fifth century resulted in the movement of the papacy from Rome and the subsequent split of the church into two separate bodies. This weakened the church's position vis-à-vis the temporal power. As a result, the interference of the emperor in spiritual matters had reached a stage where it became necessary for the Pope to make the position clear about the relationship between the spiritual authority and temporal power. It was Pope Gelasius I (ca 492–496) who developed the principle of the separation of spiritual and temporal powers.

Making a distinction between *auctoritas sacrata pontificum* (the authority if the sacerdotal pontiff) and the *regalis potestas* (the royal power), Gelasius I argued that Christ knew about the frailty of human nature and had ordained the separation of power between the two authorities. As such, there exists between them a system of checks and balances that makes interdependence necessary for them. This means that Christian Emperors need the priest for eternal life, while the priests need the imperial ordinances for the temporal affairs. The Gelasian principle did provide a workable basis for the smooth relationship between the two authorities. However, historical developments soon overtook it and rendered it unworkable. Along with some far-going changes in the constitution of temporal powers, some factors internal to the Christian community also contributed to the growing tension and hostility between spiritual authority and temporal powers. In order to appreciate this, it is necessary to have a quick look on the slow but certain transformation of the church from a loose association of believers to a formidable spiritual organization imbued with a strong power drive.

What made this possible was the complete overhaul in the substantive aspect of the term "ecclesia" (church). The I Corinthian means by it the Christ's body composed of imperfect human beings hierarchically organized according to the gift of grace. The formation of the body of believers is said, according to Acts II, to have come about with the Descent of the Spirit on the assembled community on the Pentecost day. This community was bound together by the eschatological expectation of the early arrival of the Day of Judgement. According to the Epistle to the Hebrews, the community becomes real only when its members hear and obey the word of God through his son, Christ. By hearing and obeying the word, men become "the partakers of heavenly calling." Christ is, thus, the architect of the community that forms on the basis of hearing and obeying the word. He is the lawmaker in Justin Martyr's words. And the hearing and obeying of the word constitutes a transformative act; it is a process by which "man is integrated into the community substance;" it constitutes "a tasting of the heavenly gift and as a contact with the powers of the world to come" (Voegelin 1997a: 167).

The community, then, becomes a power field and the individual believer becomes an integral part of the community through faith. Thus the act of hearing and obeying is the same thing as what Plato calls "the beholding the pattern of heaven," a mystical process by which the divine substance overflows into the beholder and transforms the soul so that it becomes part of the earthly incarnation of the city that is laid in heaven (Ibid.: 167).

In this perspective, the locus of power is the entire community which forms into a loose association. The church is simply the symbol of this power and an executive organ of the community of believers. However, the church soon turned into the head of the community instead of remaining its instrument and turned into a powerful bureaucratic organization compelled to use political means for realizing religious ends. Broadly speaking, two factors were responsible for this. In the first place, Christians considered themselves a distinct group of far greater purity having a higher purpose, "a chosen generation, a royal priesthood, a holy nation, a peculiar people" (I Peter 2:9). As a distinct group, it did not consider secular power germane to the pursuit of its coveted goal of salvation. Moreover, when this group was harassed and persecuted by the rulers of the Roman Empire, hostility to political power became quite sharp. The sharpened sense of separateness is evident when Tertulian refers to the fact that Christ rejected earthly kingdom and that it should be enough to convince the Christians that all powers and dignities were not merely alien but also hostile to God (Wolin 1960: 101).

Even when the slow realization of the importance of society, in general and the temporal power, in particular, led to the moderation of the feeling of being an alien in an inhospitable world, Christians were not prepared to give up the idea of their community being superior to all other groups in society. It considered the political order as "a second best arrangement, inferior to the promised city...necessarily condemned to rely on coercion rather than love" (Ibid.: 106). Flowing from this perception was the Christian argument that, like the political rulers, Christians too rule, but their rule is based not on coercion but on love. Gregory Nazinzen (ca 329–389), the Bishop of Constantinople, was to observe: "We also rule" and this rule is "most excellent and more perfect, unless the spirit is to be subjected to the flesh and heavenly to the earthly" (Reilly 1945: 45). The rule of love, however, soon came to be eclipsed initially by tolerance but later by the acceptance of coercion as a necessary means to salvation. Tertulian, for example, underlined that "*Timor fundamentum salutis est*," meaning "fear is essential to salvation" (Wolin 1960: 118).

By the acceptance of coercion as a means of facilitating salvation, Tetulian perhaps meant the fear of God; however, it was taken to mean coercion by the church authorities. This acceptance was based on two grounds. One of these grounds was the question of dealing with the unrighteous who refuses to hearken to the call of the promised land. According to Romans 13: 3–4:

> For rulers are not a terror to good works, but to the evil. Wilt thou then not be afraid of the power? Do that which is good, and thou shalt have praise of the same; for he is the Minister of God to the good. But if thou do that which is evil, be afraid....

Writing in 185 AD, Iraneus referred to the fall of man; as a result, man became violent. To control violence, God sent government and law so that men might know fear and be receptive to obeying. This was the basis for accepting the life after death. However, coercion was soon accepted as a proper weapon in the armoury of the church for dealing with dissidence. The life of the early Christian communities was not fixed but oscillated between the eschatological expectation of the mystical power that would bring the Kingdom of God and the understanding of the church as the apocalypse of Christ in history. This meant the abandonment of the belief in the appearance of the Messiah at a particular time in favour of the one that posited the idea that the Messiah has already appeared and that a new realm too has been established.

The new eon and the second appearance of Christ would bring the Day of Judgement. This transmutation of the eschatological community into Christian community also meant that the second coming of Christ would take place in some remote future; meanwhile, the community must adjust itself to the exigencies of existence in this world. In this adjustment, the spirit as embodied in the church would guide and help the believers.

The receding of the eschatological expectation in favour of Christ's coming at some indefinite time had the effect of transforming the church from the instrument of the community of believers into its guardian. If St. Paul was responsible for the transition of the eschatological to apocalyptic community, St. Augustine put it to rest by roundly dismissing the literal belief in the millennium as "ridiculous fables." He went further and argued that "I would not believe in the Gospel if I were not moved by the authority of the Church" (Voegelin 1997a: 216). This amounted to not only establishing the authority of the church but also to making it the sole authoritative source of justification of faith in the life after death.

This tended to create apprehension that the church would gain control over the believer's earthly life and the life after death. That this apprehension was real can be gathered from the fact that by the end of the second century the church had "ceased to be a loose association of believers bound together by the ties of doctrine and the vague primacy of the early apostles, and had become instead an institutionalized order" (Wolin 1960: 106). The church had by then developed formal procedures of regular recruitment, formalized creed, hierarchy of authority, uniformity among scattered churches and had acquired properties that had to be managed.

In short, then, the church had gradually transmuted into an ecclesiastical polity in no way different from a political order in need for leadership, governance, discipline and settled procedures for conducting its business. With this transmutation, the power shifted from the community of believers to the church, which now came to be identified as *Corpus Christi*. If the Christian community underlined *power* in the ecclesia identified with miraculous working of the Holy Spirit dwelling in the congregation, it now came to be associated with unity and uniformity. And to safeguard unity and maintain uniformity, the church had to develop proper instruments to ensure that proper obedience was rendered to the authority; for this purpose, disciplinary instruments were properly handled to promote conformity.

The growing bureaucratization of the church invited the ire of Christian radicals who wanted "not a bureaucratic but a pneumatic society, a society of ascetic spirits, undifferentiated by rank or authorities, held together not by power, but by truth and forever trembling with an explosive intensity" (Ibid.: 111). However, aspirations of a pneumatic society progressively came to be shattered by the ever-growing hunger of the church for power and pelf. The drive towards power, however, continuously met a challenge from those who saw in it a certain departure from the original legacy.

In response to these challenges, the church functionaries pointed to the dilemma of an expanding community on whose behalf the church must continue making decisions in a situation where its size, complexity and variety made it necessary to ensure uniformity and fixity of practice. Opposed to this argument was the dissidents' contention that the true nature of the church could not be reconciled with a decision-making organization resting on a sharply defined concept of authority, instruments of power for enforcing discipline and uniformity and all other paraphernalia of a bureaucratic machine continually engaged in "juggling its many contradictions of love and power, truth and solidarity, transcendent goal and worldly involvement" (Ibid.: 109).

As the church introduced more routinized practices and developed settled ways of behaviour, fixing points of doctrines and evolving hierarchical system of offices, its dilemma in dealing with dissidence all the more deepened. Its response to this dilemma was ever-more doses of bureaucratization, which further provoked dissidence and made it explosive at times. This explosion took the form of schisms and was instrumental in creating fissures not easy to mend. As a result, the lines of fissures caused by atrophy and centrifuge began to appear very early in the Christian community, which, after St Aquinas, began to break it apart into several factions or sects; the Christian community began to decline both in terms of its living presence in the hearts of men and of its institutional consciousness. What explains this is "the elevation of the individual person as Christ bearing and created in the image and likeness of God and fulfilment—uniquely able to experience faith, hope and love and to enjoy the grace of God—threatened the institutionalized community from its very inception" (Hollweck and Sandoz in Voegelin 1997a: 32).

The appearance of fissures and their persistence over centuries is symptomatic of an inherent antagonism between the assumptions underlying an ordered structure with its developing sense of tradition and reliance upon routine, and the assumption of the imminent destruction of the world as it is as a prelude to the establishment of the Kingdom of Christ. If the proponents of the institutional view based their claim on the need for the performance of an institutional function and the acquisition of authority requisite for such a performance, the dissidents saw no reason to be involved with the world since its end was near at hand.

If Cyprian, an African Bishop, attributed heresies and schism to the failure to obey the priest of God, the temporal representative of Christ as priest and judge, Tertulian exhorted the believers not to obey the biblical injunction of increasing and multiplying since the last days of the last of the world were impending. The antagonistic perspectives did give rise to schism as exemplified by the Donatist and Monatist movements; however, the institutional view prevailed but heresies and schisms continued to agitate the community of believers. Most of them, however, were absorbed within the church framework.

III

One of the important consequences of the prevalence of the institutional view was the fateful shift of gravity from the community to the church. With it, the locus of *Corpus Christi* too shifted from the community to the church. The church now emerged the representative organization of the Christian community as well as its governmental authority. And as the church gradually acquired the attributes of an ecclesiastical polity, the eschatological fervour dimmed, but did not totally evaporate. As an ecclesiastical polity, the church had, however, to contend in its power drive with temporal power since both were driven by the aspiration of unchallenged political domination.

As a result, the relationship between them was marked by rancour and conflict where goodwill and cooperation should have prevailed. The Gelasian principle of the separation of powers did suggest a mode of behaviour adherence to which would have ensured cooperative relationship between spiritual authority and temporal power and would have helped realize the medieval ideal of *sacrum imperium*. However, changes in the factual order affecting both the spiritual authority and the temporal power rendered this ideal quite unattainable. The papacy had gradually grown into a huge dominant administration and had acquired the characteristics of a temporal principality. Similarly, the Holy Empire had assumed certain spiritual powers that constituted a deep incursion into the area of church authority.

These changes in the factual order went a long way to erode the basis of cooperative relationship between spiritual authority and temporal power. Moreover, the exigencies of the Carolingian foundation coupled with the migration had produced the atrophy of the spiritual centre. The Pope was, therefore, looking for an appropriate occasion for reasserting his dominance. The occasion was provided by what is known as the Investiture controversy. Its origin lay in the practice of simony signifying the exercise of temporal power over the lay investiture of statesmen-bishops, particularly by the purchase of ecclesiastical preferment regarding Episcopal promotions from feudal lords.

The controversy involved the purity of sacerdotal sacraments administered by simoniac bishops. Principally religious in nature, the controversy soon assumed a political hue. Under the canonical law, the papacy had control over the bishops and this control would not be exerted if the ecclesiastical appointments were due to lay influence. A reform, asserting church investiture was, therefore, necessary. This meant the curtailment of the power of the temporal authority which it was not at all prepared to tolerate. It was unwilling to surrender the power it had acquired because if the church getting weak.

The resolve of the church to regain its lost power found its expression through Pope Gregory VII (ca 1075–1085) who for the first time decided against lay investiture and provided excommunication for layman as punishment for violations. This, in effect, meant extending the control of the church over its own hierarchy. This step towards reform raised not only practical problems but also provoked opposition from the ruling monarchies. The practical problem concerned the fact that bishops had become heads of temporal administrative bodies.

As such, the assertion of papal control would have severely damaged the system of government by which medieval feudal society existed (Voegelin 1997b: 67–68). Politically, a compromise between the church and the temporal power was worked out; however, it proved to be short-lived.

The Investiture controversy was, however, instrumental in raising an intellectual debate revolving around some important issues impinging on the relationship between spiritual authority and temporal power.

One of these issues concerned the status of the sacrament administered by simoniac bishops. Another issue involved the question of who enjoyed primacy, the Pope or the prince. The question was whether the validity of the sacrament depended on the worthiness of the priest or not. If the answer to this question affirmed the objectivity of the sacrament, irrespective of the personal character of the priest, then, the stand taken by the princes was strengthened. If, on the other hand, the purity of the sacrament was seen to be violated by the personal character of the priest, then the case of the papal authority was strengthened. No matter which way the ruling opinion veered, one of the parties to the controversy was sure to lose influence and power.

It was Peter Damien (d. ca 1072) who set the tone of the debate. He argued that the spiritual life of the church emanated directly from Christ, the head of the mystical body. As such, the sacrament was immune to pollution, no matter who administered it. The charisma of the sacrament was always pure; however, unworthy might be the hand that administered it. What was essential in this regard was that the receiver must meet it in the appropriate state of spirit. Damien's observations laid the foundation for an elaborate theory of sacraments and their administration; they also led to certain reforms which formed the basis of reconciliation between the church and the prince. However, the practical problem of the effectiveness of the measures that the papacy had to take to make the reforms effective if the princes did not cooperate still persisted. Sanctions had, then, to be taken against the offending princes. It was this contingency that provoked the debate about who enjoyed primacy, the prince or the Pope?

Supporting the primacy of the spiritual authority, Cardinal Humbert (d. 1062) affirmed not only the precedence of the spiritual authority vis-à-vis the temporal power, but also eased, to a great extent, the eschatological tension by making the historico-political reality, with its material equipment, a firm part of the Christian order of things. In making these two cardinal points, Humbert identified the spiritually free simoniacally affected body of Christ as *corpus diaboli*. For him, the temporal authority, too, represented the Holy Spirit and if this authority encouraged the practice of simony, it gets corrupted and, in turn, corrupts the spiritually free body. Thus while Damien insisted on the objectivity of sacerdotal sacraments that remain pure irrespective of the worthiness of the person administering them, Humbert found the worthiness of the agency affecting the charisma of the sacraments.

Humbert pronounced simony not as an abuse, but as heresy since the defence of simoniac practices implied that the Holy Spirit could be compelled to enter the soul "at the beck of slavish and commercial hands" (Voegelin 1997b: 92). He underlined the fact that the mystical body of Christ would be spiritually free only when the members participate in free actuality in the spirit of Christ. As such, the practice of simony corrupts the temporal power and deprives it of the majesty of imperial function. Thus, what Humbert did was to transform the *civitas diabolic* into an element of evil which could be combated, if not overcome, by appropriate reforming action.

Humbert did not simply argue the need to ensure the purity of sacerdotal sacraments by assuring their administration by spiritually worthy persons. He also argued that temporal power can in no way enjoy precedence over the spiritual authority. In making his case, Humbert developed a theory of Christian political order that incorporated the whole structure of temporal history into the manifestation of the Holy Spirit. He does so by arguing that "sacerdotal dignity is inseparable from the administration of the church property." This signified that property is as sacred as the spiritual structure of the church and the former cannot be separated from the latter without harming it. And if property is an integral part of spiritual pursuit, it means that the worldly power cannot have precedence over the spiritual in investiture. Thus, the continued practice of simony would prevent the true order and function of the members of the mystical body.

IV

Aquinas, too, had admitted that material riches are absolutely necessary for man's well-being. However, he did not assign primary importance to them. Material riches along with other related things constituted, for Aquinas, only the outer aspect of man's existence, while his inner aspect was meant to acquire the vision of the essence of the divine, the transcendent entity. Material riches or property were, for Humbert, something more than the instrument; they became co-equal with spiritual quest. In his thinking, "the sphere of the material goods came to be integrated into the realm of the spirit; the realm of God was not the realm of persons only but comprised the physical dimension of the world also" (Voegelin 1997b: 94). This is testimony to the great weight that the world has gained since Roman-Christian's time. A thing which was condemned earlier was made quite respectable and desirable by Humbert's time.

By incorporating the realm of material goods into that of the spirit, Humbert signalled the emergence of a new attitude towards the world of politics which became quite visible in the *Tractatus Eborcences,* an anonymous series of tracts, better known as *York Tracts* written during the English investiture struggles. While Humbert sought to enhance the dignity of the sacerdotium, the Anonymous emphasized that of the *regnum.* The Anonymous advances a new paradigm of history which posits three different ages in the realm of God underlining the gradual advance towards the flowering of full reality. Three ages are distinguished on the basis of the degree to which the full participation of mankind in the realm of God is fully realized.

The first is the age of the Old Testament prefiguring the general priesthood and kingship of Christ, while the second age is of the New Testament with the true and general priesthood of the believers and the true priesthood and kingship of Christ. The third age stands for the true realm of God in which the believers reign as kings with Christ in his glory. In this paradigm of history, the king is superior to the priestly redeeming function because Christ as king is equal to God while the priest is his inferior. The king reflects the divine nature of Christ, while the priest only his human nature.

The *York Tracts* represents more than the mere defence of the jurisdiction of the temporal power against the encroachment of the ambitious Pope. Such a defence remains within the Gelasian framework of the separation of power between the spiritual authority and temporal power since it treats the function of the Church of Rome as an usurpation that arose, according to it, out of an emergency in early Christianity. Thus, the particular sacerdotium "shrivels away into an emergency measure and the *regnum* formed in the image of Christ the king remains the superior power over the Christian nation" (Ibid.: 99). And yet the *York Tract* does not completely do away with sacerdotium since in the third age every Christian becomes a participant in the mystical body and attains a priestly function ushering in a kind of spiritual democracy. It is this eventuality that makes the function of the Church of Rome an act of usurpation. However, when we come to John of Salisbury, he weaves his political theory around the man of the world. As he declares, "I am not speaking here of man whose hearts are wholly cleansed and who rejoice in continual subjection, declining to be set over any in this life, my task is rather to analyse the life of man in the political state" (1927: Book vii, Chapter 17). In characterizing such a man, John presages Hobbes when he notes that man, ignorant of his true status and the obedience he owes to God, "aspires to a kind of fictitious liberty, vainly imagining that he can live without fear and can do with impunity whatever pleases him" and "somehow be straightway like God" (Ibid.: Book viii, Chapter 17).

Driven by the impulse of pride, every man, John notes, has the inborn tendency of becoming a tyrant insofar as he is prone to use force with a view to ruling over others. Not only the king but also the man who occupies the meanest station is likely to become a tyrant "if not over the whole body of the people, still each man will lord it as far as his power extends" (Ibid.). Thus, every man who has not cleansed his heart is pushed by his ambition to subdue others. John traces the source of this character trait to the psychological state that signifies that "there is none who can help taking joy in liberty, or who does not desire the strength wherewith to preserve it…. For slavery is as it were the image of death and liberty is the assured certainty of life" (Book vii, Chapter 7). Thus, the political state that John talks about comprises ambitious men competing among themselves for establishing their hold on others and seeking not to lose hold of it. Thus, too, *amour dei* gives way to *amour sui;* this paves the way for the appearance of the political man simply as a pure intra-mundane figure.

True, John is not yet free of the older pattern that concedes priority to the spiritual over the temporal as testified by his organic analogy of the commonwealth. The commonwealth, as John sees it, is an organism, a body that is endowed by divine favour with life, the priesthood is its soul, the prince its head, the public officials correspond to other parts of the body, down to the peasantry who have their feet on the soil. However, the use of this analogy is quite different from the Christian one which treats the Christian mystical body as not the community but the community as the body of Christ. In contradistinction to this, in John's organic analogy, the community is seen as a body standing firm on this earth, as a unit of this earth.

Thus John's commonwealth is not in any sense the *sacrum imperium* of the Christian community; nor is it something like the modern commonwealth with its institutional body fully grown. With different organs of the government still missing, the community that John has in his mind is comprised of individuals. This is evidenced by his theory of tyrannicide which charges the individual to use his own judgement on governmental acts to take appropriate steps, even to the extreme of tyrannicide if the monarch is adjudged a tyrant.

John firmly located the commonwealth, the *regnum,* on the de-spiritualized *terra firma.* Unlike the Roman-Christian *sacrum imperium,* John's commonwealth is untroubled by the considerations of any supernatural agency interfering in the affairs of man. It is inhabited solely by proud, ambitious persons who are driven by *libido dominandi* to establish their sway over others. They are absolute in the sense that each of them is the sole judge of the worthiness of the ruler and can go to the extent of tyrannicide if the ruler turns out to be unjust in his/her view. The irrupting of intra-mundane forces that is characteristic of John's theory reappears in greater strength in the Constitutions of Melfi of the emperor Frederick II (ca 1211–1250). In the Prooemium of the constitutions of Melfi (ca 1231), he made a complete break from the tradition grounded in the idea of *sacrum imperium* by providing a legal basis to the governmental order in the state. Making use of the Christian symbolism of the Fall of Man, the Prooemium referred to the transgression of God's law which still continues since man inherited the attribute that caused the Fall. As a result, men fell out among themselves and the God provided rulers to preserve order in human society.

By linking the formation of the governmental order to the act of punishment for man's transgression of God's law, the moral dimension of the myth of the Fall of Man has been completely overshadowed by a legal construction. This is symptomatic of a total disregard of the spiritual dimension of man's existence. Its place has been taken over by a perspective that celebrates intra-mundane forces as the determinant of human existence.

This view of the function of the government is rooted in a perspective that envisages the positive order of the world as the evil order that became inevitable after the fall. And the ordering function of the ruler arises out of the *necessitas rerum,* the necessity of the world: quarrelsome men need the ruler and the ruler's actions restore the meaning of creation. Thus, the Prooemium "advances a naturalistic theory of government, deriving the function of the ruler from the structure of intra-mundane human reality" (Voegelin 1997b: 153).

When the role of the sacred in structuring social reality and guiding human action has been ruled out, the question of what takes its place raises its head. This question was undertaken by Siger de Brabant (ca 1255–1286) who, in answer, raises intellect, *uno in numero,* to the highest position and claims for it the role of guiding humanity through the exigencies of existence. He does acknowledge that in the case of conflict between the truth of faith and the result of philosophical cogitation, the former must prevail. However, in the last analysis, he puts his faith in the authority of reason in challenging the established and elaborate spiritual system. As he puts it:

> This, we say, is the opinion of the philosopher concerning the union of the intellective soul with the body, but if the opinion of the Catholic faith is contrary to the opinion of the Philosopher we wish to prefer it in this instance as in others. (Ibid.: 189)

The ascendance of reason is confirmed in the case of Siger by his denial of the soul as well as the *summum bonum* other than the felicity that can be reached within the range of earthly existence. These and other denials on the part of Siger confirm the status of the world as an immanent structure without relation to a transcendental reality in the Christian sense. Its place is taken by intellect as an earthly expression of the active intellect as an emanation from God arousing to activity the passive intellect. Intellect so aroused constitutes an intra-mundane force that seeks, as an absolute, to determine the standards of human existence. Given the central role of intellect, society must be hierarchically organized since participation in intellect varies from person to person.

In this hierarchy, the intellectual stands at the top by virtue of the highest degree of his participation in intellect. As such, the intellectual is endowed with a scale of values which allows him to intervene in social affairs and promote only those activities that promise to advance or safeguard collective well-being. Thus, the intellect, in Siger's eyes, enjoys objective validity and the right to distinguish between social good and social evil without regard to the values of historical growth. Siger, thus, paved the ground for the Christian meaning of life and order of society to be completely overshadowed. By the same token, the idea of *corpus mysticum*, that is, mankind as the mystical body of Christ, is replaced by the idea of human species as a collective unit existing through the process of generation from eternity.

It became very clear that secular forces had gathered formidable strength. St. Thomas Aquinas sought to arrest this trend and if possible, reverse it by emphasizing the primacy of the spiritual dimension of man's existence. Towards this, he aimed at harmonizing reason with faith. However, his attempt proved fruitless and the gap that had already appeared between reason and faith could not be filled. Two factors intervened to render this attempt barren. In the first place, the idea of *sacrum imperium* was inextricably linked with one empire. However, by the end of the thirteenth century, the Holy Empire had splintered into a multitude of national political units, each of them claiming to be a charismatic, if not spiritual power in the *corpus mysticum*. Each of them had their own national goals, was endowed with distinct socio-cultural and economic features and was animated by power drive to emerge as the foremost. In the second place, this was parallelled by the transformation of the papal spiritual power within the imperial order into the ecclesiastical organization as a distinct power unit side by side with the secular political units. Consequently, the spiritual power of the ecclesia withdrew from the community of believers and centred in the church organization ranking over a multitude of political units. And in the hands of lawyer-popes, the formulation of the spiritual order shifted from spiritual order to legal jurisdictional claims.

With these two parallel transformations, the possibility of conflict between the spiritual authority and temporal power escalated. If the secular political units were interested in unfettered sovereignty and non-interference in the management of their affairs, the church was pushing for more influence over diverse political units with a view to extracting more revenues and taxes for meeting the lavish expenditure of maintaining a large organization in style. Thus, "the physical maintenance of the church's power organization on a lavish scale and the perpetration of its political aims necessitated an international tax system and financial administration that clashed with the interests of the growing and closing national political units" (Voegelin 1998: 41).

What triggered an active conflict between the church and the national political units was the continued struggle between England and France that harmed the financial interest of the curia. This forced Pope Boniface VIII to issue an injunction in the form of the bull *clericis laicos* in 1296 to the clergy of France and England to pay no taxes to the government. This evoked strong reaction from the governments of both the countries and this created a crisis. The crisis was resolved through a series of compromises, each of which made the temporal power still stronger. However, a new clash was occasioned by the controversy about episcopal appointments. This led to the issuance of the famous bull, *Unam Sanctam,* in 1302 which asserted the supremacy of the papal power over that of the national political unit.

Unam Sanctam was a forceful bid by the Pope to regain the power he had lost to political rulers. The conflict that ensued was, in effect, concerned more with the conflict of power than the assertion of spiritual authority. It represented the use of spiritual authority for buttressing political power. The papal supremacy was justified by arguing that "every human culture is under the Roman pontiff we declare, say and define, and pronounce it necessary for salvation" (Ibid.: 43). This signified that it was the papal spiritual power that held both of the swords, the temporal and the spiritual. While it wielded the spiritual sword itself, it entrusted the temporal sword to be used for it by the princes at the will and tolerance of the spiritual authority. What is clear, then, is that the bull, *Unam Sanctam,* put aside the Gelasian principle of the separation of power and pushed for absolute power rationalizing in the process "the older Christian evocation in the direction of a hierarchical system with an absolute power at the top of the pyramid" (Ibid.: 46). The attempt, however, failed. This signalled the disintegration of the spiritual power. As a result, the several temporal political units emerged as secular powers acquiring a new spiritual status defined by nationalism.

Marsilius of Padua is the intellectual father of such a secular state by enunciating in his *Defensor Pacis* (1951–59, 1995) the idea of a supreme secular state organism. He was interested mainly in the establishment of peace and tranquillity in the world. This he thought to be difficult to achieve unless the disturbing papal spiritual power was subordinated to the monarchical secular power as the ultimate guarantor of political and legal order. In answering the question of how the secular political power is to be constituted, Marsilius refers to the only available option of the monarch as the representative authority. His authority is not derived from divine ordination but is supposed to be rooted in the commonwealth itself. But, then, where should the authority to choose the ruler be located? If the commonwealth is organic and the king is its head, the ruler as the member of that body is not apart from other members of the functioning unit whom he has to regulate. Marsilius, therefore, locates this authority in what he calls "legislator" (I.12.3).

This legislator is not the legislator of today because he is chosen under a constitution that is already in existence; he is the intra-mundane agent authorizing the constitutional order under which the ruler executes his functions, including rule-making. He defines legislator and his functions as follows:

> [T]he *populous or civium universitas* or its socially relevant parts (*pars valentio*) is the legislator or prißme and proper effective cause of the law, through its choice or will expressed in articulate terms (*per sermonem*) in general assembly of the citizens commanding or determining that something be done or not done concerning civil actions of men, by temporal punishments or penalty. (Ibid.: 89)

By positing the idea of a supreme secular state organism, Marsilius is only reflecting the essential changes that have overtaken the Western world. By the end of the thirteenth century, the tension between the papal and the imperial powers had translated into that between the former and a plurality of national secular political powers. These powers had overtaken the papal spiritual power and reversal to *status quo ante* was not possible. The growing strength of secular forces is amply reflected in *Defensor Pacis* which shows no trace of the idea of spiritually free mature Christians forming the substance of the polity. It is this fact that caused the eclipse of faith that became the dominant characteristic of the Christian community. Some thinkers thought of protecting Christianity against the virus of rationalism. William of Ockham in the fourteenth century undertook this task.

The principal danger to the preservation of faith, as William saw it, came from science which had by then come to be firmly established and could not be uprooted. As such, he felt that there was the need for developing an ontological perspective that would be capable of protecting faith from the danger of erosion without precluding a critical and free exploration of reality. This ontological perspective he found in nominal-ism, which reduces nature to something that constitutes only the outer, the external aspect of reality that can be explored and analysed by organizing empirical materials by means of the conceptual instruments of the human mind. For William, the order of the world is the creation of God; however, it owes its structure not to the divine substance, but to an act of the divine will. It can, therefore, be changed at God's will. "The order of nature does not have a structure of real universals; we cannot know any substance in itself but can know it only by its accidentals" (Voegelin 1998: 106). Since the order of nature happens to be the subject of causality, it is knowable, while reality as determined by God's *potestas absoluta* remains unknowable through the instrumentality of empirical science. As such, "the object of knowledge is not the real object, but the object as it appears and is thought" (Ibid.: 107).

William, thus, confines the scope of science to that aspect of reality as it appears to and is thought of by us. This confinement of science to the accidentals is aimed at saving faith from the encroachments of reason. In the realm of revealed faith, which is determined by God's *potestas absoluta*, science cannot have any entry. It is a realm that defies attempts at rational theology; it is a miracle of God and cannot be penetrated by natural reason. The miracle of faith is wrought by God who infuses faith in man compelling the sacrifice of intellect. William thus seeks to screen faith from the corroding encroachment of science. However, in rescuing faith from the danger of scientific enquiry, William reduces faith to mere possibility. If God did not work the miracle, there would perhaps be no faith. This is so for the reason that faith constitutes a sentiment that has its dimensions of certainty and wavering, of hardening and opening and of courage and faltering. Perseverance in faith needs the leavening of the certainty of the transcendental reality through the manifestations of miracles. With miracles of God ceasing to occur, faith falters and finally expires before the progressively accruing "miracles" of science.

Thus, William's "ominous efforts to save faith, out of the wreckage that faith itself had not the strength to save, the very symptoms of the destruction that he tries to counteract" (Ibid.: 109). What, then, William does is to present a critique of reason for establishing a dogmatic intellectual mysticism incompatible with historical Christianity. His theoretical perspective is symptomatic of the momentous situation that the Christian penetration of the world has finally come to an end. As a consequence, an intra-mundane civilizing process subsumed under the age of secular man has begun who chose democracy as the institutional expression of his earthly aspirations.

V

With the failure of the attempt to save Christianity from the encircling army of rationalism, or Gnosticism, as Voegelin calls it, Christianity ceased to be a universal spiritual movement and was reduced to a creed, to merely a dogmatic belief system. With it also came the final curtain on the worldly existence of imperial Christianity signalling the end of the efforts to integrate the life of man into the life of the *corpus mysticum*. Consequently, the burgeoning intra-mundane forces became instrumental in creating a gap between the secular world of the Western civilization and the ethos of Christianity. This gap became ever wider as time passed. The persistent gap between the two streams, the secular and the sacerdotal, was sought to be bridged over. One of those who tried to do that was Giles of Rome in the thirteenth century.

Responding to the problem of maintaining unity in Christianity, mankind split up into national political units, seeking to solve the problem by an absolutist construction of the power hierarchy under the pope. In doing so, he established the superiority of the spiritual over the temporal power (see Carlyle and Carlyle 1950: 403). Giles was not alone in this. William too, took recourse to such an approach. The difference between them lies in the fact that while Giles advocates spiritual authoritarianism of the pope, William goes beyond "the human sphere into the transcendental;

he develops the idea of an absolute authoritarian God who posits the content of faith at his will" (Voegelin 1998: 111).

Both of these attempts failed because they were incompatible with the temper of the age. Decidedly, distaste had developed for the idea of obeying the command of the papal spiritual power. Consequently, the tension between independent intellect and faith became instrumental in fundamentally changing the relationship between the sacerdotal and temporal spheres. From this point on, temporal affairs became increasingly identified with secularism and laicism. If the former paved the way for the rise of modernism as the consequence the disintegration of Christianity as evidenced by the Reformation, laicism gave birth to modern democracy. In a very important sense, democracy is nothing else than the de-spiritualized version of one of the tendencies that appeared in Christianity right at its inception. This tendency is to treat every believer as fundamentally a priest who does not need nor can tolerate any institutional intervention in the pursuit of salvation. The tension between the individual and the institutions of the state or the church is reflected clearly in the early history of Christianity as an apolitical movement. The Christian idea of the person in the immediacy of God has also proved to be a permanent irritant against institutions of any kind. The loss of vital élan helped this tension to transmute into the resurgence of the growth of radical individualism and egalitarianism.

The reflection of this transmutation, that is, the idea of the person as cast in the image of God and therefore, autonomous, can be seen clearly in *York Tracts*. In it there is not only the recognition of the immanent structure of the world and the evolution of the historical world as divinely. There is also to be found the articulation of a new function of Augustine's *lex eterna* as the general ordering principle of the world in the full dimension its immanent structure. The *Tracts* presents a new paradigm of history consisting of three ages the last of which represents for it the true realm of God in which believers reign as kings with Christ in glory. It is a clear recognition of the individual person as autonomous and Godlike, who does not, cannot bear any control over himself from any external source save Christ, the priest–king. However, when Christianity lost its hold over people's mind and Christ was pushed to the brink of forgetfulness, the individual person emerged as the de-spiritualized king and reserved for himself the glory of Christ, as the Earl of Rochester was to pen in the seventeenth century:

> Then farewell sacred majesty,
> Lets put all brutish tyrants down;
> When men are born and still live free,
> Here every head doth wear a crown.

(Hill, 1978: 413)

And it is quite uncalled for to expect the "head that wears the crown" to bow his head to anybody else when the transcendent authority has been thrown into the limbo of the private world of the individual. He can tolerate the will of others only when it has been erected on the basis of his own consent freely given. The rise of the autonomous individual is symptomatic of an unequivocal transformation of the yesteryear's subjects into today's citizens. This brought about a decisive transference of the source of political authority from the prince to the community as Marsilius of Padua forcefully affirmed. This affirmation is consequent upon his articulation of the secular state in which faith is compelled to migrate into the private, inner world. This signalled the dawning of a new age, the age of the spirit that Joachim of Fiora (Flora) talks about (for details, see Voegelin 1997b: 133–34). What this signifies is not a return to the spiritual as denoted by *sacrum imperium,* but a projection of "a vision of an era of autonomous spiritual freedom denoted by *sacrum imperium* beyond all institutional support or control" (Walsh in Voegelin, 1998: 14). It is the enjoyment of autonomous spiritual freedom that promises to ensure perfection of man. What can be seen in these developments is the appearance on the political scene of the self-governing individual strictly in the political sense. The demand of such individuals for a political order that answers to their claim of "kingship" is the basis of modern democracy.

Democracy in modern times displays two important characteristics which form its integral part. These characteristics are constitutional government and representation. Confusion is likely to arise because we tend to think that it is the constitution that authorizes not only the institutional arrangement of democracy but also is the prime source of the procedures that govern its functioning. However, before the constitution takes its birth, there must exist a prior symbol, the symbol of the people. Without a people, no constitution is possible. As such, the constitution is the product of the articulation and expression of the will of the people, whether expressed directly or through some mechanism that constitutes an operational device that helps in the realization of the ends the political community sets for itself. Thus, prior existence of the political community is essential basically for two vital purposes: the creation of an internal structure for articulating the ends for which a society forms itself into a political community, and the fashioning of an operational mechanism for realizing these ends and the determination of the manner of their realization.

Thus, the meaning and significance of the act of representation cannot be clearly apprehended without relating it to the acts of the formation of the political community that can engage in action in history, of creating an internal structure that would enable some of its members—the ruler, the prince, etc.—"to find habitual obedience for their acts of command, the acts that must serve the existential necessities of the society." In addition, the political community must determine, especially in the case of the democratic government, the basis of articulating this command and the creation of the necessary power to be exercised by the ruler(s) to see that commands are obeyed (Voegelin, 1987: 37). The articulation of a political community, the representation of various social groups and the functioning of a democratic government—all of them are intimately related. However, representation is more than an operational device through which large groups are enabled to participate in the democratic process. The idea of popular representation forms part of the modern evocation of constitutional government; it is not to be found in the incipient national kingdoms of the High Middle Ages, although representation as a device originated then.

It is interesting to note that the idea of representation did not arise as a response to popular demand as the case of England demonstrates. During a long historical period, it was the king who performed the representative function. Not only the realm of the king but also the prelates, the magnets and cities were the king's. Also, the people owed allegiance to serve him. The ordinary individual members of the society were plainly "inhabitants" or fellow citizens of the realm without, of course, any voice in the governance of the king's realm. The change over from "the people for the king" to "the king for the people" occurred over a considerable period of time. The decisive beginning of the changing articulation of

English society is said to be the Magna Carta (ca 1215) because, it is argued, it reflected the people's demand for certain liberties. However, as Voegelin points out:

> [T]he idea of the people as the substance of the political unit is a late product in Western history and was, in the English case, not politically active before the seventeenth century, the same holds true *a fortiori* for the representation of the people. (1998: 135)

The Magna Carta did not in any profound sense mark the beginning of the English constitutional government. It was principally to restore certain liberties that Henry I had granted to the people in his coronation oath along with the use of earlier grants (Stubbs 1895: 100). Moreover, it was to emphasize the need to develop economic resources of the realm, in particular, and foreign and domestic commerce and the towns in which they were centred. In effect, then, the principal object of the Magna Carta was the desire on the part of the parties to the struggle, provoked by the demand for scutage (the sum of money to be paid to the crown by the feudal lords in lieu of military service), to avoid the ultimate destruction of the realm already ripped with conflicts (Holt 1965). One immediate consequence of the Magna Carta was that Henry VIII imposed the obligation on wider strata of society to participate in the process of government.

The initiative for participation came from the top. Thus, liberties granted by kings were initially not rooted in the people's rights but a dispensation from the king "through the respect of God and love for the people." To take an example, Edward issued in 1295 writs of summons for Parliament enjoining the Sheriff:

> to have elected without delay two knights from the counties, two citizens from each city and two burghers from each borough and to have them sent to Westminster at the appointed time; the men would have to be chosen from the more discreet and fit for this kind of work (*de descretioribus et ad laborandom potentoriobus*), the delegates must be equipped with sufficient power to act for themselves and their communities so that no delay of business will issue from lack of powers. (Ibid.: 148)

The proviso mentioned in the last part of the writ is suggestive of at least three important reasons. In the first place, the delegates were to act for their communities. This means that these communities must have reached a level of political consciousness to feel as one united whole prepared to act. In the second place, there must have been some method of selecting these delegates that would satisfy not only the official procedure but also be acceptable to the community. And last, the delegates elected must have enjoyed enough power and prestige so that their act would be treated as the act of the community, that is, their decision would be felt to be binding by the community. Whatever method might have been used to select the delegates, the fact remains that the people as an ultimate community of individuals were yet to emerge. They were an aggregation of individuals who were articulated in the communes and in the realm as a whole. Thus, as Voegelin observes, "the thirteenth century development in England does not lie in the grants of liberties. It lies in the law by which the community is governed imposition of obligation, on ever wider area of strata of English society, to participate in the process of government" (Ibid.: 137).

The obligation of different strata of the society to participate in the process of government testifies to the fact that it was the king who was the sole representative of the realm. The transformation of this situation into the one in which every citizen came to wear the crown raises the question of the process through it became possible. The distinction between *dominium regale* and *dominium political et regale* that John Fortescue made in the sixteenth century assumes importance in this connection. While the former refers to a regime in which the law by which the community is governed emanates from the will of the ruler, the latter signifies a system of government in which there is a partnership between the ruled and the ruler (Fortescue 1885, Chapter II). Thus, the process of the transformation of *dominium regale* into *dominion politicum et regale* holds the key to the transition from monarchy to democracy. This transition is made possible by what Fortescue calls the process of "proruption." Using an organic analogy, he compares the constituted body politic with that of the growth of the articulate body out of the embryo. The people erupt into a realm (*ex populo erumptit regnum*).

The body politic constituted through the process of proruption is an organic whole with the ruler as its head and the people as different limbs of the body politic. Such a political order is, according to Fortesue, a mystical body (Wolin 1960: 133). The term "people" does not signify an external multitude of human beings, but the mystical substance erupting

in articulation. The immanent *logos* of such a political body are identified by Fortesue as *intencio populi*. It constitutes the animating centre
and is like the heart from which "its nourishing blood stream (supplies)
the political provision for the well-being of the people" (Voegelin 2000:
122). Through the use of the organic analogy, Fortescue implies that the
animating centre of a social body is not to be found in any of its human
members. The *intencio populi* is located neither in the royal representative
nor in the people as a multitude of subjects but is the intangible living
centre of the realm as a whole. The orientation of governance changes
radically, once the process of proruption has constituted a body politic.
Following St. Aquinas, Fortescue puts emphasis on the fact that "the king
is given for the realm, and not the realm for the king."

This change of emphasis signals the transformation of the subject
into a supposedly politically active citizen. This became possible in
England not through embracing the democratic ethos by different
strata of society, but by creating democratic ethos among them through
the imposition of the obligation of participation in government by the
crown. This made representation an essential part of the political system.
This proved instrumental in promoting articulation of different social
strata. As indicated earlier, this process occurred over a considerable
period of time. "The first and fundamental step towards the formation
of English political society was effected through the transformation of
the baronage from a group of individual tenants-in-chief, temporal as
well as spiritual, all holding from the same lord into a commune capable
of collective action" (Voegelin 1998: 137). The symptoms of collective
action became visible first in the struggle that yielded the Magna Carta.
This pattern was followed by other sections of the society when the
representatives of the shires and boroughs began to participate in the
assembly of the realm. This participation provided them the opportunity
to deliberate as groups when summoned. The process travelled lower
down from the nobility and higher clergy to the lowest strata that were
socially relevant at the time.

The factors that spurred the crown to seek the participation of different strata of English society in the governmental process were perhaps
numerous. However, the chief among these factors was financial. The
conduct of wars and the management of royal estates and affairs forced
the crown to seek the participation of those strata of society on whom the

extraordinary tax burden would fall more heavily. First, it was the landed gentry and then the knights and merchants who had risen on the scale of affluence because of the economic development that reached a higher level by the thirteenth century. As compared to the feudal lords, these new entrants to affluence had become very visible for tax purposes and consequently, came to be the major source of revenue.

This visibility must have been accompanied by a sufficient amount of consciousness on the part of the taxable social sections of their own importance to make their consultation advisable. Once these propitious conditions combined to incline the king to seek the participation of an ever-widening circle of social strata, the ground for articulation of these strata was paved and representatives from these strata, then, were selected for participation in the governmental process. The imposition of the obligation to participate in the governmental process produced the experience of affairs, the habit of communal action and the feelings of individuals that they were members of estate—all these combined to prepare the English society with the ability for effectively transiting from a monarchical polity to a democratic political order.

But before this could happen, it lacked one very important ingredient for the integration of different articulated communes into a national whole. In the initial stages of articulation, delegates from different communes used to deliberate separately as separate and distinct groups. The knights of the shires as well as the burghers and proctors of the parochial clergy, when summoned, deliberated as groups as did the barons. This centrifugal tendency persisted for some time—in the lower clergy till seventeenth century—before their amalgamation into national groups took place. The separate deliberations by different communes might have led to the evolution of separate houses with equal rights of consent to grants and statutes. However, this eventuality was avoided through the coalescence of two upper and two lower estates into the Lords and the Commons.

It is, thus, clear that the simple act of representation does not amount to the formation of a democratic polity since representation may also be a significant feature of non-democratic political systems. The problem in this respect does not lie in "the sending of delegates, which seems to be a matter of course once the political substance is formed and articulate, but rather in the formation and articulation of the community substance itself" (Ibid.: 152). The crux of the matter lies in the problem of the growth of community among separate individuals who not only claim but also insist upon exercising their autonomy in satisfying their material needs as well as in facilitating development of their nature through interaction with the external world, both society and nature. To argue that without the presence of some coherent force that enables the individual to look at the social environment from the same vantage point as a precondition of the articulation of a community is to offer only a partial explanation. Similarly to argue, as Voegelin does, that "what is new and indeed revolutionary, is the growth of the community that requires for its articulation elected representatives" (Ibid.: 152), is also not justified. What it suggests is the prior articulation of a community which, then, needs representatives for participation in the governmental process. It can also be argued that the grant of representation to a particular community may prove instrumental in its articulation. This is supported by many societies that gained independence only after the Second World War. With the advent of democracy in these countries representation was granted to various communities which, then, grew as fully articulate communes.

VI

The system of politics integral to Christianity, in general and that of St. Augustine, in particular, conceived the sphere of power and law as a realm that is intimately related with the spiritual sphere, though its foundations are natural. With the spiritual connection cut asunder by the rise of modernism, the state today does not signify anything more than a sphere of organization of power and law that is ideologically independent of the spiritual determination. Consequently, organically interpenetrating phenomena of modernism, as a perspectival dimension of human existence and democracy, as a political dimension of social and political life, have emerged as the defining feature of our times. With it, St. Paul's affirmation of the community as a unit in spirit lost its *raison d'etre* insofar as the uniting bond of the spirit was seriously frayed and was finally snapped.

With the snapping of the divine connection, the community that constituted the basis of commonality was lost. As a result, consensus as the mark of benign politics has been eclipsed by contentious politics driven by the power of competition of interests for privileged advantage. Democracy lost its moorings in morality embedded in spirituality. The consequent rise of secular politics makes concord, the basis of community spirit, hard to achieve. Secular politics is almost by definition bedevilled by the vain quest for virtue. This calls to mind Nicholas of Cusa's recognition of the inadequacy of mere institutional forms of representation and consent. Without the underlying spirit of common order common responsibility and *concordantia*, the external forms are of little use. And democracy has, in modern times, been reduced to nothing else but external forms. When the basis of what Plato calls *philia politike* (friendship among the members of a political community) is eroded, whether this base is Cusa's *concordantia catholica* or something else and there are available alternative visions about it, democracy becomes the tool of advancing sectional interests inducing in the process the war of each against all. This calls for restoring the harmony of the order in which man finds himself and which, therefore, must be the only source of harmony he can find within himself. Just as the cosmos is organized a hierarchy in which each level is joined by a bond of mutual sympathy with the surrounding levels, so the social cosmos must also be ordered by reciprocal relationship of love by which the different roles are accepted within (this) order of the whole (Walsh in Voegelin 1998: 24).

References

Carlyle, R. W., and A. J. Carlyle. 1950. *A History of Medieval Political Theory in the West.* 5 vols. *The Political theory of the Thirteenth Century.* Edinburgh: Blackwood.

Dahl, Robert A. 1991. *Democracy and Its Critics.* New York: Orient Longman.

Eusebius, Bishop. 1975. *In Praise of Constantine: A Historical Study and a New Press.* Translation of Eusebius Trancennial Orations. Trans. Harold Drake. Berkeley: University of California Press.

Fortesue, John. 1885. *Government of England.* Ed. Charles Plummer. Clarendon: Oxford.

Hill, Christopher. 1978. *The World Turned Upside Down: Radical Ideas during English Revolution.* Harmondsworth: The Penguin Books.

Hollweck, Thomas A., and Ellis Sandoz. 1997. "General Introduction," to Eric Voegelin, *Collected Works of Eric Voegelin*, Vol. 19, *History of Political Ideas, Vol. I: Hellenism, Rome, and Early Christianity.* Ed. Athanasios Moulakis. Columbia: University of Missouri Press.

Holt, James C. 1965. *Magna Carta.* Cambridge: Cambridge University Press.

John, of Salisbury. 1927. *The Statesman's Book of John of Salisbury*. Trans. John Dickinson. New York: Alfred Knopf.

Marsilius of Padua. 1951. *Defensor Pacis*. English Translation, *The Defender of the Peace*. Trans. and intro. Alan Gewith, 2 vols. New York: Columbia University Press.

Reilly, G. F. 1945. *Imperium and Sacerdotium According to St. Basil the Great*. Washington: Catholic University Press.

Stubbs, William. 1895. *Charter of Liberties of Henry I of 1100*. In *Select Charters*, 8th edition. Oxford: Clarendon.

Voegelin, E. 1987. *The New Science of Politics: An Interpretation*. Chicago: University of Chicago Press.

———. 1997a. *Collected Works of Eric Voegelin*. Vol. 19, *History of Political Ideas, Vol. I: Hellenism, Rome, and Early Christianity*. Ed. Athanasios Moulakis. Columbia: University of Missouri Press.

———. 1997b. *Collected Works of Eric Voegelin*. Vol. 20, *History of Political Ideas, Vol. II: The Middle Ages to Aquinas*. Ed. Peter von Sivers. Columbia: University of Missouri Press.

———. 1998. *The Collected Works of Eric Voegelin*. Vol. 21, *History of Political Ideas, Vol. III: The Later Middle Ages*. Ed. David Walsh. Columbia: University of Missouri Press.

———. 2000. *Collected Works of Eric Voegelin*. Vol. 5, *Modernity without Restraint: Political Religions, the New Science of Politics and Science, Politics and Gnosticism*. Ed. and Trans. Manfred Heningsen. Columbia: University of Missouri Press.

Wolin, Sheldon. 1960. *Politics and Vision: Continuity and Innovation in Western Political Thought*. Boston: Little Brown & co.

3

Democracy: The Case of Moral Deficit

Then farewell sacred majesty,
Let's put all brutal tyrants down:
When men are born and still live free,
Here every head doth wear a crown.
— John Walcot, Earl of Rochester

I

The two instances of the transformation of order (Chapter 1) signified the displacement of cosmic order by an earthly order. Both these instances brought about a fateful change in what Collins calls "the relationship between consciousness and order." Because of this shift, social order incorporated rational utilitarian authority, which would no longer be a matter of acquisition or definition. It could be only a matter of exercise. Consequently, then, society does not any longer remain "a transcendentally articulated reflection of something pre-defined, external and beyond itself which orders existence hierarchically. It is now a nominal entity ordered by the sovereign state, which is its own articulated representative" (Collins 1989: 7).

If the transformation of order in Athens helped the formation of empires, it created in the seventeenth-century England conditions that led to the installation of democratic political order. If the rise of empire is symptomatic of the bringing together of diverse societies under the banner of one centralized political authority, the rise of democracy symbolized man's endeavour to bring together diverse socio-economic forces in a particular society under one unified political order. This institutional change, that is, the change from cosmic order to earthly order, initiated far-reaching structural changes in both the interior and the exterior of man. The first major change concerns the total eclipse of Aristotle's idea of the good life by bare life. He had made it very clear that "the life according to the good is the greatest end both in common for all men and for each man separately" (*Politics* 1962: 1278b, 23–31).

The eclipse of the idea of the good life signifying the quest for something noble, something abiding and something quintessential made man an externalized creature. The significance of man as an externalized being is that interest replaces his inner being; he becomes simply the reflexive creature of external, largely material objects, which attract or repel him. In essence, then, man becomes a receptacle of interests (Wood 1972: 111). As an externalized creature, he seeks primarily, even exclusively, to fulfil his ordinary life-needs involved with the process of production and reproduction. This, in essence, signifies the fulfilment of needs that call for access to resources that are vitally necessary for sustaining a comfortable life. These needs pertain to access to and control over wealth, power and prestige.

Thus, the transformation of order from cosmic to earthly had the effect of universalizing ordinary life purposes; these purposes concerned the acquisition of wealth, power and prestige in a situation where the distribution of different capacities is extremely unequal. Man is, in theory, endowed with both freedom and equality. Pragmatically, however, his freedom is highly constrained for two very important reasons. First, if providence allows man the gift of freedom and equality with the help of which he can mobilize material resources necessary for appropriate development of his personality, nature proves niggardly and makes available to man only limited resources.

Scarcity of resources in itself is a factor in inducing competition among men. What further add to its intensity are the similarity of life goals and dissimilarity of capacities to realize these goals. Even when life goals are quite similar, each person views these goals differently. He defines for himself how the goal he has set for himself can be realized and what resources in what quantity he must have available to him so that he can realize his purposes. Moreover, since the realization of life goals must take place in the midst of others driven by the same forces, the act of the realization assumes a political character. Political action emanating from the need to realize life goals, when confronted by the phenomenon of reciprocal resistance, usually gives birth to *libido dominandi,* the passion to dominate. This creates a situation where conflict becomes a prime mode of operation bearing upon the resolution of conflict.

Thus, one of the fateful consequences of the transformation of the cosmic order into earthly order is the prevalence of social pluralism characterized by uncompromising opinions and viewpoints about matters—social and political. This situation is symptomatic of the breakdown of what Heraclitus calls *xynon* (shareable commonality) that constitutes the basis of community. When there does not exist commonality, it becomes difficult to discover a viable ground that can prop up the fragile edifice of public order. Obviously, such a situation paves the ground for conflict. As Hobbes puts it, "when everyman follows his own opinion, it is necessary that the controversies which arise among (men), become innumerable and indeterminable" (1991: 364).

Plurality of opinions that proves difficult to reconcile constitutes the background against which the question of the basis on which the practice of government could be conducted once society is no longer a community assumes importance. What must be added to it is the factual situation bereft of any divine guidance. The plurality of private opinions calls for a political system that institutionalizes both the autonomy of the individual and the making of collective decisions by all citizens. However, such a political system turns out to be composed of what Charles Taylor calls "disengaged selves" that enjoy self-determination. This signifies not only value plurality but also the refusal to tolerate any kind of domination that curbs individual freedom. Two things follow. First, the installation of political order cannot now be modelled upon the paradigm of the cosmic order since its source is trains-individual and militates against the idea of individual autonomy. Political order must now be created only out of materials readily available. These materials are nothing more than private passions, which now clamour for satisfaction after the restraints of morality have been lifted. These two factors have facilitated the coming and taking roots of democracy as a political institutional arrangement suitable to the genius of autonomous individuals.

Second, when public order is created out of private passions, the notion of the good life is given a short shrift. The claims of ordinary life then take over and shape the pattern of individual lives and social relations. This means the emergence of what Michel Foucault calls "bio-politics" which becomes the primary mode of regulating interpersonal and intergroup relations. What bio-politics signifies is that now *homo laborans* and with it, biological life as such occupies the centre of the political scene in modern times. Bio-politics requires a political institutional arrangement that can assure the facilitation of the making of collective decisions in a situation where the sense of community no longer prevails; it has been completely eroded and with it has broken social consensus.

It is this overall background to bio-politics of today that makes moral sensibility so crucial for the successful operation of a democratic political order. Moral sensibility is crucial not only for moderating the tendency towards self-aggrandizement for the aggressive pursuit of self-defined concerns of life nurtured by self-love, but also for another reason. As Agamben puts it:

> [M]an as a living being presents himself no longer as an *object* but also the *subject* of political power. These processes—which in many ways oppose (and at least apparently) bitterly conflict with each other—nevertheless converge in so far as the bare life of the citizen, the new bio-political body of humanity. (1998: 9)

This dual role of the individual, both as the ruler and the ruled, demands from him twofold care: care for the provisioning of his own bare life and care for the well-being of collective life of which he is now an integral part. In addition, since individual life is now so intimately involved with collective life, justice assumes a crucial importance for safeguarding and promoting the well-being of both the individual and the collective he is a part of. With justice becoming a central issue of bio-politics, its cause cannot be well served without self-transcendence as a necessary condition of citizen responsibility.

Both self-transcendence and self-responsibility need the nourishment drawn from moral sensibility. It is this that enables the individual to seek his own happiness along with the happiness of others. The need for such a moral sense becomes even more pressing in a situation where divine guidance to human action is unavailable and traditional norms of behaviour have atrophied under the unceasing onslaught of instrumental, calculative reasoning. Without a strong underpinning of moral values, a democratic regime is always in danger of turning into what MacIntyre calls "civil war carried on by other means" (2007: 253). This should alert us to the fact that political order, particularly a democratic political order, needs more than power, authority, law and institutions; it needs a commitment to the promotion of the cause of what is general and common. To develop this commitment, it is necessary to make a distinction between "what is right" and "what is good for me." What is even more important in this regard is to live by the principle of "what is right."

Important though such a distinction is for democratic politics and vital as it is to live by the principle of "what is right," the fact of the erosion of social consensus and degradation of political norms have meant the disappearance of that ethos that constitutes the bedrock of democracy. The common self-understanding constitutive of liberal democracy has itself been severely eroded with the result that a democratic political order experiences everywhere the phenomenon of moral deficit. It is not that philosophers, thinkers and statesmen have not been aware of this fact. Right since the Reformation, which cleaved Christianity asunder and created several cleavages into which morality dropped down, they have seen the need for bolstering the shuddering ship of the state and sought to provide a firmer moral basis to bio-politics.

Our aim in this chapter is to examine such attempts made especially by post-Reformation political thinkers and to see the extent to which they have succeeded in this. We focus in this chapter mainly on Hooker, Hobbes, Locke, John S. Mill and Alexis de Tocqueville, as a few representative examples.

II

The point of departure for discussion here is the breakdown of Western Christianity and its splintering into numerous sects, each of which insisted on the authenticity and legitimacy of its own faith as the true faith. Symptomatic as this situation was, the breakdown of cultural consensus raised the problem of salvaging order when disagreement about fundamental truth prevented agreement on issues impinging on socio-political order. This situation rendered philosophical thinking and the discussion of what is right suspect as a cloak for manipulation. Once individual opinion came to be viewed as paramount, it became the vehicle of articulating and expressing only individual interest. Moreover, interestingly enough, interest meant just material interest. Therefore, material interest came to shape individual lives and social relations.

Each of the bickering sects sought to impose on others what it considered good for all. This attempt was pursued with apocalyptic zeal reflecting a change from "[p]resbyterian sobriety to millenarian ecstasy" (Wolin 1960: 258). This apocalyptic zeal was fed upon the Reformation doctrine of "private conscience and the priesthood of all believers" (Ibid.). Groups of men were prepared to shed blood for ensuring religious uniformity, as they understood it to be. It was a situation where all were ablaze with inner light; however, it was not possible to agree upon what that inner light was. This situation threw up two important questions to be satisfactorily answered. The first question concerned the creation of a political order out of a highly splintered social universe. This question was voiced clearly by Milton when he asked: Must political societies remain content with "the forced and outward union of cold, and neutral, and inwardly divided minds?" (Ibid.: 242). Second, if they must remain so, what kind of moral support structure was required to sustain the political order built upon a cracked foundation?

These two questions needed to be answered in the face of a challenge that assumed a sharp edge when the community of Presbyters pressed for submitting the civil order to the rule of religious order. The apocalyptic vision of paradise around the corner brought to them the realization that the royal supremacy over ecclesiastical matters was subversive of the spiritual dimension of human existence. Especially for the younger generation of Puritans, the feeling grew stronger that the church was no church "when its spiritual substance was determined by the civil government" (Voegelin 1998: 80; see also Wolin 1960: 195). Reviving the older distinction made by St. Augustine between *civitas dei* and *civitas terrena,* the Puritans insisted that the scripture must be the rule of life and overrule civil law. The Puritan demanded favoured Presbyterian Church governance and asserted that the superiority of the community of Presbyters over all authorities, temporal and spiritual, must be recognized and institutionalized.

These two vital aspects of Puritan demand on English public order evoked sharp reaction from Richard Hooker towards the end of the sixteenth century. In refuting Puritan arguments, Hooker pointed out that in a situation where the universe of religious beliefs and opinions were highly fractured, the Puritan demand to make the scripture to rule over civic life was to ignore and override all other beliefs and opinions. To impose one point of view on all is to overwhelm the public order. This amounted, according to Hooker, to self-exaltation. This was tantamount to suppressing the judgement of the community and upholding just one point of view. Lacking a trans-individual standard of evaluating the merit of different points of views, the determination of a widely accepted point of view becomes difficult.

Add to it the fact that human judgement is prone to error. "Think ye are men, deem it not impossible for you to err" (Hooker 1989: 49). If men disagreed about the most important thing in life, the manner in which they should serve God, how could they trust one another in everything else? This situation called for, Hooker argued, transcending private opinions and making general public opinion the basis of governance. "What touches all, ought to be approved by all." Thus, Hooker paid homage to the democratic ideal of consulting all in the act of governance and strongly argued for the superiority of the civil authority.

Hooker's preference for the superiority of the civil authority rests upon his appreciation of the fact that when men are prone to error, their opinion lacks reliability. Differences of opinion in the absence of a strong bond of unity tend to generate controversies and conflicts. They become endless and prove deleterious for social peace and harmony. It is, therefore, necessary to safeguard peace and harmony by submitting to public law. "So that of peace and quietness there is not any way possible unless the probable voice of every entire society or body politic overrule all private of like nature in the same body" (Ibid.: 32). Moreover, the claim of the universality of the Catholic Church was itself destroyed when it was splintered into numerous religious sects. In addition, since these sects speak in different tongues, legislative enactments of the king must be understood as the action of all, of the whole society that acts through him. Thus, the voice of the king is the voice of the people.

Using a nationalist argument, Hooker points out that there is an identity in England between the membership of the commonwealth and the Church. As such, the English commonwealth represents a society comprising the people of God. Moreover, since the Church signifies just one of the associations, albeit an important one, it is only a partial community. A partial community, therefore, must submit to the authority of the whole of the community, which means the state (Hooker 1989: VIII, i.5). Hooker further argues that since England separated from the Catholic Church, the universal Catholic Church was practically reduced to the status of the mere Church of Rome. Hooker also argued that despite the Church of Rome being submerged in gross and grievous abominations, it continued to belong to the family of Christ (Ibid.: VIII, i.7), but only as a local church as was the Church of England after its separation from the Church of Rome. Even while the Church of England was equal in status with that of the Church of Rome, this symbolized only an organizational separation, not a spiritual one.

This led Hooker to redefine the catholicity of Christianity by reviving the theory of visible church. If invisible church referred to the invisibility of "election" and "salvation," the idea of visible church pointed to the entire membership of the church whether worthy of election and salvation or not. The visible church as *civitas dei* must promote the idea of visibility; this can be ensured only if the church is small to allow "mutual fellowship and society with one another." The entire body of the faithful is too large to permit this. This is so because it contains within it diverse precincts that have diverse names, so the Catholic Church is divided into a number of distinct societies, every one of which is termed a church within itself.

Thus, even while the Church is universal, its organizational format is local. It is in the sense that "the Church is always a visible society of men" (Ibid.: III, i.14). And it is the numerous visible churches that sustain "mutual fellowship and society with one another." This twist in logic allowed Hooker to establish not only the equality of the Church of England with but also independent from the Church of Rome. This, however, had the effect of reducing the representative universalism of the Church to "something like an oversized statistical collective entity and sacramental visibility is translated into special visibility" (Voegelin 1998: 84–85). Hooker is aware of the fact that the logic of the smallness of the church can be carried too far. He therefore draws the line at the level of society which he defines as "a number of men belonging unto some Christian fellowship of the place and limit whereof are certain" (Hooker 1989: III, i.14). Implicit in this definition is the idea that a society must have a state or that the boundaries of society and state must coincide.

This leads Hooker to think of three types of ecclesiastical organizations. First, organization of church as an autonomous society in a surrounding commonwealth; second, a society divided into two bodies, that is, the commonwealth and church with the latter presided over by a Bishop at Rome; and third, a society such as England where church and commonwealth are undivided (Ibid: VIII, i.7). This tripartite division suggests that church and commonwealth represent two different and distinct societies unless they are under a common head. For Hooker, England represents a commonwealth where the temporal government is also a spiritual government. Thus, Hooker elevates the kingship to the status of the visible figuration of Christ. He contends that

> they are in authority over the church...even of Christ it is that they have received such authority, inasmuch as of him all lawful powers are, therefore, the civil magistrate is in regard of this (ecclesiastical) and under the subordinate head of Christ's people. (Ibid: VIII, v.6)

Hooker adduced a wide range of historical evidence to show that the state had frequently attached public authority to the actions of the church. In short, then, he established one of the core principles of modern politics which signifies that the public authority was now concerned principally with putting into order only the external aspect of human existence. As such, religion was thus prevented from making its presence in public and was confined to private concerns of the individual. What it further signified was that if the church was to remain a concrete visible community, then it must be, out of necessity, under the political authority of the state.

In the light of this, Hooker must be seen to have confirmed or, at least, paved the way for the evisceration of all independent institutional carriers of spiritual and moral sensibilities. As a natural outcome of this, sources of morality in public life and relations progressively atrophied. By extolling the supremacy of the temporal power in religious matters, Hooker not only asserted the autonomy of the political from religion, but also promoted the dissolution of the universality of ecclesiastical organization and ensured nationalization of religious life. This went a long way to assuring that the political order must be liberated from the discipline of any superior order regulating its working (Wolin 1960: 196).

Over all, then, Hooker's formulations did retain the universal validity of the norms of Christianity; however, they led increasingly to drain their real spiritual contents. It is for this reason that Hooker can be said to have laid the foundation of progressive secularization of the state and with it, of political life and relations. Secularization that Hooker promoted has Janus-like two faces, one posturing as a Gladiator and the other, a meek and gentle animal seeking succour and support from a source not integral to it. As a Gladiator, the state slowly expanded its jurisdiction over ever larger areas of private life. However, it had to depend on religion to help it ward off the troubles it had to face in its pursuit of unchallenged monopoly on power. The state would increasingly exploit people's religious sentiments to strengthen its own power position until it could afford to jettison religion completely. Thus, while Christianity was drained of its spiritual substance, its political utility was recognized to be crucial for the continued legitimacy of the state. However, the utilitarian stance proved fatal to spiritual life, the bedrock of moral sensibilities since he justified the primacy of civil authority by rejecting the authority of the spirit.

III

Hobbes' response to the Puritan challenge to the established public order in England was quite different from that of Hooker. However, for both of them, the core of the problem posed by the Puritan challenge was two-sided. On the one hand, there is a political system that wants to maintain its established order in historical existence and on the other hand, there are private individuals within the society who want to change the public order, if necessary by force, in the name of a new truth. Hooker rejected the Puritan claim as being an attempt to impose partial will on the entire membership of the society. He considered it as an instance of self-exaltation. In rejecting the Puritan claim, Hooker established the superiority of civil authority over religious organizations. This was instrumental in paving the way for democracy to take roots. In contrast, Hobbes installed a *Leviathan*, the King of Proud Men, to curb the tendency towards self-exaltation or *pleonexia,* particularly *libido dominandi,* with a view to making peace and order secure.

What were the factors that swayed Hobbes to create a commonwealth that tolerated no dissent and that rested on the idea that there was no public truth except the law of the state through which the law of nature speaks? In answering this question, it is necessary to pinpoint Hobbes' understanding of the Puritan position. As Voegelin observes, Hobbes had to deny that the zeal of the contending churches and sects was inspired, however misguided they might have been, by the search for truth. Their struggle had to be interpreted in terms of immanent existence, "as an unfettered expression of their lust for power and their professed religious concerns had to be revealed as a mask for their existential lust" (Voegelin 2000: 234). What Hobbes saw in Puritan challenge was, as Voegelin sees it, the interplay of *libido dominandi* behind the pretence of religious zeal and reforming idealism.

Hobbes identified the corrupting element of passion in the religious-ness of the Puritan reforming zeal. He did not, however, "interpret passion as the source of corruption in the life of the spirit as the extreme of existential passion" (Ibid.). He therefore pushed the *summum bonum,* the greatest good, out of reckoning, rejecting it as non-existent for interpreting human nature or for identifying the basis on which the practice of government must rest when cultural consensus has completely broken down (Hobbes 1950: 79). When the *summum bonum* is rejected, the ground for what Heraclitus calls *xynon*, that is, the shareable commonality, also disappears. In addition, with it disappears the source of order not only from the life of the individual man, but also from life in society.

According to the classical thinking, community life was supposed to have been based on and nourished by *homonoia*, that is, participation in the shareable commonality. With the disappearance of the shareable commonality, *homonoia* is destroyed. As a consequence, society turns out to be composed of isolated individuals. One of the essential links between man and man is, of course, man's relatedness through the openness of his soul to the divine. However, when the tranquillity of the soul through what Bodin calls "*fruitio Dei*" is irrevocably lost, man is pushed into his creaturely loneliness and weakness. He must then create the image of his omnipotence. This he seeks to do through the fulfilment of his passions, which remain for him the only ground after reason has lost its moorings in the transcendental entity. His passions lead him to ceaseless action for satisfying one desire after another in a ceaseless manner.

The object of man's desire is not to enjoy once only and for one instance of time, but to assure forever the way of his future desire (Ibid.: 79). In this, there is no rest because "continually to be out gone is misery; continually to out go is felicity. And to forsake the course, is to die" (Hobbes 1928: Part I, Chapter 9, Section 21). Passion aggravated by comparison is pride. The claim to be in possession of undoubted truth is one form of pride. Such pride in excess is madness. If this madness becomes violent, then one seeks to impose his truth upon others. The result of this usually is "the serious roaring of a troubled nation" (Hobbes 1950: 60–61).

In such a situation, the individual man emerges as a power centre who seeks to aggrandize his power by eliminating competition either through domination or through extermination. This creates a situation in which "without a common power to keep them all in awe, they are in a condition which is called *warre*: and such a *warre* as is of every man, against every man" (Ibid.: 103). It may not, in fact, be actual war; nevertheless, men "are in the posture of Gladiators; having their weapon pointing, and their eyes fixed on one another" (Ibid.: 105). In such a situation, there prevails the atmosphere of "*continuall feare*, and danger of violent death. And the life of man, solitary, poore, brutish and short" (Ibid.: 104).

Certainly, there is the law of nature, which stipulates that men should seek peace and keep it. Two situations, however, vitiate this stipulation. In the first place, everyman is governed by his own reason. In a situation of war of one against all, everyman thinks that he has a right to everything, even to one another's body (Ibid.: 107). In the second place, everyone suspects each other of taking away his life and possession. As such, the second law of nature allows the retention of the right of nature, which signifies that everyone can defend himself by whatever means he has access to.

In the absence of a centralized political authority, the prevalent atmosphere of suspicion makes the first law of nature inoperative. In order for this law to become operative, a centralized political authority has to be created with a view to removing the fear of being deprived of life and liberty. As such, the installation of a super power, if not of mutual trust, then, at least, of mutual forbearance, becomes necessary for establishing peace and order in a situation of reciprocal resistance. This will by no means eliminate the possibility of reciprocal resistance. What impels isolated individuals to enter into a covenant for creating a commonwealth is *summum malum,* the fear of death. What the covenant does is to break human units of passion and fuse them into a new unit, called the commonwealth.

The coalesced souls of individual persons create a new person, the sovereign. "This is the generation of that great *Leviathan,* or rather (to speak more reverently) of that *Mortal God,* to which we owe under the *Immortal God,* our peace and defence" (Ibid.: 143). The fusion of individual wills constitutes "a real unity of them all," a unity that represents the surrender of "their wills to the will of the sovereign and their judgment to his judgment." The unity of wills, furthermore, confers upon the sovereign the authority to form the wills of all, to peace at home and mutual aid against their enemies abroad, by the terror of his strength (Ibid.). Thus, conformity to laws of nature can be assured only by a recourse to the terror of the sovereign "and covenants, without the sword are but words, and of no strength to secure a man at all" (Ibid.: 139).

Hobbes is, then, faced with the problem of constructing an order of society out of isolated individuals who are not oriented towards a common purpose or imbued with a sense of shareable commonality; they are motivated by nature to attune themselves to the call of their own passions. Driven by the fear of death, the *summum malum,* individuals are impelled to create a *Leviathan* through a covenant with each other. The termination of the state of nature that the covenant signifies did not, however, mean the abolition of mutual and common fear. What it meant was that individuals gave up their natural right. While mutual and common fear remained, the object of fear was institutionalized in the sovereign. Society did not mark the abolition of fear, but the displacement of generally diffused fear by determinate one (Wolin 1960: 273).

Hobbes, however, did something more than displacing the generally diffused fear by determinate one. By abolishing the constitution of being with its origin in divine, transcendent entity and replacing it with world-immanent order, he envisaged perfection in human action. With the abolition of the *summum bonum* only passions remained. As a result, what assumed importance was the visible world of words and deeds; the unseen realm of processes in the soul was pushed into oblivion. This had the effect of making the external aspect of human existence the locus of human action. This led in due course to externalization of man. With the externalization of man becoming an accomplished fact, the classical moral philosophical standard of judging human action against the highest good was discarded by Hobbes. For him, objects of passion are no more a legitimate subject of enquiry. With the jettisoning of the *summum bonum,* the ordering element in human life is also enfeebled and finally extinguished. What remained for man was only his passionate existence. And the passionate existence of human beings can beget only war of each against all others. This state can be terminated only by the creation of the *Leviathan* who can overawe everyone and maintain peace and order. The *Leviathan* thus represents a power over proud men and "having set for the great power of *Leviathan* called him King of the Proud" (Norman 1985: 41).

Hobbes' *Leviathan,* the mortal God, does not enjoy unfettered superiority. It has to command allegiance of the people only under the overlordship of Immortal God. But how does one have the knowledge of the immortal God? Hobbes discusses two important ways in which one could know God. One of the ways is to let reason unfold dispassionately to arrive at last at uncaused cause, whom we may call the incomprehensible God (Hobbes 1950: 88). Another way of knowing God is, of course, revelation. However, when the signs of the supernatural in the form of miracles, prophesies and "extraordinary felicity" have ceased to appear, to believe in the supernatural on the authority of someone's words is simply to have faith in private opinion. Private opinion involves private reason, which is usually swayed by the desire to seek "that which is good for him." Private opinion overlaid by private interest can create only confusion. As such, revelation cannot be relied upon since it is based on private opinion. What makes revelation reliable is what is declared by the state to be so (Hobbes 1991: 72).

If revelation has to be authenticated by the state, laws of nature too have to be authenticated because they are God's words. This is so because these laws do not actually govern human existence in the state of nature since these laws are simply dispositions. They become visible through enactments by the state and take on the authority of the state. Only when men have covenanted to submit to the command of a sovereign authority, do the laws of nature become laws of societies in historical existence (Hobbes 1950: 119). Laws of nature and civil laws, therefore, contain each other and are of all extent (Ibid.: 227). If the law of nature gains its effectiveness through the civil law, so do tenets of Christianity retain their validity through state laws. In a Christian commonwealth, the Word of God revealed in the scripture is not at variance with the law of nature. Nevertheless, canons of scriptures to be received, the doctrinal and ritual interpretations put on it, as well as the form of clerical organization must derive their authority not from revelation, but from enactments by the sovereign as the law of the land. And as Hobbes insists, there will be no freedom of debate about the truth of human existence in society because debates bring forth only private opinion that centres on individual good.

It is clear, then, that the law of nature and canons of Christian scripture both become relevant for human existence only when they are validated through state law. This means that it is the institution of government that makes morality possible. It is by becoming a law that morality becomes effective. This points to the fact that

> if human nature is assumed to be-nothing but passionate existence, devoid of the ordering resource of the soul, the terror of annihilation will, indeed, be the overriding passion that compels submission to order. If pride cannot bow to Dike, or be redeemed through grace, it must be broken by the Leviathan who "is king of all the children of pride. (Voegelin 2000: 237)

By subordinating the law of nature and the canon of Christian scripture to civil laws, Hobbes placed interest right at the centre of political association. To have made interest the arbiter of human existence was to single out what was essentially private and least capable of representation at the public level. In addition, to insist that interest is rational is to deform and degrade reason into calculative reasoning and to rob it of its public character. Once this happens, there is nothing to rein in the tendency towards becoming eminent or self-exultant. Can we, then, be assured that the fear of the state can prevent individual atoms, moving in social space, from colliding? It is not naive to believe that in a society of egotists all that is needed for erasing conflict between public and private ends is the creation of an institutionalized public ego?

The public ego suffers from two weaknesses. First, the primacy of interest and the consequences of its aggressive pursuit lead to disharmony in society. Second, the restoration of coherence is seen to be accomplished not by morality but by power. And as the supreme repository of power, the state would assign any meaning it wished to public action. At the bottom, then, a deep irrationality pervades Hobbesian society (Wolin 1960: 260).

IV

The externalization of man that Hobbes celebrated received further fillip by John Locke when he declared:

> We are not born in heaven but in this world, where our being is to be preserved with meat, drink and clothing, and other necessaries that are not born with us, but must be got and kept with forecast, care and labour, and therefore, we cannot all be devotion, all praises and hallelujah, and perpetually in the vision of things above.... (Locke cited in Fox-Bourne 1876: I, 396)

Locke's concern with things mundane derives its inspiration from his realization that what is most important for human existence is "the little spot of earth where we all our concernments are shut up" (Ibid.: 224–25). When reality is constructed around the primacy of earthly concerns, economic aspect of human existence becomes centrally important. Man emerges as *homo economicus* and social relations come to be governed primarily by economic relations. As such, economic action has come to be considered not only as fruitful but also as the paradigm of all actions. When the individual is driven by the movement of his own desire, he works to maximize his own satisfaction through his engagement in economic action. This lends primacy to utilitarian considerations. As a result, political action comes to be eclipsed by economic action. This points to fact that the tendency to treat economic phenomena as identical and co-extensive with social phenomena has become prominent (Wolin 1960: 300).

The primacy of economic action means the centrality of interest. However, when interest assumes primacy, two things happen. First, increasing wealth is seen to be the key not only to human welfare but also to the fulfilment of human beings. However, increasing wealth transmutes needs into wishes and then the economy moves from supplying subsistence goods to providing positional (status) goods (Hirsch 1971). When this happens, the economy finds it difficult to fulfil the escalating demands for goods and services that are channelled into the market. This creates scarcity, which brings into operation severe competition among consumers for access to goods and services. Competition soon is transformed into the process of reciprocal resistance and civil war carried on by other means rages in society (MacIntyre 2007: 253). This signifies a situation in which the distinction between getting ahead in life by pushing others out of the way and to have an equitable share in generalized advance, loses its salience. The result is the erosion of morality. Consequently, structures of cooperation collapse and social harmony evaporates. This situation invites Rousseau to comment that man is born as enemy and turns knave by duty.

These developments have made it absolutely essential that moral foundation must support and sustain the edifice of democratic political order when it has to accommodate the hosts of contending self-regarding action. However, democratic politics places morality in the very place that marked its decline. This means that morality is to develop out of the contention of private interests. This creates an anomaly in the sense that private interest does not tolerate any restraint except the fear of the state. It is to resolve the crisis produced by this anomaly that John Locke makes his proposals. The point of departure for Locke's discussion is the classical economist who attributes rationality to the individual when he engages in economic action. For the classical economist, the individual is rational in two important senses. One, he uses his foresight in the act of provisioning and practises thrift and abstinence. This helps in capital accumulation, a necessary condition for the expansion and enhancement of economic production. Two, the individual is rational also in the sense that he rationally determines the best way for realizing a particular economic purpose. It is true that what determines individual purposes is his passion; however, it is reason (to be specific, calculative, instrumental reason) that helps the individual realize his purpose. Thus, economic action symbolizes a happy wedlock between passion and reason. This wedlock promotes not only individual well-being but also collective good. This is very well exemplified by Mandeville's saying that private vice leads to public benefit.

Thus, what the classical economist does is to make individual passion the basis of common good. "What is designated as the common good of society is the product of passion. Similarly, the economic well-being of society occurs by way of man's attempt to satisfy his own selfish desires" (Wolin 1960: 333). The marriage between liberalism and classical economy was thus instrumental in transforming individual norm into social norm. Locke did not feel comfortable with this perspective. He, therefore, proposed to uncover the nature of common moral beliefs or consensus that society presupposes. Locke claims that there certainly exists a moral order that transcends all private opinions. "For the nature of good and evil is certain and their nature cannot be determined either by public ordinances or by any private opinion" (Locke 1954: 121). As he sees it, this moral order is embedded in the law of nature. The question for Locke then is to identify the kind of knowledge that can enable man to apprehend the law of nature.

While the law of nature is certain, yet it admits evident variability. Abandoning his earlier position that identifies conscience as the means of apprehending the law of nature, he argued that knowledge of the law of nature could not be innate since it lacks agreement. Furthermore, since human mind at birth is *tabula rasa,* such knowledge can only be an acquired one through interaction with the external world. As such, only experience can form the basis of such knowledge. However, since experience itself is variable, the knowledge of the law of nature too must be variable. Yet the law of nature exists and is binding for all. Despite the fact that knowledge is neither innate nor traditional, it is available to all (Ibid.: 125–26). What makes this knowledge possible and certain is our reflection on sense data, which yields this knowledge with the help of the process of reasoning from the existence of things to their maker.

It is true that man is endowed with reasoning faculty. However, the law of nature is far too complex for ordinary and vulgar mind. Yet the continuance of civilized existence depends on the extent to which men are capable of grasping the meaning of the law of nature. Logical reasoning is too complex for an ordinary mind; conscience, teachings of men or even tradition cannot be relied upon in this. This situation demands a solution that is simple even for the dullest of the mind. And such a simple solution is readily available in the Sermon on the Mount. This

Locke identified as the substitute for the complex knowledge required for uncovering the meaning of the law of nature. The Christian ethic is not less rational than the philosophic wisdom. It has the added advantage of being available to all as against the few who claim to have the monopoly on religious teachings. In addition, it has the backing of to an authority behind its ethical value since it has come out of the mouth of the son of God.

Speaking of the Sermon on the Mount as surrounded by the awesome miracle of revelation, Locke observes, "God seems to have consulted the poor of this world and the bulk of mankind. These are articles that the labouring and illiterate man may comprehend. This is a religion suited to vulgar capacities..." (1824: VI, 157). Locke thus claims to have found a simple means of comprehending the complex law of nature. This formed, for Locke, the moral foundation of contract that formed the basis of both civil society and political order. He was, therefore, convinced that he had found the ultimate solution to the problem of the fragility of the moral foundation of democracy. But was he successful in this? Locke's identification of consent as the foundation of political order is no doubt of great value. However, consent itself needs to be reinforced by morality especially when the political order has shunned the idea of life. And the primacy of bare life makes the inner world of contemplation abysmally poor and ineffective.

The problem of the inner void becomes all the more acute when we consider the role of Christianity itself. What Christianity did, in effect, was to de-divine the world; it focused mainly on the inner world of the individual, while Locke celebrated the concerns of the bare life. For him, increase of wealth and convenience and the knowledge that could achieve this were the only desirable things in life. However, since the tendency to acquire more and more of material goods promotes competition, it induces civil war carried on by other means; Locke had to find a solution to the problem of disorder in society. However, none of the three possible solutions—rationality, morality and the state—proves effective. When the pursuit of interest becomes central in human existence, man's orientation degrades into what Charles Taylor calls "disengaged subjectivity" and rationality deforms into what Plato calls "logizemenos," that is, instrumental rationality. Locke himself alludes to "lawless exhorbitancy of unconfined man" (Ibid.: VII; Ibid. 1963: 125, 128 and 136). The link between the good of one individual and the good of all individuals is broken because of this exorbitance and private vice eclipses public benefit.

As compared to reason, morality proves even feebler. Religion, as the seedbed of morality, used to be the force that struck a balance between self-interest and common good. However, with the decline of Christianity, morality was left without any authenticating source. By simplifying and reducing Christian doctrines to the simple principle of the Sermon on the Mount, Locke not only projected a utilitarian perspective on religious teaching but also rendered history a *tabula rasa*. That is to say, he wiped religious history clean of the developments that made Christianity what it is. Christian doctrine, as it has grown in the tradition of the church, is not arbitrary. It is the labour of generations "to find an adequate expression to the substance of faith in the historically changing environment of Mediterranean and western civilization.... In general, the history of Christianity is the process by which the substance of faith is built into the civilization of man" (Voegelin 1998: 174). Locke completely ignored this historical tradition and looked to primitive Christianity to provide the foundation necessary for supporting the fragile edifice of morality.

By implication, it was also to abandon civilizing advances. In addition, he reduced the noble religious doctrine to an ideology, that is, a set of simplified beliefs suited to the vulgar understanding and cut believe asunder from its vitalizing support base, that is, conscience. As Wolin notes:

> [D]espite the inroads of secularism and scepticism, the modern tradition has for more than several centuries taken for granted the viability of what may be called a "common Christian conscience." Both in theory and in practice, the tradition had assumed the continuing presence of a common outlook and moral response among the members of the society. (1960: 337)

What Locke did was to strike at the root of this common concern as, private judgement and therefore, divisive.

Locke characterizes Christianity as reasonable because one does not find anything in it that one cannot find without it. If this is so, why not totally abandon Christianity and depend solely on human reason? Locke does treat reason as the authenticator of God's revelation. However, his distrust of private reason robs it of its importance in forging and renewing man's linkage with the transcendent entity. When Locke refers to the reasonableness of Christianity, he points to certain universally recognized moral sentiments not only expressed but articulated in the Sermon on the Mount. What, in essence, he does is nothing more than finding an authority for these moral sentiments in Jesus Christ, an authority acceptable to most Christians. This is aimed at bolstering these beliefs when their institutional organizational base is irreparably shattered. In short, Locke's effort to enliven Christianity drains it further of its spiritual substance. Thus, Locke joins forces unwittingly with Machiavelli and Hobbes in undermining further political significance of Christian heritage and thus contributes to the further erosion of the moral basis of democracy.

V

Apart from de-spiritualizing Christianity, Locke also paved the way for the ascendance of mass democracy. Subordination of political action to the social signalled the eclipse of the politically powerful social groups, such as, aristocracy. This resulted in the lowering of the barriers that earlier had prevented the entry of a large mass of common people into political arena. Once the mass of the common man found it easy to enter the political arena, the role of public opinion in making and unmaking public policies and collective decisions became very important and decisive. This rendered the individual helpless before the Great Mass (J. S. Mill, Introduction to Tocqueville 1959: xiv). For John Stuart Mill, individual liberty was sacrosanct. As he says, "There is a circle around every individual human being, which no government, be it of one, of a few, or of the many, ought to be permitted to overstep" (1920: 30).

Mill treats liberty as most valuable because it allows individuals to cultivate nobleness of character and develop respect for one another through the recognition of one another as persons. Individuals are then enabled to subordinate their own interest to common good. Thus, for Mill, the key to happiness is liberty. If liberty is denied or curbed,

> popular institutions develop in their people not the desire for freedom, but an unmeasured appetite for place and power. This appetite diverts the intelligence and the activity of the country from its principal business to a wretched competition for the selfish pride and petty vanities of office. (Mill 1970: 314)

Thus, the loss of liberty is instrumental in severing the connection between the good of one individual and the good of all individuals, causing dissonance between self-interest and common good.

What needs to be noted here is that the search for liberty has led to the creation of a political institutional arrangement that we know as democracy. This has tended to limit the role of the government in the life of the people. However, the search for liberty has also been accompanied by an equally powerful search for equality. The search for equality has brought into operation what Tocqueville calls "permanent social revolution." This revolution has helped the government to emerge as a titular head and to expand its power and encroach upon many different areas of life, which are supposed to be private. However, Mill does not consider the tyranny of the political rulers constituting so much threat to individual liberty as "does a social tyranny more formidable than many kinds of political oppression" (1951: 87). Thus, two opposed tendencies have operated in modern times. One, if the mood of the times has called for limiting the power of the government, social reality has facilitated the expansion of its power (Ibid.: Introduction, xviii). And if liberty, as Mill argues, is threatened by the omnipotent state, it also faces the danger of being curtailed by powerful social groups, whose interest lies in protecting and promoting their well-being as against others.

These two problems, that is, the danger to individual liberty from public authorities and the overshadowing of the common good by private interest, have occupied the intellectual attention of Mill. In respect of the first problem, Mill was convinced that this problem had been solved largely by the operation of checks and balances. However, Mill was clear in his mind that the most important function of the government was to prevent individuals from harming each other. The good of the individual, either physical or moral, is not a sufficient warrant for the exercise of governmental power (Ibid.: 99).

It is necessary that individuals must, Mill insists, be allowed to live their lives as they wish. The fact that they refrain from harming one another is symptomatic not only of the prevalence of differing opinions and viewpoints but also of the need to live together without sliding into an attitude of mutual suspicion and mistrust. The realization of living together helps create an atmosphere of trust that becomes salubrious for facilitating cooperation for implementing projects of mutual necessity and benefit. This is, no doubt, a very attractive proposition. However, Mill must answer the question whether the mere recognition of differences would make the elimination of tension and its by-product, conflict, between private benefit and common good possible.

For Mill, liberty is the key not only to individual happiness but also to social harmony and collective good. As such, the state must not seek to maintain, for its own good, a population of contended consumers of private liberty. Instead, it should promote a rigorous spirit of independence; this spirit should not be negative, but positive and native insofar as it permits individuals to cultivate nobility of character. Liberty, for Mill, is not a means for establishing a zone of indifference around largely self-absorbed human beings. Rather, it is envisaged as something that would help genuine community to emerge since it is based on the recognition of one another as real persons. This recognition constitutes the bedrock of self-government and social cooperation.

We must ask, however, whether the generalities Mill associates with liberty would become operative in a society comprising egotistic individuals. The trouble is that Mill can affirm these qualities as necessary attributes of a civilized society, but he fails to supply those forces that can generate them. Mill realizes that the integration of liberty and common good is *sine qua non* for the type of society he is talking about. He also realizes that for such integration, what is needed is spiritual underpinning in the sense that it calls for "social transformation" or "change of character." However, Mill insists that such a hope of transformation must be wrought without any supernatural aid or intervention, because the language of the supernatural is, for him, not the resident of reason, but of hope and a false hope at that. For the agnostic Mill, therefore, there should be a secular alternative. Mill finds this alternative in Comte's idea of Religion of Humanity *sans* its coercive political application.

Mill fails to realize that the soil of self-interest does not bear the sweet crop of universal altruism; it can only yield the bitter crop of reciprocal resistance. It is, therefore, not surprising that Charles Taylor finds in Mill "strange contradictions;" Mill belongs to the class of thinkers who are "constitutionally incapable of coming clean about the deeper sources of their own thinking." They are motivated by the strongest moral ideals of freedom, virtue and altruism, but their very ideals seem to drive them to deny the ideal's existence (Taylor 1989: 88). Thus, Mill is unable to resolve the tension between liberty and equality. As long as this tension remains unresolved, fraternity becomes difficult to attain. Secular religion does not possess the inner strength to successfully tackle this problem.

This problem occupies Tocqueville's intellectual attention, which grapples with it and proposes a solution. For him, the core of the problem consists precisely of the question of how to make liberty into responsible liberty. He realizes that with the dawning of self-government, rulers must possess self-responsibility. The rise of mass democracy has pushed aside all those forces that used to exercise control over both individual and public conduct. It was because of the presence of powerful aristocracy and religion that arbitrariness, both at the individual and governmental levels, was checked. However, unchecked liberty without religion is an invitation to disorder. As such, "despotism can govern without faith, but liberty cannot." Religion is even more necessary in a democratic form of government than in any other form precisely because there is less in the way of political restraint on the people. "What can be done," Tocqueville asks, "with a people who are their own masters if they are not submissive to the Deity?" (1959: I, 318).

What then replaces religion when it is in decline and is not acceptable to the philosophical mind of today? Religion, even while it is not altogether dead, cannot be revived in today's climate of opinion. As Tocqueville remarks:

> Do you not see that religious belief is shaken and divine notion of right is declining, that morality is debased and the notion of moral right is therefore fading away? Argument is substituted for faith, and calculation for the impulse of sentiment. If in the midst of this general disruption, you do not succeed in connecting the notion of right with that of private interest, which is the only immutable point in human heart, what means you will have of governing of the world except by fear? (1959: I, 255)

What in Tocqueville's opinion connects right with private interest is the practice of local self-government. He finds in the American practice of local self-government the employment of liberty for counteracting the effects of equality. When men are left to govern themselves, to take charge of their affairs, they realize that they are connected in the web of interdependence. Interdependence promotes cooperation and people become engaged in cooperatively pursuing their common interest (Ibid.: II, 109). Continued cooperation obliges men to turn their attention to affairs that are not their own; "it rubs off that private selfishness which is the rust of society" (Ibid.: I, 142). Once the people have begun the journey towards transcendence, they will fully realize the transcendental constitution of order. And then, "the soul of man will have the taste for what is infinite and the love of what is immortal.... He may cross and distort them, destroy them he cannot" (Ibid.: II, 142).

The vision is, undoubtedly, grand. However, the ground on which the mansion of this vision stands is quite marshy and shifting (Roy 2012). This ground is incapable of supporting the edifice of self-government by local communities practising what Thomas Jefferson calls "elementary democracy." Note, for example, that existential conditions have basically changed because of the rise of what Charles Taylor calls "disengaged subjectivity," signifying the emergence on the social scene of the egotistic subject. Small townships and local communities have lost their economic autonomy under the press of the globalization of economic life and relations. Globalization has provided strong stimulation to the tendency towards centralization of economic and political decision-making and control.

Note also the fact that the modern times witness a serious contention between the lure of gold and the charm of the community. In this contention, gold has the better chance of winning because there does not exist any restraint on human orientation, thought-ways and work-ways other than self-interest. As a consequence of the primacy of the pursuit of self-interest, local communities have lost their coherence and therefore, the sense of common purpose is irretrievably lost too. Homogenization has made rapid inroads in the traditional pattern of living. However, it touches only the external aspect of human existence. It has not in any way brought about uniformity in opinions and viewpoints nor has it built any common perspective.

All these factors suggest that Tocqueville's proposal does not have any merit now, if it had at any time in history. Democracy therefore cannot but suffer from moral deficit. It is clear, then, that neither Hooker's suggestion of liberating politics from the constraints of religion nor Locke's reformulation of Christian doctrine nor Mill's assertion of the efficacy of the Religion of Humanity or even Tocqueville's prescription of reviving the spiritual foundation of transcendence is capable of making compensations for moral deficit of democracy.

References

Agamben, Giorgio. 1998. *Homo Sacer: Sovereign Power and Bare Life*. Trans. Daniel Heller-Roazen. Stanford: Stanford University Press.

Aristotle. 1962. *Politics*. Trans. T. A. Sinclair. London: Penguin Books.

Collins, Stephen L. 1989. *From Divine Cosmos to Sovereign State*. New York: Oxford University Press.

Fox-Bourne, H. R. 1876. *The Life of John Locke*, 2 vols. New York: King.

Hirsch, Fred. 1971. *Social Limits to Growth*. London: Routledge and Kegan Paul.

Hobbes, Thomas. 1950. *Leviathan. Everyman's Library.* New York: E. P. Dutton.

———. 1991. *Man and Citizen (De Hiomini and De Cive).* Ed. Bernard Gert. Indianapolis: Hacket Publishing Company.

Hooker, Richard. 1989. *Of the Laws of Ecclesiastical Polity.* Ed. Arthur Stephen McGrade. New York: Cambridge University Press.

Locke, John. 1824. *The Works of John Locke,* 9 vols, 12th edition. London: Rivington.

———. 1954. *Essays on the Law of Nature.* Ed. W. Von Lynden. Oxford: Clarendon Press.

———. 1963. *Second Treatise.* Ed. Peter Laslett. New York: Cambridge University Press.

Macintyre, Alasdaire. 2007. *After Virtue,* 2nd edition. Notre Dame: Notre Dame University Press.

Mill John Stuart. 1920. *Principles of Political Economy.* Ed. Sir W. J. Ashley. London: Longmans.

———. 1951. *Utilitarianism, Liberty and Representative Government.* Introduction by A. D. Lindsay. New York: E. P. Dutton.

———. 1970. *Principles of Political Economy.* Harmaonsworth: Penguin Books.

Norman, C. 1985. *The Book of Job: A Commentary.* Philadelphia: Westminster John Knox Press.

Roy, Ramashray. 2012. *Decentralized Political Order.* New Delhi: Gandhi Peace Foundation.

Taylor, Charles. 1989. *Sources of the Self: The Making of the Modern Identity.* Cambridge: Cambridge University Press.

Tocqueville, Alexis de. 1959. *Democracy in America,* 2 vols. Ed. Philip Bradley. New York: Vintage Books.

Voegelin, E. 1998. *Collected Works of Eric Voegelin.* Vol. 24, *History of Political Ideas, Vol. VI: Revolution and the New Science.* Ed. with Intro. Barry Cooper. Columbia: University of Missouri Press.

———. 2000. *Collected Works of Eric Voegelin.* Vol. 5, *Modernity without Restraint: Political Religions, the New Science of Politics and Science, Politics and Gnosticism.* Ed. and Trans., Manfred Heningsen. Columbia: University of Missouri Press.

Wolin, Sheldon. 1960. *Politics and Vision: Continuity and Innovation in Western Political Thought.* Boston: Little, Brown and Co.

Wood, Ellen M. 1972. *Mind and Politics: An Approach to the Meaning of Liberal and Socialist Individualism.* Berkeley: University of California Press.

4

Democracy: Myth and Reality

Jamhuriat ik tarz-e-hukumat hai ki jismen
Bandon ko gina karate hain, tola nahin karate.
—Muhammad Iqbal (1878–1938)

I

Democracy is a style of government in which heads are counted, not weighed (on the scale of merit).

When the seven conspirators of Persia including Darius killed the usurper Magi, a discussion took place among them about the best form of government that should be established. According to Herodotus (Herodotus 1954: 210), Otanes recommended democracy on two grounds. One, it represents a political order that celebrates *isonomia*, equality before law and two, rulers be held responsible for their official acts. The two others, Megabyzus and Darius, argued against democracy as a form of government suited to any society. The former accused the mass of the people of ignorance and irresponsibility, while the latter because it breeds corruption as well as its tendency to throw popular leaders with autocratic inclinations. Darius' argument is worth quoting at length. As he argued:

> In democracy malpractices are bound to occur. In this case, however, corrupt dealings in government services lead not to private feuds, but to close personal associations, the men responsible for them, putting their heads and one mutually supporting each other. And so it goes on, until somebody or other comes forward and breaks up the cliques which are out for their own interests. This wins him the admiration of the people and, as a result, he soon finds himself entrusted with absolute power.... (Ibid.: 211)

These strictures find their forceful echo in Plato when he likens democracy to a party in which the wine server goes on serving wine to young men who are already in a state of inebriation and are bent upon destruction and violence. Despite these strictures, democracy is still considered to be the best form of government, particularly in modern times, which has seen the rise of the autonomous self as the centre of experience and action. Historically speaking, Athenian democracy has evoked universal admiration. However, as Thucydides notes, Athens under Pericles was qualified in actual life by the fact that it was only "nominally a democracy, but actually a monarchy under the foremost man" (Thucydides 2000: II, 65.9). It was the monarchy of superior political ability. What is worth noting is the fact that *isonomia*, equality before law, does not imply equality in politics. Thucydides reports Pericles saying that in Athens every men is alike before the law, but "in politics the aristocracy of talent is supreme" (Ibid.: II, 37.1).

The implication of *isonomia* is, then, quite clear. Logically, it implies the principle that if one man is supremely valuable, he should be recognized as the ruler of the state.[1] This suggests that even while the political activity of each individual has some value for the community, people alone cannot possibly govern a large and complex state. A very emphatic confirmation of this fact is available in the mock funeral speech that Aspasia, wife of Pericles, delivered in her salon. She called the Athenian polity under Pericles an aristocracy and sought to show that it is and always was "the rule of the best with the consent of the people" (Plato, *Menexenus* 238c in Jaeger 1986).

It is not that only democracy as a system of government displays two important aspects: myth and reality. All types of governments do so. However, they differ in terms of their constitutive principles and way they are pragmatically manifested. The pragmatic manifestations of governments differ widely, even if their purpose remains constant. However, it can be asked, what is the purpose of the government? Following Eric Voegelin, we can say that "to set up a government is an essay in world creation" (1997: Appendix A, 225). By setting up a government, a world is created out of "a shapeless vastness of conflicting human desires" and then there "rises a little world of order, cosmic analogy, a cosmion, leaving a precarious life under the pressure of destructive forces within and without maintaining its existence the ultimate threat and application of violence against the internal breaker of its laws as well as the external aggressor" (Ibid.).

The application of violence, whether actual or potential, by the government is only to maintain itself in history; it is not its actual function. Its actual function is, to quote Voegelin again, "the creation of a shelter in which man may give his life a semblance of meaning" (Ibid). Thus, all types of government symbolize order, a cosmos albeit on a smaller scale. As an instance of cosmion, the government has necessarily two important dimensions. The first of these dimensions involves the rationalization of the shelter function, while the other concerns the pragmatic manifestation of this shelter function. Different rationalizations of the shelter function and their differing pragmatic manifestations represent just one way of visualizing the drama of history. On this view, we can take history as a stage on which have appeared, played their role and then disappeared in an unbroken sequence, a variety of governments. All such manifestations, that is, governments, are power-units created for action in history.

Different manifestations of the rationalization of the shelter function signify the rise and fall of one power-unit after another. Democracy is just one link in this sequence. The circumstances in which democracy appeared as a power-unit and the structure of its pragmatic manifestation have a great bearing on and relevance for apprehending the substantive aspects of democratic theory and practice. We have, thus, to take into account the circumstances in which the appearance of democracy was made possible. Along with it, we have also to take note of the character, the circumstances governing the appearance of democracy stamp on the theory and practice of democracy for understanding how these shelter function works. Only then, we can appreciate the functioning of the shelter function. Before we do so, it is necessary to clarify a couple of points. In the first place, the rationalization of the shelter function implies a primordial insight into the structure of order, which, when systematically developed into a theory, represents just one aspect or dimension in the tradition of theoretical thinking. However, when this rationalization enters the stream of history, that is, when it assumes concrete institutional shape, it becomes vulnerable to pollutions that existential conditions of man engender. Then a gap between what the theory prescribes and what pragmatically happens or is possible appears. It is not, however, to deny that the theoretical formulation itself may suffer from certain lacuna.

In the second place, democracy happens to be just one instance of political order. As a particular instance of political order, it may signify a creative and innovative imagination; however, it is nonetheless a finite system of order. Yet it is an example of the cosmos writ small, a cosmion. As an instance of order, it must be "considered to be the perfect exemplar of order and at the same time, the cause of all order in particulars which only in degrees can approximate the whole" (Jonas 1968: 242). Clearly, then, the term "cosmos" signifies not simply that it is fully ordered but also that this order is also the source of disciplining and regulating human conduct. It is precisely in this sense that the terms "praxis" and *shastra* are used to exemplify the process of both contemplation and regulation of conduct by the principle derived from the process of contemplation. The two meanings of the term *shastra—shansanam* and *shāsanam*—signify just this.

Given this signification of the term "praxis," can we say that the democratic order that prevails today constitutes both the exemplar of order as well as the source of disciplining and regulating human conduct? The apprehension of the significance of the term "order" holds the key to the understanding of the relationship between democratic theory and praxis. One complicating factor in facilitating this comprehension is, of course, the universal acceptance of democratic form of government and, consequently, the claim of every type of regime to being democratic or, at least, a necessary stage on its journey towards the esteemed goal— democracy. One reason for this is that democracy today has no rival; it has gradually vanquished all other types of regimes. That is why Alexis de Tocqueville referred as early as 1835 to the advent of democracy as a governing power in the world's affairs, a power, which he recognized as a universal and irresistible force. It has overthrown the feudal system, vanquished mighty kings and stymied communism in our own days. In its onward march since its inception, democracy has been universally and invincibly victorious.

Modern democracy made its appearance late in the eighteenth century. And Benjamin Franklin announced its appearance as the rising of a new sun. This sun has now mounted the highest peak of political firmament and its rays are illuminating even the darkest corners of the world. They fill the heart of mankind with a new hope, a hope that excites it with pleasurable expectations. "For the world over, it is increasingly the focus of hopes for a brighter future and aspirations for a life of freedom and dignity" (Baechler 1998). Undoubtedly, the hopes it has raised, the expectations it has created and the desires it has stimulated—all of them have made democracy a universally desirable political system. As a result of the respectability it enjoys, democracy has come to be applied to different situations, evokes different images and works differently in different political climates. It seems to have become an honorific term and creates in its trail a bandwagon effect prompting all kinds of regimes to ride the wave of current fashion of opinion.

It is no wonder, then, that George Orwell painted a very attractive picture of democracy when he refers to the ambiguity of its significance. As he says:

> In the case of a word like democracy not only that there is no agreed definition but the attempt to make one is resisted from all sides.... The defenders of any kind of regime claim that it is democracy, and fear that they might have to stop using the word if it were tied down to any one meaning. (Roy 2005: 1)

The multiple signification of the term "democracy" prompts Tocqueville, an ardent advocate of democracy, to point to the confusion that prevails in the use of such terms as "democracy" and "democratic government." As he notes, "Unless these words are clearly defined and their definition agreed upon, people will live in an inestimable confusion of ideas, much to the advantage of demagogues and despots" (Ibid.: 3). This confusion impels Juvenile de Bertrand to complain: "Discussions about democracy, arguments for and against it, are intellectually worthless because we cannot know what we are talking about" (Sartory 1965: 8).

The multiple signification of the term "democracy" is not the only complicating factor. What complicates further is the nature of the idea of democracy. As it has evolved over the long stretch of history, the idea of democracy evokes three different images. These images do not gel together to produce a well-integrated homogeneous concept of democracy. It creates confusion whose source, as Burzio points out, lies in the fact that it means different things to different people. As he says: "In a democratic whole we must make a distinction between three diverse elements: (a) a reality, that is, rapid circulation of elites; (b) a desire, that is, equality and (c) an illusion, that is, direct government by the masses" (Ibid.). What is interesting to note is that this illusion is further reinforced by Abraham

Lincoln's characterization of democracy as the government "of the people, by the people and for the people."

This characterization of democracy conceals the wide gap that exists between the expectations democratic political order builds and the reality that underlies it. Democratic theory locates sovereignty in the people and declares them the ruler, masters of their own destiny. This signifies not only that sovereignty has been transferred from the monarch to the people, but also that it is the people who now hold the reins of governance either directly and if it is not for any reason possible, then, through their representatives. Thus, while sovereignty is still nominally with the people, political power has, in reality, shifted to their representatives. Veogelin has designated this shift in the location of political power as "the articulation of society." With the collapse of the medieval civilization—a civilization that was inspired by and embodied the ethos of Christianity—a radical change took place in both thought-ways and work-ways. The rise of secularism not only put paid to the idea of *civitas dei* that was so laboriously put on its feet by Saint Augustine. It also put a question mark on the ground of legitimacy of the ruler, whether constitutional or not. In addition, it also led to the assertion of the right of those who are considered politically conscious sections of the community to have a share in the management of public affairs. This is what Marsilius of Padua argued. This led gradually to the inclusion of different sections of society into the process of government.

In this process, the content of articulation of society changed until it ended up by drawing in every person in the governmental process. If earlier, the realm was in the service of the ruler, now the ruler was charged with the responsibility of serving the realm. The direction of articulation thus shifted its focus from the "realm for the ruler" to "the ruler for the realm." This process found its culmination in democracy. Lincoln's formulation of "government of the people, by the people and for the people" is perhaps the grand affirmation of the shift in the locus of power. As Voegelin puts it, this shift continues

> until the limit is reached where the membership of the society has become politically articulate down to the last individual and, correspondingly, the society becomes the representative of itself. Symbolically the limit is reached with the masterful dialectical concentration of Lincoln's "government of the people, by the people and for the people." (1987: 37)

This dialectical concentration of power into the hands of the people, however, failed to become factual for several reasons, all of which it is not possible to discuss here. The failure of the ideal of democracy to become real is a fact that has a serious ramification for the existential condition of millions of people all around the world. It is this failure that Manicas refers to as "the victory of democratic ideology over democracy" (1988: 137). And it is democratic ideology, not democracy that rules over the destiny of the people in the world today. It is interesting to note that this victory could become possible by the same forces that made the appearance of democracy possible in the first place. These forces were released by the revolution of modern self-defining subjectivity. What this revolution did was to release the individual from all the constraints that customs, conventions, tradition and society had placed upon him. It made individual the centre of experience as well as the agent of the regeneration of the institutions. This revolution was the inevitable consequence of the snapping of man's connection with the divine ground of being and the withdrawal of the spirit from public institutions.

This also meant that withdrawal of the divine shelter that previously provided sanctuary to men from the uncertainties and irritations of the inhospitable world, the individual had no alternative but to rely on his own powers to refashion the conditions of his existence. The process of refashioning must follow the dictates of man's nature not as he ought to be but as Giambatista Vico insists, as he is. And what man's essential nature has come to be understood in modern times is as a being of appetites. Having lost his spiritual mooring, man emerged only as a truncated being, *homo economicus* or the economic man because his material needs received primacy. Once his material needs assumed primacy, man had to transform/manipulate nature for satisfying his ordinary life-needs involved with production and reproduction. In order to be able to do so, the individual must have freedom to plan and execute what he plans. However, freedom is vacuous if it is not accompanied by equality. It is only when the individual is equipped with both freedom and equality that he can be expected to be able to realize his self-defined purposes. Only when these purposes are realized can man hope to grow to his full stature and ensure his flourishing, not only as a social being but also as a political man.

The realization of self-defined purposes is, however, dependent upon the individual's capacity to see clearly what his interests are; also, he must have sufficient courage and self-respect to press for them by speaking up by actively involving himself in the determination of policies that the state does or proposes to pursue. Thus, there are three different but interrelated values that modern democracy celebrates. These values are freedom, equality and popular rule. But prominent among these values is, of course, equality. Tocqueville considers equality as of momentous importance so much so that other values are derived from and on which they converge. As he says, "the gradual development of the principle of equality is a providential fact, it is universal, it is durable, it constantly eludes all human interference and all events as well as all men contribute to its progress" (Tocqueville 1959).

Several consequences have followed because of the squeezing out of the spirit from personal lives and social relations. First, de-divinization of the world symbolizes what Max Weber calls "disenchantment of the world:" this signifies value subjectivity as well as value plurality. As Weber makes it clear, we live in a disenchanted world: the meaningfulness of "a meaningful cosmos" centres around interests, particularly material interests. The ground for meaningful cosmos is, Weber insists, rationalization, the capacity to control the world through calculation (Weber 1958: 17). Diversity of interests creates value pluralism and value pluralism cannot be negotiated based on the supremacy of any one principle (Shils and Finch 1949: 17) or one interest.

Given the fact that value plurality precludes the negotiation of interests based on the supremacy of any one principle, the way for making public decisions has to be found. And the way that was finally identified was the rule of all. The trouble with the rule of all, however, is that it does not automatically translate into the transformation of divided and fragmented space of opinions of individuals and groups into consistent, effective domain of public policy. Moreover, given the sheer size of a political entity occupying a large territory, it is not at all possible to involve every individual in the making of public choices. Moreover, industrial capitalism has pervaded most aspects of people's life. This has conspired to make public issues and policy making very complex making the role of expertise, science and technology indispensable (Giddens 1972: 45).

This has further reduced the role of the common man in democratic decision making.

The only solution, therefore, is representative democracy signifying the fact that instead of the demos directly participating in the making of public policies, their representatives, elected through periodical elections, will make collective decisions. However, this device is instrumental in dividing the citizens with the right to vote into politically active and politically passive elements (Schumpeter 1950: 285). This division signifies the reduction of the power of the sovereign people to the function of selecting representatives and it is the representatives that now stand proxy for the sovereign people and act in their name and on their behalf. It is this division, again, that establishes the principle of majority as the arbiter of who among the contending political parties is authorized to rule. By the same token, democracy has been robbed of its noble purpose of making it possible for the people to rule; it emerges simply as an institutional device that somehow facilitates the making of collective decisions. In short, then, democracy has been shorn of all its moral purposes; it is only an instrument of policy making in a situation of value plurality.

The downgrading of democracy as an ideal to an instrument without any moral significance is in stark contrast to Plato's idea of the state as a moral entity charged with the responsibility of making men moral or at least, keeping them on the path of virtue. The status of the state as a moral entity underlined the fact that the state and spirit mingled and merged in order to serve the community of men. However, when the form of government called democracy was reduced to the status of merely an instrument, the state and spirit not only separated but also became stranger to each other. As a result, the community of men lost its wholeness.

The transmutation of the state as a moral entity to merely an instrument has been the result of several factors and has passed through several stages of ideological and institutional developments. It is not possible to deal with all of them here. However, we can identify three crucial stages for our purpose. The first stage in this transmutation is the change in the substantive meaning of the term "community." Note, for example, that Plato talks of *philia politike* (love among men in a political community) as the ingredient that makes a political system just and salubrious; such a political order is capable of safeguarding *homonoia* (originally signifying the absence of factional fighting). However, the substantive meaning of community undergoes a slight change because of the introduction of Christian charisma. Every one of the diverse members of community possesses dignity and as individuals they so complement one another as to form all together through baptism the body of Christ (*corpus mysticum*). The ethics of the community are determined by the Ten Commandments and the new law, the law of love described in chapter in the Bible: "Thou shalt love thy neighbour as thyself. Love worketh not ill to his neighbour. Therefore, love is the fulfilling of the law." This evocation of community underlay the institutional arrangement of church and empire along the lines developed by Saint Augustin.

Again, a change came about in the substantive meaning of community when John Fortescu (d. 1476) detached the notion of *corpus mysticum* from Christ and imputed it to the community of men without their grounding in any transcendental entity. For Fortescu, a political order is an organic whole with the ruler as the head and the people as different limbs of the organic body politic. The political order signifies a mystical body (*corpus mysticum*) with its immanent logos, which he identified with *intencio populi* (intention of the people) (Fortescu 1885). For him, *intencio populi* is the heart from which "its nourishing blood stream (supplies) the political provision for the well-being of the people" (Voegelin 1959: Preface). *Intencio populi*, the animating force of a social body cannot be found in any of its human members. It is located neither in the royal representative nor in the people as a multitude of subjects but in the intangible living centre of the realm as a whole. Fortescu thus breaks the link between political order and the cosmic order; he paves, as such, the way for the creation of an absolute cosmos out of the finite forces of human desire and will.

Second, with the snapping of the link between political order and the cosmic order, the concrete community of men came to be the locus of the mystical element of community based *intencio populi*. However, the community could not retain its organic quality for long because of the proliferation of economic interests imposed on the previously existing divisions of ethnic and/or racial differences. Thus, society, whether small or large, inexorably came to be divided into numerous competing interests, each of them vying for articulation, ascendancy and control. However, the numerous socio-economic interests entered the political arena not all at once; their entry into politics was determined by the extent to which they happened to exercise control over different power resources. Thus, when interest became the primary impulse in man's life, justification for inducting various socio-economic interests were not far to come. For example, Marsilius of Padua made, sometime in the fourteenth century, a differentiation between the common man and what he called *pars valentior*, that is, those sections of society whose weight—intellectual, social or political—cannot be ignored.

The process of the inclusion of various socio-economic interests did not stop here. With the inclusion into the political process of more and more socio-economic interests, contesting for access to scarce material resources aggravated the opposition between freedom and control. When liberty combines with diverse interests, factions form. Each of these factions is driven by a common impulse of passion or interest that proves adverse to the right of others. In such a situation, full participation by the common man infuses in the body politic the moral disease of conflict, instability, injustice and confusion. Such an eventuality cannot be prevented when the pursuit of interest becomes aggressive and as a result, the good of the whole community is lost sight of. Thus, the community, which valued *homonoia* came, slowly but certainly, to be invaded by the disease of factional fights. Consequently, the relationship between the good of one individual and the good of all individuals was irrevocably broken.

And last, with a view to endowing the political system with institutional resources to effectively deal with emergent problem either of the opposition between freedom and control or of the possibility of one major interest either singly or as an aggregation of several interests spanning a large territory exercising political power, the political system came to rely on artificially creating and maintaining an institutional device. Machiavelli, for example, argued that conflict is a necessary characteristic of an organized political system. However, it can be controlled. What is necessary is not recourse to any God-given framework for ordering political and social relations, but to employ a political artifice. It is what Machiavelli proposes for establishing a proper balance between the powers of the state and the powers of the citizen. And it is what Hobbes delineates in his *Leviathan*.

For Machiavelli, liberty must be preserved; however, its adverse consequences must be contained and controlled by an appropriate political institutional arrangement. This arrangement is nothing else but a mixed government combining the elements of monarchy and democracy. Such an arrangement would permit, Machiavelli argued, the balancing of interests of rival social groupings, particularly those of the rich and the poor. When drawn into the political process, these interests would find legitimate political expression and encourage mutual accommodation. Each watchful of its own position, both would expand greater efforts to ensure that no laws are passed that are detrimental to their interests. As a consequence, a body of law would develop to which everyone will agree and obey. This is what Machiavelli prescribes for ensuring *homonoia*.

Obviously, Machiavelli puts his faith either in deterrence because of the possibility of the clash of interests or in the goodwill of interests in opposition. He overlooks the possibility of the failure of deterrence or fails to take into account the quicksand nature of goodwill. Moreover, Machiavelli also overlooks the fact that the tendency of the factions to gain unchallenged political supremacy has a much more deleterious effect on the political system. It is what James Madison came to realize and proposed to deal with the help of political artefact.

Madison treats factions as the prime source of distortion in the political system. The source of distortion inheres in the possibility that a faction might emerge as very powerful and become a durable majority. If and when this possibility turns into actuality, "the form of popular government... enables it to sacrifice to its ruling passion or interest both the public good and the rights of other citizens" (Hamilton, Madison and Jay 1982: no. 10). It is, therefore, necessary to control the effects of factional competition. In Madison's view, delegation of authority through representation and extension of territory in order to prevent a durable majority from emerging would perhaps protect the rationality of politico-administrative decision-making by separating it from what Habermas calls "legitimizing political will formation" (Habermas 1975: 86). These two devices, Madison believed, would ensure the election of those "whose wisdom may best discern the true interest of the country and whose patriotism and love of justice will be least likely to sacrifice it to temporary and partial considerations" (Habermas 1975: 86). And finally, if the respective legal powers of the executive, legislative and judiciary are separated, both at national and local levels, freedom can best be protected.

All the three factors, that we noted earlier, led bit by bit to the victory of democratic ideology over democracy, as Manicas has reminded us. It also makes it clear why Burzio speaks of the three dimensions of democracy as a whole. All these developments, that we have only briefly sketched, have paved the way for the degeneration of a noble aspiration into a mere institutional device, a device that has been disrupted from its sustaining moral sensitivities. And this device has been assigned the onerous task of producing, out of a myriad of conflicting interests and incompatible political perspectives, a wholesome, well-integrated policy domain reflecting the true interest of the country. For doing so, the democratic political regime has available to it (a) a score of disjointed, partial and particularized interests, (b) power-hungry elites grouped into rival political parties with pronounced tendency towards promiscuity and (c) a passive, politically ill-educated and divided body of citizenry. This body of citizenry is made responsible for nurturing and sustaining a democratic system of government, which does not bear any weightier responsibility than selecting every five year the persons who are going to rule over them. It is with the help of these resources that a democratic regime is expected to tease what Rousseau calls "General Will" out of the bitter contests of particular general wills.

Three factors intervene to make the process of the transformation of particular general wills into general will not only difficult but also defective. First, as Schumpeter points out, because of the expanding influence of industrial capitalism, politics has been transformed into business; this reduces the role of the citizen to that of what he calls acclaiming the selection of "ruler-managers" (Schumpeter 1950: 285). If this is so, there is nothing surprising about it. After all, even the social order, as Macpherson shows, is inspired by possessive individualism (Macpherson 1966) and underlines the crucial role of contract in social life and relations. Thus, social order, too, resembles a market and can do no better than to give birth to a market-made democracy. As Hirsch puts it, "the political arena …is akin to the market mode for the fulfillment of personal wants. It is an extension of departmental store—and the problem is to find managers who can undersell the rest of the street" (Hirsch 1977: 93–94).

Second, given the fact of market-mode democracy, it is not surprising that there is so much accent on the wisdom and sagacity of the "ruler-managers" for producing a general will out of the contesting, conflicting particular general wills as well as to pull the political system back from the brink of disaster, where it often gravitates. However, this raises the most difficult question of who governs the governors. Like the Olympian gods, "ruler-managers" are above the mundane affairs of the world;

however, they have also vital stakes in how these affairs are run insofar as their interests might be harmed if things do not work in the way that protects or at least, does not harm their own interests. Moreover, they are easily swayed in managing public affairs by their own selfish ends of acquiring and securing power resources with a view to enjoying unchallenged political ascendancy and supremacy. For this, they have no compunction in violating procedural safeguards. When this happens, watchdogs turn into dangerous wolfs.

And last, if the role of the citizen is simply to acclaim the selection of "rulers-managers," it follows that the citizen does not participate in the making of political decisions and has, therefore, much less interest in what happens in or to the political system unless it impinges heavily on his own small world of everyday routine. Moreover, to restrict democratic participation proves dysfunctional when the system finds it difficult to satisfy the increasing demands of the people for a better life, demands stimulated by the system itself. As a result, the lack of the people's participation in a situation of frustrated hopes and aspirations of the people, promotes alienation of the people from the system, which becomes widespread.

All these factors have conspired to expose democratic government to a variety of threats. These threats range from jeopardy of procedural safeguards by governing elites seeking to perpetuate their power, to the pressing of popular demands that exceed what the system can provide (Bachrach 1969). It is no wonder then that democratic government is, in fact, of the people; it is, however, not run by the people nor does it usually work for the people. This can be empirically verified by a reference to Indian experience of democracy (Roy 2009). And since people's hopes and aspirations remain unfulfilled and an extreme inequality prevails in the distribution of societal resources, justice suffers. "A realm may have a legal order and the power to enforce it as well; it may even observe correct procedures, but what is such a realm but a *latrocinium* (a band of robbers), if justice is missing" (St. Augustine 1957–72)?

Modern democracy, insofar as it makes representation the key to its functioning, represents a system that is based on alienation. As Collins argues, "man self-consciously articulates secular order and chooses to transfer responsibility from self to state in representation" (Collins 1989: 168). This leads to alienation: at the same that the demos transfer his responsibility, he alienates himself from his representative. It is true that, as Collins suggests, by the nature of his articulating capacity, he retains original authority for social order. However, this authority is only symbolic, not real and, therefore, vacuous. These two instances of alienation combine to produce what Brown calls "vicarious satisfaction:" "the deed is both theirs and not theirs. On this self-contradiction, this hypocrisy, this illusion, representative institutions are based" (Brown 1989: 117).

Note

1. Aristotle suggests that the *spudaios,* the mature man, as the one who surpasses all others in virtue, must be treated "like a god among human beings" (*Politics* 1962: 1284a: 3–11). He must, therefore, be made a permanent king. However, he scuttles the idea on the ground that "the rest of the citizens will necessarily be debarred from honours since they will not occupy civic offices" (Ibid.). For a useful discussion, see Roy (2002: 52–56).

References

Bachrach, Peter. 1969. *The Theory of Democratic Elites.* London: University of London Press.

Baechler, Jean. 1998. *Democracy: An Analytical Survey.* New Delhi: National Book Trust of India. Preface.

Brown, Norman O. 1989. *Love's Body.* New York: Random House.

Collins, Stephen L. 1989. *From Divine Cosmos to Sovereign State.* New York: Oxford University Press.

Fortescu, John. 1885. The Governance of England. Ed. Charles Plummer. Oxford: Clarendon Press.

Giddens, Anthony. 1972. *Politics and Sociology in the Thought of Max Weber.* London: Macmillan.

Habermas, Jurgen. 1975. *Legitimation Crisis.* Boston: Beacon Press.

Hamilton, A., Madison J., and Jay John. 1982. *The Federalist Papers,* Bantam Classic Edition. New York: Bantam Dell.

Hirsch, Fred. 1977. *Social Limits to Growth.* London: Routledge and Kegan Paul.

Herodotus. 1954. *The Histories.* London: Penguin Classics.

Jaeger, Werner. 1986. *Paideia: The Ideals of Greek Culture,* Vol. 2, second edition. Oxford: Oxford University Press.

Jonas, Hans. 1968. *The Gnostic Religion: The Message of the Alien God and the Beginning of Christianity.* Boston: Beacon Press.

Macpherson, C. B. 1966. *Possessive Individualism.* Oxford: Oxford University Press.

Manicas, Peter T. 1988. "Foreclosure of Democracy in America," *History of Political Thought*, IX(1) (Spring).

Roy, Ramashray. 2002. *Political Order: The Vedic Perspective*. Shimla: Indian Institute of Advanced Study.

———. 2005. *Democracy in India: Form and Substance*. Delhi: Shipra Publications.

———. 2009. *Economy, Democracy and the State: The Indian Experience*. New Delhi: SAGE Publications.

Sartory, Giovanni. 1965. *Democratic Theory*. Calcutta: Oxford and IBH Publications.

Schumpeter, Joseph A. 1950. *Capitalism, Socialism and Democracy*. New York: Harper.

Shils, Edward, and A. Finch. (Eds). 1949. *Max Weber: The Methodology of Social Sciences*. Glencoe: The Free Press.

St. Augustine. 1957–72. *The City of God against the Pagans*. 7 vols; Civitas Dei IV. 4. London: Haineman.

Thucydides. 2000. *History of the Peloponnesian War*. London: Penguin Books.

Tocqueville, Alexis. 1959. Preface to the 12th edition of *Democracy*, 2 vols. New York: Vantage Books.

Voegelin, E. 1987. *The New Science of Politics*. Chicago: University of Chicago. Press

———. 1997. *Collected Works of Eric Voegelin*. Vol. 19, *History of Political Ideas, Vol. I: Hellenism, Rome, and Early Christianity*. Ed. Athanasios Moulakis. Columbia: University of Missouri Press.

Weber, Max. 1958. "Science as Vocation" in *From Max Weber: Essays in Sociology*. Eds H. H. Girth and C. Wright Mills. Gleane: Free Press.

5

Fault Line of Democracy

And democratic government is nothing but a device to organise the most freedom possible, and to maintain it.
—Herbert Agar, *The Perils of Democracy*, 1965: 10

I

In the latter half of the eighteenth century, Benjamin Franklin talked of the appearance on the horizon of the globe of a new sun. This new sun is, of course, democracy. In the words of Frederico Mayor, the Director General of the UNESCO, democracy has become the focus of the people's hope for a brighter future; it ensures the fulfilment of aspirations for a life of freedom and dignity. Democracy has, as Alexis Tocqueville attests, conquered all opposition, received universal admiration and won adherents all over the world, so much so that even those regimes, which do not qualify as democracy, claim to be democratic.

Democracy also made its appearance in India after independence. A new body of politic came into being which framed a constitution that established a democratic republic. The constitution promised, in the name of "we, the people of India," justice, social, economic and political to all citizens. This promise finds concrete expression in numerous provisions of the constitution and is reflected in the policies and programmes of social justice of the government of India.

Social justice in today's world means essentially the removal of gap between rich and poor in the distribution of material resources. This forms the basis of the possibility of realizing slumbering human potentialities. The stress on the removal of poverty emanates in modern times from two different sources: one, the realization that poverty is not inherent in human condition and two, life on the earth can be based on abundance.

This is symptomatic of coming into prominence of the economic motive as the driver of politics. As such, the claim of justice must be weighed against the actual elimination of the gap between rich and poor. With it, necessity, in the Aristotelian sense of the term, becomes the main driving force of politics today.

It is against this background that various policies and programmes of social justice in India assume central importance. The thrust of these policies and programmes has been to transform Indian society radically. They aim at creating a new social order that would realize the much sought after goal of the struggle for freedom movement, that is, freedom with dignity. The appearance of democracy, albeit in a modified form, that is, as a representative democracy, initiated a new era, an era that would turn its back, irrevocably, to millennia of Indian civilization and its cultural and institutional attributes.

The newly founded body politic was expected to initiate a new age full of promise and excitement, the promise of equality, dignity and self-determination and the excitement of participating in the task of building a new, vibrant and vigorous society. Jawaharlal Nehru voiced this when he talked in the Constituent Assembly about the moment when "we step out from the old to the new, when an age ends and when the soul of the nation, long suppressed, finds utterance..." (1947).

The transfer of power transformed the people of India from subjects to citizens and they acquired the status of sovereign people. As the sovereign, "we, the people of India" became the source and repository of political power—the power necessary not only for founding a republic but also for conserving it to make it durable and stable. It was to be a foundation that would make all earlier foundations obsolete and cancel all their features, characteristics and consequences. It would bring into being a new social order, which would make freedom secure for all and obviate fixed odds in the struggle for life.

India as a democratic republic was to usher in a new era, an era that envisaged democracy not only from the political but also from the social standpoint; that is, it envisaged "not only a democratic form of government but also a democratic society" infused with the spirit of "justice, liberty, equality and fraternity" (Basu 2008: 23). In short, Indian society was to be reconstructed in a manner that would allow it to be hospitable to the ethos of modernity. It was to be a society that made it possible for all, especially the deprived and depressed sections of Indian society, to achieve the goal of self-determination, dignity and equality, all these denied to them for centuries. It is in this sense that democracy in India represents a profound revolution.

It represents a revolution not merely in the political sense but also, and more profoundly, in the social sense, since it aims at getting India "out of medievalism based on birth, religion, custom and community and reconstruct(ing) her social structure on modern foundations of law, individual merit and secular education" (Santhanam 1946). How far has this objective been realized? How do we test the advance the Indian political system has made in the last six decades? What should be the basis of this test? Does this test lie in the efficiency and effectiveness with which the Indian political system has successfully carried out the important function of forming and sustaining governments during the last six decades? Can the electoral performance alone be the ground of evaluating the performance of democratic republic in India?

It is true that elections in India have wrought profound changes and have firmed up the foundation of what we know as representative democracy. Electorally, India has done remarkably well both in terms of popular participation and peaceful and orderly change in government. However, electoral performance alone cannot be a sufficient ground for evaluation because it reduces democracy merely to the status of an instrumental device that facilitates the making of public choices in a situation of value subjectivity and interest plurality. Democracy has other and more important dimensions, the dimensions of equality, dignity and self-determination, the dimensions against which can be measured what it has achieved in terms of increasing the welfare of the people, the people who founded the republic. This suggests that the evaluation of the functioning of democracy in India cannot be limited to electoral performance alone.

The founding of a democratic republic is not sufficient in itself. After all, it was founded to realize what the people of India set for themselves to realize through the instrumentality of the newly established body politic. In this, the political system is guided in its movement in history by a constitution. The constitution is the product of the articulation and expression of the will of the people. It is the will of the people that creates an operational device for the realization of certain ends that the political community aims at realizing. It is what Voegelin calls the existential aspect of the political system (1981).

Thus, the act of beginning is not an act that is arbitrary and random; it is an act that is pregnant with both principiul and principle (or *arche* which, again signifies both the beginning and the principle). It is this principle that has to be conserved through augmentation and this constitutes *auctocritas*, a word derived from *augere* meaning to augment, increase and enlarge the foundation as it has been laid down. "The uninterrupted continuity of this augmentation and its inherent authority could come about only through an unbroken line of succession, of the principle established in the beginning" (Arendt 1965: 201).

It signifies a coincidence of authority, tradition and piety (towards the principle). Without this piety, the act of conserving through augmentation is not possible. All these three simultaneously spring from the act of foundation and must be preserved for sustaining the revolutionary spirit. Moreover, it is piety that links conservation with augmentation; it signifies *religare*, that is, to bind oneself back to the beginning and in the process to augment and preserve it in the present. Thus, the Indian Constitution constitutes the beginning of a new story, started by freedom fighters, which must be enacted further, to be augmented and spun out by posterity (ibid.: 47).

Thus, the criterion of the evaluation of the working of democracy in India cannot be formulated in terms of anything external to it or with reference to any absolute standard for that matter. The criterion, if it lies anywhere, lies in the beginning itself. However, what are in the beginning are the constitution itself and the principles that are contained in it. In addition, the principles that are contained in the constitution underline heavily the need for justice in the envisioned new social order that grants equality, dignity and self-determination to all. Individual freedom and equality of status of all citizens are central to this vision. According to modern sensibilities, all these components are essential ingredients of making man's life noble and materially comfortable.

It is therefore necessary to go beyond electoral performance and focus on the substantive aspect of the newly created body politic. For this, it is necessary to follow Filippo Burzio's suggestion of making a distinction between three different elements of democracy. These are: democracy as (a) a reality, that is, rapid circulation of elites, (b) a desire, that is, equality and (c) an illusion, that is, direct government by the masses (quoted in Sartory 1965).

Leaving aside the first dimension, our evaluation must focus on the extent to which equalization of life conditions of different social groups has been achieved. This we do through exploring the extent to which (a) economic well-being of different social groupings has been achieved and (b) provisioning of public health care services have been accessible to the depressed and deprived sectors of the Indian population. These two components are important for carrying forward the revolutionary élan of democracy in India. These two components are important for carrying forward the revolution of democracy in India.

In case Indian democratic republic lags behind in equalizing life conditions, a necessary prerequisite for equalizing life chances of different social groupings, the reasons for this must be identified and explanation for it must be advanced. This necessitates the mapping, even if only selectively, of the theoretical domain for identifying the possible factors responsible for this state of affairs.

How has India performed in terms of these two components? As a recent, very important study, *Caste in a Different Mould: Understanding the Discrimination 2010 by* Rajesh Shukla, Sunil Jain and Preeti Kakkar (2010) shows that India's demographic structure is still heavily tilted in favour of the upper castes—whether in terms of the income they earn or jobs they hold. This is reflected in a set of four very disturbing patterns of inequality and disparity. The first pattern indicates that higher we go in caste hierarchy, larger the income becomes. Second, within each caste group inequality prevails and makes for differential incomes for different castes.

Third, this inequality is greatly accentuated as the level of educational attainment rises higher. Last, different social groupings receive larger income in states with higher GDP. For instance, upper castes in India comprise just 34.1 per cent of the population, but earn 45 per cent of income. In contrast, Scheduled Castes (SCs) comprise 16.8 per cent of the population, but account for just 11.8 per cent of income and Scheduled Tribes (STs) constituting 8 per cent of population have just 5 per cent of income as their share.

This is simply a rough and ready indicator of the persistence of inequality and disparity in the availability of resources to different social groupings. However, the ramification of this inequality goes deeper and farther.

Access to economic resources is the gateway to education, which opens the gate to better life conditions and utilization of health care services. Furthermore, the government of India recognizes health and education as constituting two important elements of the good life of modern conception.

Education constitutes the central axis around which modernity is constructed. Almost all the central values of modernity such as democracy, equality, mobility and the ability to define oneself depend upon access to education. In addition, educational achievement facilitates migration, which, in turn, ensures higher income, especially in urban centres and more developed states. However, access to education is still unequally distributed and highly skewed in favour of upper castes.

Inequality can be observed not only across social groups but also within each of the social groups. As we go up in caste hierarchy, not only the income level rises, also the level of education goes up. Note, for example, that the proportion of households with at least one member having completed secondary school is 11.7 per cent for the STs, 12.6 per cent for the SCs and 18.6 per cent for the Other Backward Classes (OBCs) but it jumps to 20.4 per cent for the upper castes.

The same pattern is observable in the case of graduate-level education: 8.9 per cent for the STs, 13.8 per cent for SCs, 16 per cent for the OBCs and 34.4 per cent for the upper castes are graduates and above. This inequality is repeated also in the case of per capita income per household: ₹8,456 for the STs, ₹9,109 for SCs, ₹11,931 for the OBCs and ₹17,318 for the upper castes.

There is greater inequality across education levels. For instance, the difference of 1.4 times between what an upper caste illiterate and an illiterate ST or SC earn (₹31,511 versus ₹22,456 per year) as compared to a difference of 3.7 between an illiterate ST and a graduate ST (₹22,456 versus ₹85,023) and 4.2 between an illiterate upper caste and a graduate upper caste (₹31,511 versus ₹136,086).

And here too inequality in access to education in two senses—utilization and cost—is characteristic of Indian society even after six decades of intense economic growth. It is true that there has been a great expansion in educational institutions at all levels. Yet the distribution of educational benefits remains highly skewed favouring those groups that occupy the higher terrains of the social order. For instance, only 1.5 per cent of the upper caste persons are illiterate as compared to 8.6 per cent of both the STs and SCs. In terms of graduate and above, the difference is almost three times.

There is, of course, a great demand for education. However, even though children of STs/SCs go to school, they have to dropout in large numbers because of economic necessity. Also, the poor are forced to spend out of their pockets for education over ₹5,000 annually in urban areas where educational facilities are concentrated. This simply means that the poor people, belonging especially to STs/SCs, save less and are therefore more vulnerable to contingencies of life. Also interesting is the fact that as the level of education rises, the proportion of expenses also rises.

An illiterate ST household spends 2.5 per cent of its income on education as compared to 10 per cent of a graduate ST household. Add to it also the fact that there is a strong relationship between expenditure on education and health. As the expenditure on education rises with the rising level of education, the expenditure on health falls proportionately but not in absolute terms. It is clear, then, that the age-old inequality and disparity among traditional social groupings has not by any means been eradicated, even while some of its stings may have been taken out.

The situation gets murkier when we take into account the provisioning of public health care services. Despite impressive economic performance after the introduction of economic reforms in the 1990s, progress in advancing the health care services has lagged far behind. It is slow, tardy and uneven. In fact, economic growth has been accompanied by deceleration in health care services after 1990s. This is despite heavy expansion over the years in health services, both public and private.

The National Family Health Survey (2005–06) reveals sharp regional and socio-economic divides in health outcomes with the lower castes, the poor and the less developed states bearing the burden of mortality and malnutrition heavily. High rates of infant mortality rates and under-five mortality are, in general, inversely related with income. This means that the occurrence of child mortality is higher in poor families. The risks of mortality before the age of five years are higher in girls than in boys among the SCs, the STs and OBCs as compared to others.

As the World Bank report, "The Economic Impact of Inadequate Sanitation in India" (as reported in the *Times of India,* 21 December 2010), estimates, inadequate sanitation cost India in 2006 was about $64 billion or 6.4 per cent of the GDP. Over 70 per cent of the economic impact was health-related with diarrhoea followed by acute lower respiratory infections. Moreover, it is the poorest of the people and children in poor families who have to bear the major brunt of inadequate sanitation. For instance, more than four-fifths of the preventive mortality related economic losses are due to deaths and diseases in children under five years of age. Diarrhoea among them accounts for a little over 47 per cent of the total health-related impact.

Insofar as the poor are concerned, the poorest fifth of the urban population bears the highest per capita economic impact of ₹1,699, which is much higher than the national average per capita loss of ₹1,000. It is not surprising in view of the fact that a large part of the countryside still serves as open latrine. In rural areas, where half of the population has no access to improved sanitation, about 575 million people defecate in the open. Even in urban area, 54 million people are estimated to go to open spaces for latrine. Moreover, over 60 per cent of the waste water is discharged untreated.

There are other darker sides of inequality and disparity. However, the preceding discussion is enough to highlight the impact of various social and economic divides on differential access of different social groups to societal resources. Social, economic and regional differences in economic well-being still persist. The persistence of socio-economic inequality and disparity is indicative of the failure of the Indian body politic to fulfil the constitutional promise of ensuring justice to all and especially to the poor and the needy.

This failure is related to still a larger failure of keeping the "pre-independence revolutionary spirit" alive; it is also, by the same token, symptomatic of the fateful failure of the post-independence phenomenon of the loss of remembrance of the revolutionary spirit that inspired pre-independence political upsurge and emerging out of it, the exalted dream of a new India. This is well illustrated by the post-independence obsession with civil liberties, the welfare of the individual even at the cost of his fellow men and the public opinion as the greatest force ruling an egalitarian democratic republic. There is in operation a tendency to equate, erroneously, civil liberties with the exercise of freedom. In short, it is, for the same reason, symptomatic also of the diminution of liberty under the pressure of necessity.

This underlines the fact that the initial revolutionary élan was lost, perhaps irretrievably and the phenomenon of *religare* was drowned in the clamour of hot, focused contests for privileged access to societal resources. Democracy that raised hopes and aspirations of millions of people for the good life seems to have lost its way in the crooked lanes of affluent and powerful self-seekers. We must then ask: Where does the fault line lie? How do we explain the fall of the great political ideal? These questions clamour for answer.

Where do we look for answers? Can the explanation be found in the nature of Indian culture that is usually credited with the quality of dampening the spirit of innovation and creativity? Alternatively, can it be successfully maintained that the mostly peaceful revolution that paved the way for the mighty British Empire to transfer power and quit was principally the consequence of the endeavour of a class of political elite, a class that was deeply imbued with the western, liberal ideas and dreams.

Perhaps, there is something in these arguments; however, to treat these as sole factors responsible for the loss of collective memory about the pre-independence revolutionary intent is to lose sight of the great awakening of the Indian people, especially during 1920s and 1930s, when the Indian people did not hesitate to make sacrifices to attain freedom and enjoy its fruits. Has the élan created by that upsurge been exhausted?

Where does, then, the source of the failure to bind oneself back to the beginning and increasing it lie? It is interesting to note that the large part of this failure can be attributed to the success of the revolutionary movement itself. "The act of founding the body politic, of devising the new form of government," notes Arendt, "involves the grave concern with the stability and durability of the new structure" (1965: 224). Undoubtedly, the act of founding is emblematic of the revolutionary thinking of the founders, of their progressive mindset for creating a new India. This mindset propelled them to fight for realizing their ideals and their concern to make what they had founded durable and stable, pushed them towards conservatism.

Thus, the interplay of two opposite concerns led them to seek to combine meaningfully the idealistic thrust of the revolutionary spirit and the practical, this worldly, secular concern for durability and stability of the newly established political order. The founders opted for the republican form of government with a view to combining both these concerns. This they did not because of its egalitarian character but because of its promise of great durability. By doing so, they created a structure of institutions that would give greater preference to power than to liberty, since freedom, when unchained, tends to turn into the rule of passion. And herein lies some of the important factors that are responsible for creating a fault line in the structure of democratic republic.

The answer to these questions does not lie anywhere else but in the intimations of the act of beginning itself. These intimations did lead to the initiation of the process of the reconstruction of Indian society. However, this process seems to have lost its way or, alternatively, have been waylaid in its movement onward. Two sets of factors, one psychological and the other structural, have played a major role in the development of the fault line in Indian democratic republic.

The revolutionary intent inherent in the act of founding the republic made it necessary to combine judiciously freedom and power. The former was necessary not only for enabling the people to resist tyranny against which they waged a relentless war for a long time. It was also necessary for stimulating and sustaining people's capacity to meaningfully participate in the building of a new India. The latter was essential for defending national sovereignty against external aggression.

It was also necessary for making the authority of the state effective in guiding and supervising national endeavour of ushering in the age of abundance. This was *sine qua non* for ensuring people's happiness, the foundation of the nation's strength. Independence, however, also brought forcefully to the consciousness of the country's leaders the depressing realization that liberation from the colonial rule spelled freedom only for the few and was hardly felt by the many who remained loaded down by the misery of their poverty.

Poverty is more than deprivation; it is a state of constant want whose ignominy consists in its dehumanising force. It puts men not only under the dictates of their body, that is, the absolute dictate of necessity. It also robs the poor their capacity of independent action and prevents them from actively participating in public affairs. It was, therefore, necessary to introduce in the national economy some dynamic elements to stimulate rapid economic growth as well as ensure equitable distribution of the benefits of development. Several factors intervened to lead astray the strategy of growth with justice (for details, see Roy 2009).

First, the consciousness of the poverty of the Indian people was felt most deeply by those who themselves had least experience of poverty and deprivation. Thus, they confronted the spectacle of poverty they did not themselves share. They had, therefore, to have in their efforts to eliminate poverty not only a sympathetic understanding, *verstehen* as Weber calls it, but also and more importantly, the capacity of raising their sympathetic understanding to the rank of supreme political passion and of the highest public virtue, as Robespierre called it (Arendt 1965: 74–75).

While the combination of these attributes in any leader is essential for keeping the revolutionary spirit alive, the difficulties in stimulating rapid economic growth because of the operation of the low-level growth trap, makes the task of radical economic changes to stimulate growth, very difficult, indeed. Add to it the political factor of the need of the leaders in power to keep intact their political support base for remaining in and returning to power. Large-scale changes in a society still under the influence of its traditional ways of looking and doing things are, by definition, unthinkable.

This meant the establishment of a proper strategy of dealing with the people and taking care of their existential problems. However, the term "people" has three different significations; this multiplicity of signification makes for confusion and a perplexing ambiguity. The term "people" has two different significations. If, on the one hand, it refers to the constitutive political body of citizenry as a unitary body politic, it also refers, on the other hand, to the class(es) that is needy and excluded de facto, if not de jure.

If this is not enough, the third signification of the term "people" in the sense of "many-ness," especially, diversity of socio-economic interests, complicates the matter further. To serve the cause of one of these categories is bound to leave the other discontented and unhappy. This, in turn, means depletion in the political capital of a representative. This inherent ambiguity makes possible dialectical oscillation, in political lexicon as well as in political action, between the people as a whole and people as a fragmentary multiplicity of needy and excluded bodies as well as people as the aggregate of diverse socio-economic interests.

It is true that with the French Revolution, sovereignty was entrusted solely to the people; however, people became an embarrassing presence and poverty along with exclusion an intolerable national scandal. That is why development assumed such a central place in overcoming this scandal. Development in this context means primarily, even exclusively, economic development, which, it is claimed, lays the foundation of all kinds of development including the growth in moral sensibility. This is well reflected in Lord Keynes' proposition that "economic development is the possibility of development."

On this view, economic development assumes a centrality as a prime value in human existence, a value that engenders and sustains other values without the assistance of any transcendent divine authority. The presumption behind this supposition is the resolve to engage in the secular enterprise of creating a human order in which the question of God has become obsolete. In this order, the enjoyment by all of equality, dignity and self-determination would ensure human flourishing. Human flourishing signifies, in this context, both material affluence and high morality, in short, virtuous materialism as the basis of happy life.

What is important to note is that with the recognition of poverty as the major problem to be solved, the issue, which previously used to be subsumed under social category became a political issue. As a political issue, politics ceased to be the apt instrument in removing poverty. Politics is instrumental only in evolving a policy frame and programmatic structure through persuasion and decision. The task of working out policies and programmes devolves on administration. However, apart from bureaucratic apathy and inefficiency, the impingement of politics on administration is likely not only to engender corruption but also to create lag in development.

It should also be added that what, essentially, development signifies is technologically induced and sustained economic growth. This finds impetus in the ever-increasing proliferation of needs. As such, needs become endless not only in the sense that they are de-linked from any higher end but also in the sense that they proliferate endlessly. And once the possibility of making good materially in life becomes real, the poor man's wish no longer remains restricted to "[t]o each according to his needs" but are transformed into "[t]o each according to his desires."

As Arendt (1965) points out, this has led to a situation in which the political has been overwhelmed by the demands of the social. The overwhelming of the political by the demands of the social symbolizes the dominance of production and consumption, which arises when politics admits the exigencies of man's physical necessities as its primary concern. Such an invasion is, of course, invited through compassion, but it becomes virtually irresistible under the pressure of the modern technological reduction of all activities to their instrumental value.

Several things happen as a consequence of this; we would take note of only a few of them. First, modern perspective on development underlines the inexorability of the satisfaction of ordinary life-needs. For this, access to and control over societal resources becomes *sine qua non*. However, scarcity of material resources induces intense competition among individuals and groups. This competition becomes all the more intense and pervasive because with the collapse of commonality, there remains nothing for the individual to share with others except for the common existence inspired by the same goal of privileged access to societal resources. It is the loss of commonality that prompts individuals and groups to get a larger share in scarce resources. As such, a scramble for scarce resources becomes unavoidable. To take part in this scramble is both natural and rational. However, it tends to erode the distinction between what is available because of getting ahead of others and what is available from a general advance shared by all. The individual who wants to have a larger share in the available material resources must engage in the game of beggar your neighbour. This is what everyone tries to do even though not everyone can. This erodes morality, eclipses interdependence, shatters structures of cooperation and destroys social concord (Hirsch 1977: 10).

What adds to it is the mingling of two not very compatible goals as preferred objectives of the newly created body politic. The constitution makers set the achievement of growth with social justice as the systemic goal. However, as Harvey points out, values of individual freedom and social justice are not, however, compatible. Pursuit of social justice presupposes social solidarity and a willingness to submerge individual wants, needs and desires in the cause of some more general struggle for, say, social equality or environmental justice (Harvey 2005: 41).

If the goal of social justice is to distribute material resources more equitably, the benefits accrue to individuals, not to the group as a whole. And since access to wealth, a key resource in modern times, is essential for promoting and securing human flourishing, the element of sharing wealth with others is eroded. In fact, insistence on privileged access to wealth becomes stronger. Thus, the fusion of freedom and social justice becomes instrumental in disrupting social solidarity, as is evident from extreme fractionation of Indian society today.

Second, it is true that economic development does increase, to an extent, material well-being. It is also true in the case of India where the floor of the standard of living has been raised a bit, in general and lessened the pains of deprivation of millions of people, in particular. However, there is no relationship between development and welfare. The increasing wants necessitate the production of more and more goods and services. However, with increasing resources, wants, too, increase correspondingly. As Hirsch argues:

> [I]ncrease in resources (and thereby in the availability of goods) does nothing to increase welfare since wants increase correspondingly. The extent to which existing demands are satisfied may never increase welfare because wants rise commensurably with resources. So, economic advance appears as one of those hoax races that leaves the participants in the same place. (1977: 60)

The story of the race in Alice in Wonderland is repeated in real life.

Third, central to liberal democracy has always been the philosophy of economic growth in one form or another. Given this, liberal democracy can hope to purchase relative quietude in any considerable degree only through a growing economy. Political conflicts over wealth can be less divisive and dysfunctional when the fund available is an expanding one rather than the one that is static or contracting. But growth always includes decline and instability, which translates into real human suffering. However, democratic government as well as the people who it rules over has neither mastered the self-discipline nor risen to the challenge of evolving mechanisms of confronting economic uncertainties; rather it destroys all such mechanisms that traditional societies had made available to them. And with the persistence of inequality and disparity, discontent is bound to mount and adversely affect the legitimacy of the legitimacy of the ruling coalition as well as of the political system.

And last, as John Stuart Mill's statement underlines, behind a liberal government, there must exist a liberal society (1910). A liberal society must be built up on the solid foundation of freedom-loving citizens who recognize and respect the freedom of others. The idea of "freedom" includes the indispensable conditions for realizing human potentialities.

Generally speaking, "man is free when he is not impeded by material or social or personal factors, in fully employing his uniquely human resources" (Cassinelli 1967: 135). Apart from the fact that a large number of the Indian people still lack requisite material resources and social deference, there is also the fact of the lack of public space where individuals could develop the attributes of citizenship. And the basic characteristic of a citizen is to transcend his own narrow self-interests and link his destiny with the collective he is a part of. The lack of public spaces where freedom can make its appearance has made it quite difficult to attain.

In their apprehension of disastrous consequences of fissiparous tendencies operating in the country for the integrity of the nation, the founders created a strong central government and turned their back on the idea of making local communities the loci of self-government and the seats of freedom and power. As such, democracy was deprived of vital and vibrant organs that could have promoted self-confident citizenship on a sustained basis. What it meant was the victory of democratic ideology over democracy. Lacking concrete organs, democratic republic also lacked the space "where the voice of the people could be fairly and peacefully discussed and decided by the common reason of the citizens" (Jefferson 1816).

It can be argued that certain structural factors are inherent in a democratic form of government, such as separation of powers, the party system, rotation in government, civil rights, etc. They are enough of the guarantee to safeguard individual freedom. Agar is quite confident of it when he says that "the problem of freedom is institutional: we must tame the government without diminishing it. The executive must have all powers needed to safeguard and to promote the well-being of the people, yet powers must not be used except by permission" (Agar 1965: 55). This is precisely what representative democracy, as Agar claims, does.

That this argument lacks force is evident from the fact that it invites the criticism of David Hume when he says, "political writers have established it as a maxim that, in contriving any system of government, and fixing the several checks and controls of the constitution, *every man ought to be supposed to be a knave*" (Ibid.: 52). Also note that, as Manent argues, separation of power means divided power and the "organization of powers in fact sets up a kind of generalized powerlessness" (2003).

Similarly, rotation is merely the device of "preventing the governing few from constituting themselves as a separate group with a vested interest of their own" (Arendt 1965: 238). Civil rights cannot be equated with the exercise of freedom because they stand for safeguards against the misuse of power by either the government or any other agency, not the positive power of doing something meaningful and beneficial by reasoned exercise of freedom.

To look at it from another perspective, it is often argued that the power of the citizen to oust a government by exercising the right to vote keeps the ruling coalition within the bounds of political propriety and makes it conform to the democratic rules of the game. This argument does not stand a scrutiny. As Walter Lippmann warns: "Merely to enfranchise the voters, even to give them true representation, will not in itself establish self-government; it may just well lead, in most countries it has, in fact led, to a new form of absolute state" (Quoted in Agar 1965: 51).

Alternatively, it is forcefully argued that political parties can, in the absence of direct participation of the people, be the best vehicle of not only preventing the possibility of the emergence of an absolute state, but also of ensuring the installation and continuity of democratic government by linking the demos with governing institutions. Political parties ensure political participation. This argument lacks persuasive power for three different reasons.

First, the very essence of participation is so watered down that citizens are denied all powers but one, the power to vote, merely a formal act. Second, the elite that springs from the people has nowhere enabled people *qua* citizens to make their entrance into political life and become true participants in public affairs. Third, as Arendt (1965: 277) argues, the lack of public spaces to which people would have entrance and from which the elite would be selected prevents the appearance of freedom and therefore true citizenship.

The trouble is that politics has become a profession and a career, and the elite is, therefore, chosen according to the standards and criteria that themselves are profoundly apolitical. "It is the nature of the party system that authentically political talents can assert only in rare cases and it is even rare that the specifically political qualifications survive manoeuvres of party politics with its demands for plain salesmanship" (Ibid.: 278).

Add also the fact that the hope that the members of the parliament would exercise free and well considered views on any particular issue being discussed in the House is belied because of strict party control over what its members speak and do. They are instructed to act according to the instructions of their respective parties. They become only rubber stamps. They may object to become rubber stamps, but they, however, continue in their humble duty of stamping.

No institutional devices can stand proxy for the active exercise of freedom; freedom gets nourishment from a share in public power. However, in the lack of more public space than the ballot box and more opportunity to make their voice public than the Election Day, the people are deprived of their share in public power. Thus, the ultimate aim of the struggle for freedom movement, that is, freedom, was defeated early in the life of the new democratic republic. The result has been that the failure to create "village republics" denied public space where freedom could appear. This has made it very difficult for individuals, groups and local communities to resist encroachment by state and federal governments on their private space. Also, these governments have grown so large and unwieldy that people find it very difficult to influence their thinking and action.

It can be argued that the belated introduction of the Panchayati Raj system in the country has surely provided the much-needed public space for the appearance of freedom. However, this argument does not carry much weight since Panchayats have become the arenas where private or partisan interests count and collide (Roy 1993). Moreover, they are so shackled by their necessity to depend upon the state for mobilizing financial resources for implementing state-planned, not self-determined plans and projects. In essence, then, the decentralization of the type that India has does not pave the way for the appearance of freedom because allowing a degree of local autonomy is only in the interest of the overall efficiency of the system.

Such a situation, as Jefferson was to argue, leads people to sink in "lethargy, the forerunner of the death to public liberty," or brings into play "the reserve power of revolution" (Jefferson 1787). However, only this power bursts forth and that usually chaotically. Moreover, the system robs the people of their power to resist. This is evident from Tocqueville's writings on democracy in America. As he points out, liberal democratic revolution posited the idea of freedom and equality as essential attributes of man in modern times.

Essential though they may be, dynamic interaction between them has, however, led to a perversion; the perversion of the emergence of the danger of equality being purchased at the cost of freedom, which, in the first place, made equality a fundamental tenet. Liberal democracy treats all men alike. However, "when men are alike, all are weak." Similarly, they are all equally powerless, poor in the resources for taking care of themselves. Unable to find means of satisfying their needs in themselves or in others, they have to turn to the government to seek protection as well as care and succour from the state.

Consequently, the state becomes too powerful and emerges as a titular head that increasingly encroaches upon what is profoundly private. It professes to work for the happiness of the people; however, it becomes the sole agent and arbiter of that happiness; it provides for their security, foresees and supplies their necessaries, facilitates their pleasures and manages their principal concerns. Not much remains for the people themselves to do since the government as a titular head spares them all the "care of thinking and the trouble of living" (Tocqueville 1958: 336). In short, liberal democracy seeks to make them men but succeeds in only keeping them in perpetual childhood. The heavy reliance on the government for getting equality ends up in the loss of real manhood.

The overwhelming of the political has produced three very adverse consequences. One, the unitary character of the people is destroyed by the claim of autonomous separate existence made by the multitude of fragmentary needy and excluded bodies. With it, the consensus underlying the political order breaks down. Two, the very meaning of the term "political" undergoes a sea change. The original meaning of the term *politiei*, as the constitutive principle of political order, loses its salience and, as a result, the political surrenders its controlling authority to politics, that is, those considerations that determine who gets what, when and how. Principled politics degenerates into bio-politics. And, last, with the competition for getting access to societal resources becoming highly contentious (Cassinelli 1967: 114) what Alasdair MacIntyre calls "civil war carried on by other means" comes to characterize democratic politics (2008: 253).

The second ambiguity concerns the idea of democracy itself. Just like the concept of people, the idea of democracy, too, has two significations. The first signification refers to its instrumental role in the sense that it renders the making of public choices possible in a situation of value subjectivity and interest plurality. In its instrumental role, democracy does not pretend to make men moral; it only allows negotiation between conflicting interests with a view to preserving order. As such, formal instrumental democracy, better known as representative democracy, is associated with the politics of fragmentary socio-economic interests. With the erosion of commonality, language, that links one person to another in the ties of what Plato calls *philia politike* (friendship among members of a political community), degenerates into individual voices. The upsurge of civil war carried on by other means is the natural consequence of this transmutation of language into voice.

In contradistinction to this, there is another sense of democracy, which underlines what Ambedkar used to call social democracy inspired by the recognition of equal worth, dignity and equality of the other. Such a democracy is naturally associated with the unitary body politic underpinned by the values of interdependence, cooperation and social harmony. Political lexicon and, by the same token, political action oscillate between these two significations of democracy and lends democratic politics with uncertainty, latency and high expectations without allowing these expectations to get realized.

It is true that the state becomes very powerful. However, two factors conspire to rob it of its role of neutral watchdog and a jealous and passionate guardian of the needy and the excluded. One, like the expansion of monetary value to practically all areas of life, democratic politics tends to extend the formality of contractual relations and centralized powers of social control to the entire range of social and commercial activity.

Two things then happen: one, representative democracy tends towards formalization and abstraction; the state is separated and isolated from the people it purports to govern. This leads, slow by slow degree, to what Guy Debord calls "society of spectacle." This tendency has become stronger with the emergence of the executive branch of the government as the dominant partner. This produces the danger of what Sheldon S. Wolin calls "inverted totalitarianism."

The second factor involves the coming of age of the corporate power and the collusion between the state and free market forces. This has tended increasingly to eclipse the good of those who lack economic and political power. As Colin Crouch notes:

> By the late 1990s it was becoming clear that in most of the industrialized world, whatever the party identity of the government, there was steady

consistent pressure for state policy to favour the interests of the wealthy—
those who benefited from the unrestricted operation of the capitalist
economy rather than those who needed some protection from it. (Crouch
2004: Preface)

Thus, the Lincolnian understanding of democracy as a political institutional arrangement created by the people for working for their welfare
has remained just a tantalizing ideal without any substance. The vaunted
ideal of freedom degenerates into the preservation of its outward form
and the quest for equality that aims at creating what Tocqueville calls
"virtuous materialism" succeeds only in enervating the soul and noise-
lessly bending the spring of action. People wish to remain free, but they
do not mind being led. They erroneously believe that they are not being
controlled because they have elected their controllers.

The interplay of all these factors is instrumental in the degeneration of
the democratic ideal into the harsh struggle for power and pelf. This is
symptomatic of the lurking of oligarchy, the rule of the few over many,
beneath the appearance of democracy. Democratic politics, thus, yields for
the citizens only what Norman O. Brown calls vicarious satisfaction: the
deed is theirs and not theirs. On this self-contradiction, on this hypocrisy
and on this illusion, representative institutions are based. However, it is
argued that this is a part of the democratic game; the voter is assumed to
be represented and the assumption, it is claimed, as Winston Churchill
had to point out, is complete humbug, which is a small price to pay for an
orderly constitutional system (Agar 1965: 52). The result of this humbug
cannot, therefore, be anything else than the betrayal of the democratic ideal.

Does not all this underline, rather emphatically, the need for us to
look to Mahatma Gandhi for guidance in establishing true democracy?

References

Agar, Herbert. 1965. *The Perils of Democracy*. London: The Bodley Head.
Arendt, Hannah. 1965. *On Revolution*. Hammondsworth: Pelican Books.
Basu, Durga Das. 2008. *Introduction to the Constitution of India*. Nagpur: Lexis-Nexis
    Butterworth.
Cassinelli, C. W. 1967. *The Politics of Freedom: An Analysis of the Modern Democracy*.
    Cambridge: Polity Press.

Crouch, Colin. 2004. *Post-democracy*. Cambridge: Polity Press.

Harvey, David. 2005. *A Brief History of Neoliberalism*. Oxford: Oxford University Press.

Hirsch, Fred. 1977. *Social Limits to Growth*. London: Routledge and Kegan Paul.

Jefferson, Thomas. 1787. *Letter to Colonel William Stephens*. 13 November.

————. 1816. *Letter to Samuel Kercheval*. 12 July.

MacIntyre, Alasdair. 2008. *After Virtue: A Study in Moral Theory*. Notre Dame: University of Notre Dame Press.

Macro International and International Institute for Population Sciences. 2007. *National Family Health Survey (2005–06)*. Mumbai: International Institute for Population Sciences.

Manent, Pierre. 2003. "Modern Democracy as Separation," *Journal of Democracy, 14*(1) (January), 114–25.

Mill, John Stuart. 1910. *Utilitarianism, Liberty and Representative Government*. London: J. M. Dent & Sons.

Nehru, Jawaharlal. 1947. *Address to the Constituent Assembly*. 14 August.

Roy, Ramashray. 1993. "Decentralization: Some Unresolved Questions," in *Captive Vision*. Delhi: Ajanta Publications.

————. 2009. *Economy, Democracy and the State: The Indian Experience*. New Delhi: SAGE Publications.

Santhanam, K. 1946. "Editorial," *Hindustan Times*, New Delhi, 8 September.

Sartory, Giovanni. 1965. *Democratic Theory*. Calcutta: Oxford and IBH Publishing Co.

Shukla, Rajesh, Sunil Jain and Preeti Kakkar. 2010. *Caste in a Different Mould: Understanding the Discrimination*. New Delhi: B S Book.

Tocqueville, Alexis. 1958. *Democracy in America*, 2 vols. New York: Vintage.

Voegelin, Eric. 1981. *New Science of Politics: An Introduction*. Chicago: University of Chicago Press.

6

Making Sense of Social Justice

The worst form of inequality is to try to make unequal equal.

—Aristotle

Only a world ungoverned by purposeless order leaves principles of justice open to human construction and the conceptions of the good to individual choice.

—Michael Sandel
Liberalism and the Limits of Justice, p. 175

The hard truth is this. There is no moral meaning hidden in the bowls of the universe. ... Yet there is no need to be overwhelmed by the void. We may create our own meanings, you and I."

—B. A. Ackerman
Social Justice in the Liberal State, p. 368

I

The question of social justice is embroiled with unequal distribution of talent and assets. The strategy of ensuring social justice in such a situation has, therefore to contend with the problem of promoting social justice without eradicating natural and social endowments. Three different approaches, one in currency and two others still to be tested, to the solution of this problem vie for ascendance and unchallenged recognition. The currently preferred and in vogue in India in addition to other states is the strategy of state welfare that promises to take good care of the problem of social justice. The two other strategies of ensuring social justice are two variants of the principle of trusteeship.

One version of this strategy has been advocated by John Rawls, while the other is associated with the name of Mahatma Gandhi, who formulated it long before Rawls did. The point that needs to be forcefully argued is that only Mahatma Gandhi's principle of trusteeship has any hope of tackling the problem of social justice in a situation of unequal distribution of talents and assets. In order to appreciate why this conclusion must be arrived at, it is necessary to (a) take a close look at the Indian experience in the area of implementing programmes of social justice; (b) to examine the theoretical status of group rights; and (c) to discuss the proper way of securing social justice in a situation of inequality when inequality cannot be eradicated no matter what one does.

The question of social justice assumes importance and becomes highly relevant when certain groups of people who have been excluded from and discriminated in respect of access to certain key societal resources that a society generates and distributes. The question of social justice remains muted when exclusion associated with social structural factors is seen as either a god-ordained phenomenon or naturally evolved social system. However, when these explanations advanced to justify discrimination in the matter of the distribution of societal resources are successfully challenged, the question of exclusion assumes central importance. This challenge puts forward the idea that the universe is ungoverned by a purposeful or nature-imposed order. In this situation, it is left to human beings to evolve principles of how to ensure social justice. When it happens, lines of social divisions, the basis of exclusion, are viewed as segregating and exclusionary. Social practices associated with such divisions are adjudged discriminatory.

This is what happened when liberal worldview, sweeping aside traditional cultural perspectives on man and his world, came to the fore and assumed dominance some 300 years ago. What it did was to make the material aspect of man's existence the foundation as well as the effective means of human well-being. Two things—economic growth and fair and equitable distribution of societal resources—became pivotal. A setback in the former and distortions in the latter came to be considered fatal for man's well-being. They, therefore, became the driving force of social and political movements in modern times in almost all parts of the world. At the heart of most of these movements stands the vital issue of social justice. And social justice means equitable share of all social groups not only in the available stock of societal resources but also in the benefits that the growth process yields without discrimination. As the Eleventh Five-Year Plan of India documents: "Inclusive growth demands social groups have equal access to the services provided by the State and equal opportunity for upward economic and social mobility. It is also necessary that there is no discrimination against any section of society" (2008).

It also refers to two sources of practice that usually lead to discrimination. First, there are certain groups, such as the SCs or Dalits as they are popularly called STs and OBCs and minorities, that are the victims of exclusion because some features of the social order make them so. If the SCs are considered historically disadvantaged and vulnerable, the STs, even while they are not untouchables, are isolated and, therefore, excluded. Second, certain other groups may be discriminated against because of their lowly social and educational status; they therefore may suffer from certain handicaps. In these cases, the question of social justice comes to the fore.

Concern for social justice is by no means a new phenomenon in Indian politics. What adds to its contemporary relevance and sharpness is material well-being, which occupies today the centre-stage in human existence in general and political arena in particular. It is believed to hold the key to human well-being. Lord Keynes's observation that "economic development is the possibility of development," constitutes an ample confirmation of this. That is why the removal of economic deprivation, supposed to be the cause of blocked development, must assume centrality in political thinking and action. Two things, therefore, assume importance. The first thing is the removal of obstacles that hinder the weaker sections of society from taking advantage of societal resources and the second thing concerns a concerted effort to remove all obstacles that prevent or delay rapid economic development.

What assumes significance is the persistence of structural inequality, which distorts the pattern of economic growth and tends to perpetuate cumulative inequality. This is most likely to happen in a society where social hierarchy coincides with ritual gradation and allows the hierarchical ordering of society to determine the pattern of the distribution of wealth, power and prestige. In such a social situation, some social groups tend to be excluded from the benefits the society generates. Exclusion causes economic deprivation, which, in turn, becomes a political problem to be solved.

Cumulative inequality prevents the excluded social groups from gaining access to societal resources. Without such an access, individuals fail to take full and fair advantage of the new opportunities opened up by the process of economic development. The removal of these obstacles becomes necessary in order to enable individuals and groups to shape their life patterns in the light of liberal values that support modern political systems. However, the legal guarantee of equal treatment, even the removal of some of the impediments facing the disadvantaged groups, may not prove adequate. The interplay of dispositional factors and skill deficiency may incapacitate disadvantaged groups from utilizing and benefiting from the available opportunities. Thus, to go beyond the mere outlawing of discriminatory practices or extending constitutional assurance of equal opportunity assumes great importance. This may push the state to cross the boundary of formal affirmative action and to undertake substantive measures aimed at ensuring equal start.

These considerations have made the question of social justice not only very relevant but also a politically pressing issue. In India, too, the issue of social justice has been a major politico-administrative concern right from the days of the colonial rule. The colonial policy of social justice was guided mainly by two major objectives: (a) the establishment of a political balance between communities through representation and (b) the creation of fissures in the nationalist movement by provoking differences among social groups. In contrast, measures of social justice in independent India have been motivated by the resolve to uplift the social groups traditionally excluded and to give them, as far as possible, an equal start so that they can compete effectively for access to available societal resources.

Commitment of Indian leaders to the principle of social justice has been inspired largely by three factors. The exposure of the Indian elite class to Western, liberal worldview and its fundamental tenets that define the basic characteristics of man and his place in this world, as a result of the rapid spread of Western education in India, was one major factor. It exposed them to the new currents of thought-ways and work-ways contemporaneously prevalent in the West. This exposure instilled in them the fundamental ideas of the liberal worldview. What bewitched them, in particular, was the centrality and primacy of the individual person in the liberal worldview. The celebration of such values as freedom, equality, dignity and self-determination was the necessary corollary. These values emphasize the need to preserve and promote individual autonomy in shaping his life conditions and life chances. The liberal values relating to individual autonomy are pivotal within a context in which they are the critical preconditions for personality development, skill acquirement and human well-being. And since human well-being is linked with and is dependent upon economic growth, liberal worldview makes the philosophy of economic growth, in one form or the other, its central concern and treats it as a necessary condition of individual well-being.

Second, the tremendous advances made by Western societies in different areas of life have gone a long way to convince Indian leaders of the superiority of the liberal worldview. This perception shaped their attitude towards their own society. What they saw in their society were a series of depressing and disheartening elements. These elements were instrumental in forming the understanding of Indian leaders of what India as a civilizational unit substantively meant. They saw India marked by social fragmentation, lack of political unity as a glue of social unity,[1] depressed economic condition causing periodical famines or famine-like situations and backward-looking and superstition-laden traditional worldview. Looked at from the perspective of liberal ideas, the traditional Indian social order came to be viewed not only as backward but also demeaning for human dignity. The feeling of humiliation, engendered by the onset of what Trautmann calls "Indophobia" (Trautmann 1997: 99), did impel most of them to look back and reconstruct the past of India in many different ways. This reconstruction did highlight some of the commendable, salient features of Indian civilization. However, most of the intellectuals and leaders were largely, if not completely, alienated from their own tradition and culture.

The third factor had to do with their consciousness of a deplorable present, a present that was humiliating not simply because of degrading political subjugation but also of the sense of perceived cultural inferiority. This did impel them to bring the colonial rule to an end, but most important was their resolve to undertake the onerous task of social creation by launching a peaceful social revolution. The task of social creation received the utmost priority in view of the extreme backwardness of the Indian economy, which produced adverse social, economic and political consequences for what the modern sensibility treats as "the quality of life." This, the Indian leaders felt, applied especially to Indian people. In addition, the principles that would guide the process of social creation were not available in the Indian tradition since it was the Indian tradition that, they believed, was responsible for the ills affecting Indian social order. These principles could be derived only from liberal ideas.

All this provided them with a vantage point from which they could view, assess and evaluate their past as well as derive their vision of the future of India. The vision that they came out with projected a socio-political order whose source was the liberal worldview; it aimed at refashioning Indian psyche and reordering social institutional set-up. The social revolution they were to launch and eventually they did launch, was, as K. Santhanam, the editor of the *Hindustan Times*, noted long ago, to get India "out of the medievalism based on birth, religion, custom and community and reconstruct her social structure on modern foundations of law, individual merit and secular education" (1946).

The social revolution that was launched was, of course, to make the law the prime regulator of social relations as well as to make merit, not ascribed identity and status, as the basis for the purposes of what Aristotle calls "distributive justice." However, they realized that equality in and before law is no guarantee against discrimination and exclusion. They, therefore, refused to put their faith completely in individual merit. Going beyond it, they recognized group rights as the fountainhead of social creation with a view to bringing to an end the cumulative and systemic deprivation that certain lower castes suffered from. The Indian Constitution made group rights the basis of preferential treatment of excluded or discriminated groups the main driving force of bringing about social justice.

The Preamble to the Constitution, the keynote to the whole Constitution, as Sir Ernest Barker puts it, therefore, speaks of securing "to all its citizens social, economic and political justice." While political justice could be ensured by the enjoyment of freedom and equality, that is, equality of opportunity, economic justice called for redistribution of wealth with a view to removing inequality and banishing poverty. Formidable barriers, however, have impeded the achievement of the goal of social justice. In the hierarchical social order marked by multiple inequalities and disparities, numerous communities were forced to exist as ritually polluting; they also became socially degraded and economically depressed. The end result has been political silence of these hapless and helpless communities. This has perpetrated violence in the sense Aristotle understands it.

Confronted as the Indian leaders were by all these deficiencies of the Indian social order, it was easy for them to be convinced of the need to create a new India that must be animated by the values of liberty, equality and fraternity. As such, the Indian leaders found it necessary to mount a conscious and concerted effort to shape personal lives and social relations in the light of these values. That is why Indian democracy aims at securing both formal and substantive equality. As India had to address the cause of historically disadvantaged groups, on an urgent basis, the Indian Constitution has made room for both individual freedom and group rights. Both of these commitments—one to give freedom to individuals stripped of differences or in John Rawls' sense, unencumbered persons and the other to recognize rights of groups differentiated on the basis of primordial identities—are essential features of new, modern India.

Thus, the Indian Constitution is not merely a set of procedural rules laying down how political decisions are to be reached—perhaps more precisely, the conditions that must be fulfilled for a political decision to be binding for both officers and for its ordinary citizens. It also lays down what Jasay characterizes as substantial rules. These rules contain specific provisions about the admissible content of political decisions (Jasay 1997: 148).

The inclusion of substantive rules in the Constitution is the recognition that procedural democracy and formal equality are not enough to bring about substantive outcomes insofar as improvement of the socio-economic condition of the groups is concerned. Substantive rules become necessary in order to transform legal equality into factual equality. What President Lyndon Johnson, responding to the movement of civil rights in the USA, said best expresses it:

> You do not take a person who, for years, has been hobbled by chains and liberate him, bring him to the starting line of the race and then say, "You are free to compete with all the others" and still justly believe that you have been completely fair. This is not enough to open the gates of opportunity. All our citizens must have the ability to walk through those gates.... We seek not just freedom but opportunity—not just legal equality as a right and a theory but equality as a fact and as a result. (Rainwater and Yancey 1967: 126)

Indian democracy is committed to removing man-made inequalities and enabling the disadvantaged groups to gain the full stature of citizenship. To achieve this objective, the Indian Constitution incorporates some two dozen articles, providing for compensatory treatment to these groups, protecting them against discrimination and promoting their development. Indian constitution thus represents "an intriguing instance of using law to reshape recalcitrant patterns of social practices" (Galanter 1984: preface, XXII). And it is here that we find the powerful expression of human choice and preference in remaking Indian society, in general and refurbishing the destiny of the deprived and the dispossessed, in particular.

If the Preamble to the Constitution assures social justice to all the citizens, the Directive Principles of the State Policy require the State "to promote, with special care, the educational and economic interests of the weaker sections of society, and, in particular, of the Scheduled Castes and Scheduled Tribes." The State is also directed to protect them from social injustice and all forms of exploitation (Article 46). This direction is reinforced by the constitutional ban in Article 15(1). This ban does not permit discrimination against any citizen "on grounds only of religion, race, caste, sex, place or birth or any of them." The Constitution, however, goes beyond legal equality and permits the State, through Article 16(3) to make provisions for the reservation of appointments or posts in favour of any backward class of citizens which, in the opinion of State, is not adequately represented in the services under the State.

Further, Article 15 makes it quite clear that nothing can prevent the State from making any special provision for the advancement of the socially and educationally backward classes of citizens or for the SCs and the STs. The logic of these constitutional provisions underscores a political orientation that would not hesitate to create equality of life conditions. This would, it is hoped, ensure a fair start to all individuals so that everyone, irrespective of his or her place in the social universe, can have equal access to scarce societal resources. However, two considerations inveigle against this. If everyone will have equal access to good things of life without putting requisite effort, why should one use his talent and skill in producing them? However, if talent is ignored, it may slow down the production of those good things and services that promise to make human life pleasurable. When talent is ignored, it is bound to slow down the growth process and perpetuate a low level of economic growth and is sure to force upon society the need to tolerate low standards of living, which, by definition, is anathema in modern times.

These considerations have inclined Indian leaders to stop short of equalization of life conditions. However, they have certainly moved away from formal to substantive equality. A clear line of progression can be discerned from non-discrimination to equal opportunity to equal outcome. Undoubtedly, the Constitution reflects this progression, which is evident when it sanctions three types of preferential treatments. The first of these involves legislative bodies, government jobs and educational institutions. Later on, OBCs were added to this category. Second, SCs and STs are preferred in respect of certain expenditures, services and ameliorative schemes such as scholarships, grants, loans, land allotments, health care, legal aid as well as some anti-poverty measures. The third type of preferences includes measures of special protection intended to safeguard vulnerable groups from oppression and exploitation.

Three social groups have been identified by the Constitution for receiving preferential treatment. The SCs constitute the first group identified based on being deemed untouchables, they constitute 16.3 per cent of the population. The second group, the STs, amount to 8.2 per cent of the population; this group is distinguished by its tribal culture and physical isolation. A large part of this group is settled in specially protected scheduled areas. 92 per cent of the STs still live in rural areas. The last group is constituted by the OBCs, a heterogeneous category composed, for the most part, of castes (including some non-Hindu communities) that are low in traditional social ranking but not as low as the SCs. Their population ranges between 25 and 52 per cent. The OBCs are considered backward because of their peasant status and lack of education and access to public institutions.

The criterion for identifying social groups for preferential treatment has evoked a great deal of debate[2] going back to the colonial period. The point of contention has been whether reservation should be extended to backward classes, who have escaped the stigma of being pronounced untouchables. This, is effect, has boiled down to the question of whether to identify groups on the basis of social and economic backwardness or with reference to specific criterion of ritual and social exclusion, exclusion that becomes the cause of economically depressed condition.

The Indian Constitution explicitly considers caste as the determining factor for identifying excluded groups. Accordingly, the Constitution has identified the SCs as the target of preferential treatment. However, caste identification does not apply in the case of the STs. Here, what seems important is their social and cultural isolation from the mainstream of national life coupled with their extreme poverty. In the case of the OBCs, however, the criterion again shifts, as Article 15 (4) makes it clear, the backwardness of the OBCs has to be determined on the basis of social and educational achievement or lack of it. This makes it possible to causally link, as did the Mandal Commission,[3] social backwardness to educational backwardness and both to economic deprivation.

What is clear from all this is the refusal of the framers of the Indian Constitution to accept the criterion of economic deprivation and depression and the consequent backwardness as the sole criterion of identifying groups for preferential treatment. They attached the greatest importance, even after some resistance, to social backwardness and economic deprivation. In the case of the SCs, they were considered to be the unfortunate victims of the caste system and its exclusionary practices. With a view to removing this historical injustice, the Constitution provided for compensation, taking recourse to the argument of justice on the principle of restitution. In the case of the OBCs, educational and economic factors enter into the definition of backwardness. The term "OBCs" represents an all-encompassing category; it includes all underprivileged and marginalized castes. As such, the term "OBCs" is not a class category and as Galanter points out, it has been understood to mean certain castes (1984: 166).

India has been implementing programmes of social justice for more than six decades now. Note, for example, that the bane of untouchability has been completely removed at least legally, if not socially. In addition, there is, for the SCs and the STs, the Scheduled Castes and Scheduled Tribes (Prevention of Atrocities) Act, 1989. Since the Eighth Five-year Plan, there is in operation a multi-pronged approach for the socio-economic development of the targeted groups. Social empowerment of these groups has been sought to be achieved through educational development, while economic development is to be fostered through income and employment avenues and holistic development is expected to be achieved through the earmarking in Five-year plans of funds proportionate to the population of these three groups. Schemes for providing coaching facilities to students coming from these three groups for competitive examinations, hostel facilities, scholarships, etc., are in operation. In order to promote economic development of the SCs and STs, there is the provision of separate development plans to ensure for them a fair share in the benefits of economic development in a more equitable manner. In addition, finance and development corporations, both for the SCs and the STs, have been established to provide financial aid and other support for members of these groups to take on various income-generation activities.

In respect of the OBCs, in pursuance of the Supreme Court judgement, *Indira Sawhney and Others versus Union of India* (1992), the National Commission of the Backward Classes was set up in August 1993 under the National Commission of Backward Classes Act 1993. Thus, after a gap of 46 years of independence, the OBCs were recognized as a separate group and given 27 per cent of reservation in jobs in government and public sector undertakings. Programmes for the development of the OBCs were initiated from the Eighth Five-year plan. The National Backward Classes Finance and Development Corporation was set up in 1992 with an authorized capital of ₹200 crores, which was raised to 700 crores in the Ninth Plan. Several schemes for the improvement of the educational status of the OBCs are in operation, which include scholarships, hostel facilities, coaching services, etc.

It cannot, therefore, be denied that after half a century of expanding and extensive concern with social justice, something substantial has been achieved. There has been of course, a steady enlargement of the liberal guarantee of rights over an ever-widening range of activities, individuals and groups. Nor can it be denied that the expansion of civil rights, enforcing the liberties of those who had not hitherto enjoyed the full protection of the laws, has enlarged the domain of the development of a network of welfare and security arrangements. Undeniably, these programmes have recorded commendable success in reducing the pain of deprivation and dispossession; they have uplifted a large number of persons from economic distress and social humiliation. All these measures of social justice have instilled in them some degree of the feeling of self-confidence.

However, these programmes have not made any significant dent in the structure of exclusion or even blunted the sharpness of its process. Even while the progress in securing social justice is remarkable, it is not potent enough to effectively undermine the structures of discrimination. This is evident from a recent survey of the socio-economic condition of the targeted groups. A large number of persons falling in the excluded categories are not yet able to stand on their own feet. As has been discussed

above, there is enough evidence to indicate that the large range of preferential treatment has been meted out to the targeted groups. We must ask,
however, how effective have these different programmes proved to be.
If anyone expected miraculous results, he must be greatly disappointed.
Referring to a classified report of the Scheduled Castes Commission for
2004–2005, Vikram Pathak of the *Hindustan Times* notes that 21 Dalit
women are raped and 11 Dalits murdered every week. More than half of
Dalit students drop out before they reach class VIII. In many hostels built
for the Dalits, children do not know the taste of milk and untouchability is
still rampant as of 27 July 2009. According to another report, the National
Human Rights Commission receives more than 78,000 complaints in
a year. The National Crime Bureau registered 27,000 cases of violence
against Dalits in 2006 (Saxena 2009). It is true that literacy rates for the
SCs and the STs have gone up. However, the gap between the literacy rates
of the SCs and the STs and that of the general population remains almost
constant. Both the SCs and the STs are largely rural dwellers earning their
livelihood from their brawn power and are compelled to live at the margin
of subsistence. In the case of the tribal, it should be noted that Eleventh
five years plan focuses that development has done more damage to them
(Eleventh Five Years plan 2008).[4] In addition, discrimination against them
in employment, wages, credit, etc., is still rampant. More than 40 per cent
of the SCs and STs are below the poverty line. This is based on the head
count method, which does not take into account educational, medical
and other developmental expenses. If we add these, the proportion of
the SCs and the STs below the poverty line will jump up tremendously.

What is most disturbing to note is the lack of real concern for the well-
being of the disadvantaged groups. To take one example, the Scheduled
Castes Commission, mandated by the Constitution to highlight the sufferings of the Dalits, has not bothered to file its annual report for the last
four years, although the Constitution commands it to do so regularly. In
the past seven years, it has filed reports only twice. However, no reports
of the Commission have been placed before the Parliament since 2001
even when the Constitution prescribes the tabling of the report every year
along with a memorandum detailing the action taken or proposed to be
taken against the complaints received. In addition, the central and state
administrative machinery is indifferent to programmes of social justice;
it always plays the game of passing the buck and does not hesitate in

blaming state governments for the lack of concern about social justice. All this underlines the fact that, as a professor of sociology at Jawaharlal Nehru University, New Delhi, Vivek Kumar, who specializes in Dalit affairs, emphatically notes, "All talks of justice is just that, talk."

This reinforces the suspicion voiced by Jaffrelot that the Directive Principles of State Policy, claimed to be a revolutionary principle by Granville Austin, are merely diversionary. Instead of emancipating the subaltern groups, they aim at defusing their mobilization (in Bhargava 2008: 249). Yet, the very act of defusing creates a greater uproar for getting more of the same that is said to prevent their mobilization. As a result, their integration into the larger society is stalled. Moreover, measures of social justice have proved nothing better than palliatives. It can be argued that these very palliatives have freed the excluded groups from the bondage that the traditional social order had forged for them. However, we must take note of the cost they have had to pay for this. These palliatives do not emancipate them; what they do is to deaden their spirit and enervate the spring of their action. They have failed to kindle the fire of self-responsibility or self-dependence in the beneficiaries of affirmative action.

II

Our discussion underlines that the possibility that we can never actually aspire to, let alone realize, the vision of social justice within the framework of liberal worldview, is never entertained. It is not to denigrate the idea of social justice; it is only to highlight some of the inadequacies, both pragmatic and philosophical, of the liberal perspective on social justice. These inadequacies flow from its inability to resolve the conflict that arises between individual rights and collective good. It has neither the resources nor the power to transform what John Rawls calls "reasonable pluralism" into the overriding social concern. This is well illustrated by the utter failure of his bold and brilliant effort to reconcile inequality of talent and assets with social responsibility.

Admittedly, the liberal vision of social justice must be credited to have achieved a lot and that is precisely the point of its limitation. Rapid economic development was expected to ease up the pain of deprivation, if not completely eradicate it. However, the pattern of economic growth during more than the last six decades has failed to do so. On the contrary, it has added to the problems of those people whose lives have been affected by development projects. It is especially true of the tribal people, who have been dispossessed and displaced without adequate compensation and rehabilitation.

India still has a large number of the disadvantaged people. Structural inequality persists, poverty is rampant, basic food-security is still lacking,[5] the satisfaction of basic needs still eludes, universal education is still a far dream, the poor quality of school education continues unabated, and the enlargement of access to education and employment across different social groupings is sluggish. The result is that exclusionary practices have been reinforced. Exclusion from control of assets, exclusion from the benefits of economic growth, exclusion from the impact of physical and social infrastructural expansion and exclusion from education and from income-generating opportunities (Mahbub-ul Haq, Human Development Centre 2008: 48).

The various measures of social justice have surely helped the deprived groups, to a significant degree, to join the mainstream of national life. However, it has achieved success, as Galanter points out, only partially and at a cost great (1984: 551). The result is an uneven distribution of benefits in beneficiary groups. This is reflected in what Galanter calls "substantial clustering," meaning that the benefits of social justice have not been available to all equally in recipient groups. A few members of these groups have not only gained more from affirmative action, but also these people have utilized the benefits to create more opportunities for their own progeny. Clustering has also promoted cumulative inequality both within the beneficiary groups and in the society as a whole. In addition, there is also an evidence of two undesirable consequences of preferential treatment for politics in India.

In the first place, the focus on caste, as the basis of identifying groups for preferential treatment has intensified competition for receiving the benefits of affirmative action among the disadvantaged groups and fermented resentment among those who have been left outside its pale (Hasan 2009: 113). This has led to a copious flow of demands in the political arena for receiving the benefits of affirmative action on the part of those disadvantaged groups that have been unfortunately left out of the circle of the beneficiaries.

This has lent to the question of social justice a political colouration and has made politics the most important mode of socio-economic status mobility. It amounts to, as Hannah Arendt puts it, "the overwhelming of the political with the demand of the social." The latter represents the dominance of production and consumption, which arises when politics admits the exigencies of man's primary, even exclusive concern of human existence. Politics, then, leaves aside the question of the good life and focuses on bare life. When this happens, politics is reduced to what is characterized as bio-politics.

It has also, in the second place, added to the fragmentation of social space into myriad groups, all competing and contesting for privileged access to scarce societal resources. Politics of social justice often resembles what MacIntyre describes as "civil war carried on by other means" (1984: 253). The politics of social justice seems to be designed to destroy commonality or what Heraclitus calls *xynon* (shareable commonality), of social existence and preserve as well as accentuate the separate identity of groups by promoting and fostering their key distinguishing features. These markers of separate identity become coins to be used as exchange value in the marketplace of democratic politics.

Affirmative action is expected to restore to the disadvantaged persons their citizenship rights and thereby facilitate their integration in national life and relations. However, it has encouraged fragmentation. To recognize these social fragments as wholes in themselves, as B. R. Ambedkar had done in the case of the Dalits, is to celebrate pluralism as a basic characteristic of particularly a democratic polity. To do so is to admit that we share less and less of common understanding of things with one another. With the decline of what is common, there is less of a community. Similarly, it is to treat collective good as the sum-total of individual goods. Aristotle pointed out long ago that common good could neither be broken down to nor derived from an account on interests and preferences of each of its constituents. We may disagree about what the public good is or how it can be achieved. However, "it is not any kind of game-theoretic equilibrium in which each does as well as he can consistent with everyone else doing so" (Jasay 1997: 145).

Equally worrisome is the growing dependence of especially the benefi-ciary groups on the state for enjoying the benefits of equality. The spread of democratic ideals has fostered a widespread passion for the equalization of property, power and status within the spheres of state and civil society. The passionate struggle for equalization has reached dizzying heights. However, while the disadvantaged groups can and do often exercise liberty to fight for equality, the lack of resources prevents them from making any headway. It seems that equality is possible only through the shrinking of man to the status of interchangeable atoms, no one exercising any more power, influence and prestige than the other does. However, this also means that they are equally poor in resources for taking care of themselves. Unable, therefore, to find the means of satisfying their needs in themselves or in others, they are left with no other protection than that provided by the state.

This is especially true of those who have been dealt a cruel hand either by fate or by society. This has divided civil society into those who are resourceful enough to make substantive choices for themselves and those unable or indisposed or ineffective for doing so. Thus, substantively speaking, two classes of persons inhabit the social universe: those who can and do and those who cannot even if they wish to do. Oakeshott puts the latter in the category of "individual manque" (1975: 275). Such individuals are incapable of sustaining individual life; they, therefore, long for the shelter of the community. However, since the community is in disarray, dependence on the state for such a shelter becomes unavoidable. This longing for the state's shelter and the consequent dependence that it breeds have been reinforced by the dissolution of the old certainties of belief, of understanding, of occupation, relationship and status because of the onset of modernity. With it, the belief of these individuals in their self-enactment has also been dissolved.

This situation has helped the state to take on what Oakeshott calls "managerial engagement" in some important areas of collective affairs in respect of the lives of the disadvantaged social groupings. This has meant that the state must have command of resources in order for it to provide substantive benefits to assignable groups. The result is that the state looms large in the lives of individuals, in general and of the individual manqué, in particular, who has less independence over against the state. Add to it the fact that when the material aspect of man's existence assumes centrality, intervention of the state in economic life and relations becomes unavoidable. Economic growth always includes decline and instability. To prevent society from sliding into severe dislocations because of the physical and human factors caused by the fluctuations in the growth process, the state has to take corrective actions. By performing this role, the state safeguards the legitimacy of the governing institutions and of the ruling class as well as to tighten its grip on the social universe. The search for material well-being thus causes people to surrender their independence and become the unconscious accomplice by aiding and abetting the dominance of the state. As Tocqueville observes:

> Day by day citizens fall under the control of the public administration, to which they insensibly surrender ever-greater portions of their independence. These very citizens, who periodically upset a throne and trampled on the feet of kings, more and more submit themselves, without resistance, to the smallest dictate of a clerk. (1996: II, 379)

The expansion of state power has unleashed "a new series of oppression that menaces democracy." To quote Tocqueville again:

> Above the race of men stands an immense tutelary power, which takes upon itself alone to secure their gratifications and to watch over their fate. Their power is absolute, minute, regular, prudent and mild.... It seeks to keep them in permanent childhood (Ibid.: 336).

This despotism degrades them without tormenting them. It has created a paradoxical situation in which every man allows himself to be put in leading strings, because he sees that it is not a person or a class of persons but the people at large who hold the end of its chain (Ibid.: 337). Unlike the older varieties of despotism, modern despotism does not destroy life or tyrannize; it only perfects and "civilizes" its techniques of control and is, therefore, rendered less odious and degrading in the eyes of its subjects. It transforms citizens into passive subjects who invest their trust in "benevolent" power and busy themselves with their humdrum life, the life of everyday-ness. The more the state enhances its power, the more it gets involved in providing public services and less the civil society can cope with without state intervention and direction and so the need for state intervention constantly grows.

Undoubtedly, this does not constitute the only threat to democracy; there is yet another equally potent source of danger that manifests itself in what is known as consequentialism. It signifies the assessing of the worth of an action by its results, not by its merit that reason can detect in it. "It tells us always to take from a set of mutually exclusive options the one that will bring about the best consequence unless there is a sufficient reason for doing otherwise" (Jasay 1997: 147). Measures of affirmative action conform to this characterization. They are frequently directed to either remove historical injustice or empower disadvantaged groups. Such actions unfailingly represent examples of consequential-ism. We can dismiss Rawls' claim that the ground of such actions is moral, not utilitarian insofar as such actions are aimed, not infrequently, to advance electoral fortunes of the party in power. As such, consequential-ism, grounded, as it happens to be in the utilitarian calculus, makes it incoherent to wish to limit the scope of government. As a result, consequential-ism suffers from three major flaws: it limits the scope of majority rule, it suppresses freedom of choice and it brings about a disjunction between outlay and output.

Substantive rules in the Indian Constitution define the nature of preferential treatment and thereby render certain procedurally irreproachable decisions inadmissible. It amounts to restricting majority rule insofar as these rules make the content of certain political decisions beyond the reach of the majority. This is undesirable for two reasons. One, democratic politics is, for all practical purposes, a non-unanimous politics; it is designed to "make one view, one interest, one order of preferences prevail over others, most of the time by the application of established rules, peacefully without recourse to violence" (Ibid.: 1). Non-unanimous decisions are not neutral for the substantive content of such decisions that are likely to be taken by this procedure. It is not neutral because it allows the winner in the electoral battle to impose his/her will on those who have lost out. The winner can then take recourse to redistributive measures that transfer resources from one class of the people to other classes.

Redistribution is justified on the ground that though it imposes costs on some, it brings benefits to numerous others. Two variants of this justification are: one, that policy benefits more people (voters) than it imposes costs upon and two, that the benefits in terms of money or "wealth" exceed the cost. Both of these arguments are problematic not only because they limit choice but also because those who pay the cost for the benefit of others do so involuntarily. Burdens and obligations are imposed by collective choice rather than assumed voluntarily for the sake of benefits to their bearers. This forces us, sometimes with great severity, to do what we would not freely choose to do and forbear from what we would choose. It is done not at some finely drawn moral margin, but over a major part of our feasible choices. In particular, it takes the lion's share of individually earned and owned resources and uses them in ways that the individual in question would not have chosen (Ibid.: 11).

Further, the state acts in the belief that whatever affirmative action it takes or proposes to take will produce beneficial results. However, the fact is ignored that such actions may also produce unintended consequences, which may prove harmful in time. In effect, it amounts to a vow that not to do certain things even if, one day, there was sufficient "on balance" benefit from doing them. There is also the adverse relationship between outlay and outcome. The deficiencies of redistributive politics become evident not only in everyday sense that taxes of some go to supplement the resources of others, but also in the sense of severing the link between costs, material and moral and benefits they produce (Ibid.: 4).

It also severs the link between the selection of a preference ordering and its justificatory ground, insofar as most selections are conjectural. This is because their usefulness is determined not by rational calculation but supposedly by their potential success. It is prompted usually by the consideration of what may prove useful and helpful in electoral battle. As such, political value of such programmes, that is, programmes of social justice, outweighs their economic merit. There seems to be very little concern about what programmes of affirmative action cost and what benefits they yield to whom and to what extent. Public expenditure goes on mounting and tax burden on the taxpayer keeps on increasing. The most recent example of this is the Right to Education Act, which promises to add enormously to state expenditure; it is estimated to be 37,000 crores annually.

The mismatch between cost and benefit has resulted in a horrendous increase in public expenditure. The Union Government has, according to a report that appeared in the *Hindustan Times,* Delhi, 20 August 2009, spent ₹1,519 billion in the past four years under just three anti-poverty schemes. Another report shows that out of the total expenditure on welfare programmes for relieving the distress of the poor, only 10 paise out of hundred really reach the needy persons (Shah and Soumya 2004). In addition, for every one rupee transferred to the poor through the public distribution system, the government has to spend ₹3.65 (National Centre for Advocacy 2005: 33). What is most invidious is that huge expenditures invite waste and corruption, but they are justified in the name of such terms which can be twisted as "fairness," "justice," "welfare," "account-ability" and so on. No doubt, these terms are politically appealing, but they are substantively variable and empirically not testable.

Apart from adverse pragmatic consequences that are produced by consequential-ism, there are conceptual and theoretical/philosophical flaws as well. Provisions of social justice are meant to enable the deprived and the dispossessed to manage their worldly affairs as well as to play their citizenship role effectively. In this, the sole reliance has been placed on social rather than economic factors as the cause of discrimination and deprivation. However, discrimination does not respect any boundary and affects those who are economically weak and therefore, vulnerable too. Moreover, the caste as a homogeneous category is a myth. Economic distress is *varna*-and-caste blind; it grips people in every social situation. To exclude those who do not fall in particular castes is tantamount to tolerating injustice. This is precisely the point Zoya Hasan makes. As she points out:

> The idea that India has succeeded in creating public spaces that are equally shared by members of diverse communities or that various disadvantaged groups have access to and actively participate in governance is a distant one because the trend towards inclusion and empowerment does not embrace all groups equally. (2009: 5)

This forces us to ask: Can group membership, as a primary condition of receiving the benefits of affirmative action, be justified theoretically or philosophically? Also, are the measures taken to serve the cause of social justice adequate? To take the first question, to make group as the basis of identifying beneficiaries is to treat it as a recognizable unit of agency. As Dworkin notes, "a recognizable unit of agency must be equipped with sufficient power, functional unity and legitimacy to stand for, commit and 'represent' the collective entity in question" (1992: 211–12). However, a collective entity chooses a course of action, exercises a right assumes and fulfils an obligation only in a metaphoric sense. Anthropomorphism happens to be the standard metaphor in this regard. Also, to ascribe agency to a group in an age, which is not comfortable with the idea, is to artificially boost up a group and allow some self-appointed and self-perpetuating decision-making organ to make decision on behalf of separate individuals. In the process, it tends to override the liberties of dissenters and the idly indifferent anti-activists within the group. We should also ask: What does it mean that a group such as SCs, STs and OBCs decides, acts, claims or expresses a right? Only separate individual members of a group can exercise "group rights." As Epstein puts it:

> Statements about groups of individuals must be translated into statements about individuals.... No independent rights of the groups attach to the corporate forms.... At all points the rights of groups depend on the rights of their members. No group has a right, which is more than the summation of its parts. (1985: ix, 13)

To make the group as the basis of rights is to raise the problem of the Russian Doll; we unscrew it and we find several dolls one inside the other till we come to the last one. This is also the case with the idea of a group. Individuals in a group, no matter how we define it, can be differentiated in numerous ways. A group will have subgroups of other kinds, differing in class, wealth, education and so forth. However, these differences are ignored for the purposes of affirmative action. It amounts to virtual personification of the group; it liberates at one stroke the concept of group rights and liberties from their major vice, the agency problem that must be ignored or circumnavigated in the passage from individuals, their minds and wishes to the group mind and group wish. However, this passage entails distribution of benefits in undetermined and unequal proportions.

Given the heterogeneity and plurality of groups, the claims both for the grant of more rights and receiving the benefits of affirmative action by more and more groups are lengthening. In the process, certain pseudo-rights, such as the right to work, the right to be educated, the right to livelihood, to food, etc., are also raised in the political firmament. These imitate genuine rights but only partly in the sense that they cannot be exercised by the claimant group or individuals without some body or some group agreeing or being forced to perform a matching service, that is, to play the role of someone who obliges. However, the resemblance is hollow because no one offers to provide the necessary matching service nor is anyone put under the obligation to perform and provide it.

Such claims initiate a disoriented search for an elusive accommodator. They are, as such, "manifesto rights," as Feinberg calls them (1980: 130–43). In any case, the search usually stops at the doorstep of the state. As for the lack of someone to oblige in the non-governmental sector, the state has to provide the necessary services. Obviously, this increases the tax burden on the taxpayer who has to bear the cost of such services. The transfer of wealth from taxpayers to the beneficiaries is seldom transparent. Those that pay for these services are "often unaware that they are paying for some benefit that accrues to others and that they, in ignorance of its cost to themselves, do not begrudge—this is what makes the notion of group rights slippery and holistic language about them dangerous" (Jasay 1997: 225).

What is also noteworthy is that the goal of mitigating disadvantages and deprivations slips from the people's hands at the very moment when they seem to have grasped it. And here we confront the question: Can the liberal vision of justice for all be ever realized? Alternatively, can satisfactory results be obtained from the prevalent strategy of assuring social justice to those who are the victims of discrimination, either historical or any other? As we noted earlier, a progression in terms of upgradation in measures of social justice is observable. These measures have ranged from making discrimination constitutionally invidious to equal opportunity to equal start or equality in life conditions. However, equal start is beyond the ken of liberal politics because it is sure to throttle talent and capacity. Thus, inequality in talent and assets has to be tolerated. However, the cause of social justice cannot be allowed to suffer or lapse through indifference or design.

Since inequality cannot be eradicated nor the measures of social justice benefit all equally, the problem that has somehow to be tackled is to secure social justice in a situation of inequality of talent and assets. But it has to be in a way that deprivation resulting from discrimination does not become a problem either for those who suffer it or for the society. Rawls offers a solution that deserves our attention. He identifies three distinct possible principles by which the distribution of social and economic benefits might be regulated or assessed. These principles are natural liberty, liberal equality and democratic equality. Natural liberty signifies the full play of formal or legal equality; it assures equality before law but reinforces inequality of talents and assets. Rawls, therefore, considers this principle inadequate because it tends to reproduce the initial mal-distribution of talent and assets. To remedy injustice inherent in it, liberal equality requires going beyond formal equality and correcting, wherever possible, for social and cultural disadvantages.

Concretely, the mitigation of social and cultural inequalities is sought to be realized through the provision of equal educational opportunities, certain redistributive policies and social reforms. However, the purpose of providing equal start is defeated because the arbitrariness of initial endowments is not fully corrected by these measures, although redistribution of assets does take place to some extent. Admittedly, liberal equality represents an improvement over natural liberty since it aims at providing to all equal start by neutralizing, at least to some extent, the effects of social contingencies. However, it still permits the distribution of wealth and income to be determined by the natural distribution of talent and capacities.[6] And the influence of natural contingencies is as abhorrent to democratic equality as that of social contingencies.

This calls for a conception that could nullify the effect of natural, social and cultural differences while acknowledging their intractability at the same time. And this conception, for Rawls, is democratic equality. This may mean, for many, the taking of the next step of moving from equality of opportunity to equality of results. However, the equality of results, Rawls argues, is by no means the only democratic alternative to meritocracy. As he insists, it is not at all necessary to eradicate unequal endowments; what is necessary is to arrange the scheme of benefits and burdens so that the least advantaged may share the resources of the fortunate. This means that "social and economic inequalities are to be arranged so that they are both: (a) reasonably expected to be to everyone's advantage and (b) attached to positions and offices open to all" (Rawls 1971: 60). And here we come across the Rawlsian formulation of what we know as the principle of trusteeship.

The Rawlsian principle of trusteeship does not rely on transforming the conditions under which people utilize their talents. It is claimed to rest on the moral principle that underlines the need to regard the distribution of natural talents as common asset and to share in the benefits, whatever it may turn out to be, that the utilization of talent produces. By socializing talents, Rawls obviates the need to equalize life conditions. It is in general interest, he insists, that talents and capacities must be cultivated and society must provide incentives and resources for this. However, the benefits that are generated should also be utilized for satisfying the legitimate expectations of those who find themselves in a disadvantageous position. Realizations of this principle will, Rawls believes, institute justice as fairness in society. As he says:

> By arranging inequalities for reciprocal advantage and by abstaining from the exploitation of the contingencies of natural and social circumstances within a framework of equal liberty, persons express their respect for one another in the very constitution of their society.... Another way of putting it is to say that the principles of justice manifest in the basic structure of society (that is) men's desire to treat one another not as means only but as ends in themselves. (Rawls quoted in Sandel 1998: 77)

What we see in Rawls' principle of trusteeship is undeniably a very strong reflection of Mahatma Gandhi's formulation of the same idea. However, Rawls shrouds it in a thick cover of deontological ethics. Deontological ethics, nevertheless, rejects the idea that man has any connection whatsoever with any transcendental, trans-individual divine entity. We must question therefore, the chances of the translation of the realization of a principle into reality that refuses to accept any divine entity as the anchor of human existence. The distinctive mark of Rawls' formulation of the idea of trusteeship is his refusal to derive the idea of justice from the notion of the good life.

The refusal paves the way for the installation of the reign of the material interest and is, therefore, symptomatic of the explicit acceptance of the idea of pluralism within the framework of bio-politics. And what is inherent in pluralism is the element of conflict that grows out of the clashes of antagonistic interests. The social fact of what Nozick calls "our separate existence" makes it necessary to find a median point that represents an acceptable principle of justice either by consent or by tradition that is independent of all interests. Such a median point is impossible to evolve or discover in a society that lacks the idea of the good life or what Heraclius calls *xynon*, the shareable commonality. Rawls recognizes that people differ, sometimes very ardently and occasionally violently, in their understanding of who they are and what their world signifies to them. However, he insists that somehow they come to agree about the meaning of justice. This is nothing but an example of sheer logical legerdemain. This is what Sandel argues effectively and what Amartya Sen misses out completely.

Sen, in his recent book, *The Idea of Justice* (2009), gives the example of three girls with only one flute among them. One girl owns it, the other wants it and the third is an expert at playing it. The question, then, is: Which of the girl should have the flute? Sen concludes that there is no such thing as perfect justice and that justice is relative to a particular situation. As such, rather than searching for an "ideal" justice, the stress should be on removing the more manifest forms of injustice. "The idea of justice demands comparison of actual lives that people can lead rather than a remote search for ideal institutions. That is what makes the idea of justice relevant as well as exciting in practical reasoning" (Suroor 2009).

It is surprising that Sen overlooks the simple fact that any situation as good or bad, desirable or undesirable, does not reside in the situation itself; the standard for judging anything as good or bad, desirable or undesirable, is prior to and above the specific characteristics of an evolved situation. "Prior to all reflections is the sense of a right order that must be defended through its articulation. Without that pre-analytic sense, there would be neither a reason nor a direction for the unfolding of moral reflection" (Walsh 1997: 69). Deontological logic loses sight of this important truth. It aspires to ground the idea of justice in pure logic; however, it lacks internal resources to make it vigorous enough to survive the test of harsh reality. One has to go beyond the givens of situations and seek the source of such a standard and in some conception of the good life (Roy 2007). And the idea of the good life has to be grounded in a trans-individual source, especially the divine entity. Without the formative spiritual orientation that produces order in the soul, the idea of trusteeship, such as Rawls', seems to produce the outer shell that conceals the hollowness within. He fails to appreciate that it is this source that supports and nourishes the strength of belief and commitment.

In contradistinction to Rawls' formulation of the idea of trusteeship, Mahatma Gandhi embeds it in an entity that resides in all beings, the *Purusha*, the entity celebrated in the Vedic literature. It is the entity that Mahatma Gandhi considers the anchor of human existence, the buckler of all. The whole gamut of man's activities—social, economic, political and religious—constitutes, for Mahatma Gandhi, an indivisible whole. And all these activities must be impregnated with love for God. Only then, man's activities receive a moral basis; otherwise, they would reduce "life to a maze of sound and fury signifying nothing." And morality is cultivated when man's soul is attuned to the divine ground of reality.

Without it, economic activities, which are organically linked to the problem of inequality of talents and assets, turns out to be nothing but Mammon worship. As Mahatma Gandhi puts it:

> An economics that inculcates Mammon worship and enables the strong to amass wealth at the expense of the weak, is a false and dismal science. True economics, on the other hand, stands for social justice. It the good of all equally including the weakest, and is indispensable for decent life. (1954: 14)

And it is the good of all under the shelter of God that is the objective of the principle of trusteeship that Mahatma Gandhi enunciates. He is fully aware of the fact that it is only through the love of God that we come to love our fellow-beings. Rawls fails to understand this and, therefore, his idea of trusteeship lacks not only originality but also authenticity.

Notes

1. Extreme social diversity and lack of political unity—these were the two themes that the Viceroy Lord Northbrooke emphasized in his welcome address on the occasion of the visit of the Prince of Wales to India in 1875. See Griffith (1957: 17). Indian leaders had no difficulty in accepting this appraisal of Indian society.
2. There exists a large body of literature in this area. However, see Galanter (1984) and Hasan (2009) and references cited therein.
3. What the Mandal Commission did was to identify backwardness among the Hindus. Four of the 11-point indicator the Commission evolved pertains to caste, three to education and three to economic condition. However, it treats both educational and economic backwardness as derived elements of social backwardness.
4. As the Eleventh Five-Year *Plan,* however, notes:
    Ancestral land, villages, habitations, environs belonging to the tribal people have been made available for various development projects as tribal areas possess 60–70 per cent of the natural resources of the country. In such cases, though primary displacement, however, appears small due to low population density, secondary displacement has

been extensive, encompassing common property resources that provided supplemental livelihoods, particularly to those with low or no dependence on farming. (2008: 112)
5. This has been taken care of by the passage of the Food Security Act.
6. For a fuller discussion, see Sandel (1998: 67–77).

References

Dworkin, R. 1992. "Liberal Community," in *Communitarianism and Individualism*. Eds S. Avinery and A. Shalit. Oxford: Oxford University Press.

Epstein, R. A. 1985. *Takings: Private Property and the Power of Eminent Domain*. Cambridge, MA: Harvard University Press.

Feinberg, J. 1980. *Rights, Justice and the Bounds of Justice*. Princeton: Princeton University Press.

Galanter, Marc. 1984. *Competing Equalities: Law and the Backward Classes in India*. Delhi: Oxford University Press.

Gandhi, M. K. 1954. *Sarvodaya*. Ed. Bharatan Kumarappa. Ahmedabad: Navajivan Publishing House.

Griffith, Percival. 1957. *Modern India*. London: Ernests Benn Ltd.

Hasan, Zoya. 2009. *Politics of Inclusion: Castes, Minorities and Affirmative Action*. Delhi: Oxford University Press.

Jaffrelot, Christophe. 2008. "Containing the Lower Castes: The Constituent Assembly and the Reservation Policy," in *Politics and Ethics in the Indian Constitution*. Ed. Rajeev Bhargava. New Delhi: Oxford University Press.

Jasay, Anthony de. 1997. *Against Politics: On Government, Anarchy and Order*. London: Routledge.

MacIntyre, Alasdaire. 1984. *After Virtue*, 2nd edition. Notre Dame: University of Notre Dame Press.

Mahbub-ul Haq Development Centre. 2008. *Human Development in South Asia: A Ten Year Review*. New Delhi: Oxford University Press.

National Centre for Advocacy. 2005. *Parliament Digest, Labour, Governance, Agriculture, Social Development*. Winter Session. Delhi: National Centre for Advocacy.

Oakeshott, Michael. 1975. *Human Conduct*. Oxford: Clarendon Press.

Planning Commission, Government of India. 2008. *Eleventh Five-year Plan 2007–2012*. New Delhi: Planning Commission.

Rainwater, Lee, and William Yancey. 1967. *The Moyanihan Report and the Politics of Controversy*. Cambridge, MA: MIT Press.

Rawls, John. 1971. *A Theory of Justice*. Cambridge: Harvard University Press.

Roy, Ramashray. 2007. *Life against Good Life*. Allahabad: G. B. Pant Institute of Social Science.

Sandel, Michael. 1998. *Liberalism and the Limits of Justice*, 2nd edition. Cambridge: Cambridge University Press.

Santhanam, K. 1946. *Hindustan Times*, New Delhi, 8 September.

Saxena, Sibban Lal. 2009. "A Billion Indians and Millions of Injustices," *The Times of India*, New Delhi, 26 July.

Sen, Amartya. 2009. *The Idea of Justice*. London: Allen Lane.

Shah, Parth J., and H. B. Soumya. 2004. "Who Pays for Welfare Programmes?" *The Economic Times*, August 19.

Suroor, Hasan. 2009. "Amartya Sen and his Idea of Justice," *The Hindu*, New Delhi, 16 July.

Tocqueville, Alexis de. 1996. *Democracy in America*, 2 vols. New York: Harper and Raw.

Trautmann, Thomas R. 1997. *Aryans and British India*. Berkeley: University of California Press.

Walsh, David. 1997. *The Growth of the Liberal Soul*. Columbia: University of Missouri Press.

7

The Elusive Search for Community

Our ability to reach unity in diversity will be the beauty and the test of our civilization.

—M. K. Gandhi

The passing away of the medieval civilization in the seventeenth century ushered in a revolution. The after-effects of this revolution are still felt throughout the world. This revolution put paid to the organic perspective on social organization and changed the idea of "who man is." The impact of this change has also been felt on the way we look at society. Earlier, society represented a great chain of being in which each individual person was linked to another individual person and all individual persons were linked in turn to the whole. As an organically organized institution, society displayed a hierarchical order of status and function and had a definite place for everybody and all were functionally related to each other. The revolution that took place after the passing away of the medieval civilization signalled the end of the organic society, and the individual was freed from all bonds that tied him to others and all to the whole. This has completely eclipsed the sense of community, the hallmark of traditional societies. Efforts to revive this sense are mounted, to be sure; however, such efforts, for reasons detailed below, do not meet any success.

It is this revolution that Charles Taylor designates as the revolution of "modern, self-defining subjectivity." This revolution celebrates the gaining of pre-eminence by the liberal worldview in the seventeenth century. This revolution, which still shows vigour, brought in its wake a social order that is quite distinct from the one it displaced. It is distinct from the traditional social order not only in terms of the idea of the person but also in terms of the nature of social organization. It is also distinct in the sense that in displacing the traditional social order, it paved the way for its own eclipse. The traditional order was grounded in some conception of cosmic order. As such, it lent meaning and, therefore, legitimacy to differentiation based on caste, class or status. Differentiation was justified as a reflection of a hierarchical order of things. This justification and tolerance of differences installed, in effect, a great community, which contained within its fold several little and partial communities.

Despite the existence of numerous partial communities, differences among them did not jeopardise social harmony; rather the larger community gave meaning to differences between social groups and knit them together in a larger whole generating in the process loyalty to itself. Traditional societies were thus characterized by a sense of significant differentiation which enabled partial communities, whether geographical, socio-cultural or occupational, to be treated as important centres of concern and activity for their members in a way which connected them to the whole.

The rootedness of traditional societies in some world-transcendent divine entity was articulated and celebrated through myths, symbols, rites and rituals. They symbolized a particular explanation concerning the meaningfulness of man's sojourn on this earth. Members of these societies interpreted existence and their relations with the world above and beyond themselves in terms of these myths and symbols. These myths and symbols expressed the experience that man is fully man by virtue of his participation in a whole, which transcends his particular existence. The articulation through a constellation of symbols (Voegelin 1952: 27), myths and rites of the meaning of human existence is what gave a unique character to traditional societies. It also constituted the self-interpretation of societies, ordered them, shaped and sustained the consensus based on the sense of a shareable commonality, the *xynon,* in Heraclitus' term. These symbols are expressive of both the widespread social consensus and popular participation in fundamental social affairs

> communicating the fundamental consensus of the society and shaping the fabric of its institutional life and the public and personal lives of the people. It forms the belief structure which is the distinctive foundation of association in society and it also shapes the essential humanity of the individual members of the society by supplying meaning in their existence as participants which they experience in transcending merely private existence. (Sandoz 1981: 98)

The revolution of modern self-defining subjectivity put paid to traditional societies and all that they signified. It installed in its place a society that is nothing more than a mechanical aggregate of self-defining subjects. Man is considered, in the emergent ideological perspective, to be the subject of egoistic desires, and nature and society are expected to provide the means of realizing man's self-defined purposes. This is considered the basis of his self-fulfilment. Thus, the mainline enlightenment view of man "advanced a philosophy which is utilitarian in its ethical outlook, atomistic in its social philosophy, analytic in the science of man and which looks to a scientific social engineering to reorganize man and society and bring men happiness through perfect mutual adjustment" (Taylor 1979: 1).

With the search for ever-rising levels of material well-being, desires assumed central importance in man's existence and the fulfilment of desires became essential. This, in turn, made rationality subservient to appetites, which became, in essence, their handmaiden. Assigned only an instrumental role, reason simply meant "reckoning"—practical, prudential reasoning—responsible for intelligent calculation of how to encompass ends and means when ends are considered to be beyond the arbitration of reasoning or social determination. In effect, then, it emphasises the strategic role of making choices on the basis of calculative reasoning in discerning and determining the course of action the individual chooses for appeasing his appetites.

Whatever the chosen course of action, it leads, willy-nilly, to the denigration, even rejection, of the idea of the sacred,[1] which is not the only casualty of the ascendancy of self-interest as the regulator of personal lives and social relations. The wholeness of man is also adversely affected by the single-minded pursuit of self-interest involved with the acquisition of wealth, power and prestige. If it makes freedom *sine qua non* for realizing self-defined life purposes, it also makes equality, especially in economic terms, as important as freedom for enabling individuals for charting out routes of their self-development. And development is considered possible only when individuals have access to societal resources that are believed to be essentially vital in the fulfilment of needs. In the process of the fulfilment of needs, however, needs multiply and proliferate endlessly. This makes it necessary to expand and enlarge the resource base in order to meet the proliferating and fast growing needs. This, in turn, makes it imperative to push the frontiers of economic development. It is not surprising then to find Lord Keynes asserting that "economic development is the possibility of development."

Human existence has, because it now turns on the pivot of the satisfaction of ordinary life-needs, what MacIntyre calls "goods of effectiveness." They have become strategically important in man's life. Such a life has as its end pleasure, *apolaustikos,* a life devoted to the quest of pleasure, as Aristotle reminds us. Man becomes, in Iris Murdoch's words, a "broken totality," since his motivation, aspiration and behaviour get segregated from his higher, nobler nature posing the danger of distortion, both internally in man's psyche and externally in his relationship with the external world, both society and nature.

As a result of these distortions, what is harmonious continuity is transformed, both conceptually and existentially, into antagonistic dichotomy. Cut off from his higher nature, man is forced to prefer worldly pleasure or what Glaucon in Plato's *Republic* calls "relish." But the search for relish introduces in man's life elements of irrationality because such a life does not respond to or accept the claim of certain rationally determined ends. In this sense, life becomes, to use John M. Cooper's felicitous term, "open-ended" in the sense that "it lends us to maximize in our lives as a whole the amount of certain good, but without specifying at all what this maximum may be" (1975: 83).

An open-ended life lacks fixed principles that should guide how a man must live his life. As a result, everyone has his own idea about who he is and what kind of relationship he must have with the external world. Everyone has his own separate world. The result is that his experience of the sense of what Heraclitus calls *xynon* (shareable commonality) is deadened. While *xynon* remains actively operative or actively acknowledged, man remains awake and aware of his essential relatedness with his maker and his destiny. "Only one cosmos...exists for the 'waking' alone, while the sleepers each have their private world of dreams" (Jaeger 1930: I, 180).

When individuals become self-defining subjects, society is reduced to an aggregate of separate individuals. Social relations, then, come to be based on antagonism and mutual forbearance. Radically separate individuals are forced to struggle against each other, even when their antagonism must be tempered by forbearance and collaboration. When the necessity of social bonds is recognized, they are treated as both precarious and threatening to individuality. They are precarious because they are fragile in the absence of shared ends; they are threatening because greater the sharing of ends, the more the substance of individuality is likely to be eviscerated (Unger 1975: 155). Thus, self-defining subjects are essentially lonely beings. As Alexis de Tocqueville puts it:

> Each of them living apart is a stranger to the fate of all the rest; his children and private friends constitute to him the whole of mankind As for the rest of his fellow citizens, he is close to them, but he does not see them; he touches them, but he does not feel them; he exists only in himself alone; and if his kindred still remain to him, he may be said at any rate to have lost his country. (1956: II, 336)

If shareable commonality is lacking, *homonoia* (harmony) is hard to conceive and even harder to achieve. If there is no *homonoia*, there cannot be what Plato calls *philia politike* (love among men in a political community). And if *homonoia* is destroyed, order in society reflecting *philia politike* is disrupted. The destruction of *philia politike* is indicative of man becoming egocentric, who is always on the lookout for gaining freedom from the pressures of the surrounding society. Freed from the restraints of society, every individual tends to pursue his own ends without taking into account whether the end he proposes to pursue has benign or malignant consequences for others. Thus, when ordinary life-needs, or the pleasure of the body, become the pivot of man's life activities, the conception of the good necessarily assumes a private character. Private goods come to edge out the notion of collective good and arrogate to themselves the dominant, even exclusive role of arbiter of the guiding principles of individual action. The consequence of this situation is the disruption of the link between the good of one individual and the good of all individuals.

Consequently, both society and the political institutional arrangement that goes by the name of democracy are transformed into market-mode organs. If society is reduced to a simple aggregate of separate individuals, democracy, too, as Pierre Manent notes, is characterized by differences and separation. The only foundation to liberal democracy then must be the aggregation of private valuations of individuals. "There can be nothing approaching a shared worldview, because being liberal means that we do not have to share a worldview. In the absence of a commonly shared worldview, everybody must follow his own opinion" (Walsh 1997: 16). In such a situation, "the controversies which arise among them will become innumerable and indeterminable" (Hobbes 1991: 364). This breeds "among men, who by their own natural inclination do account all dissensions an affront, first hatred, then brawls and wars, and thus all manner of peace and society will vanish" (Ibid.: 365).

With pleasures of the body claiming preference and precedence on everything else in man's existence, power, not any consideration of promoting the common good, becomes the principle instrument of gaining what one wants and retaining what one has. The reason for this lies in the fact that when pleasures of the body takes precedence over non-bodily concerns and become the substratum of all other activities of life, effectiveness in acquiring and retaining the resources that make pleasure possible become strategically important. Access to and control over resources, then, depends on the extent to which the individual succeeds in generating/ mobilizing power in concert with others, if necessary. Resistance to the power-drive of one group by another leads to conflict and then, conflict to war. This then becomes the war of one against all; sociability is lost and peace cannot be regained.

The wars of one against all can, it is argued, be prevented from breaking out or restricted and harmoniously resolved by altruism, which constitutes one of the core characteristics of human beings. If this fails, the state, which represents the collectivization of individual wills, could intervene to do so because it wields the powerful weapon of law. Rousseau, however, reminds us that we are told that personal interest tightens "the bonds of society place them all in mutual dependence and gives them reciprocal needs...obliging each to concur in the good of others to achieve his own." Yet the prominence of interest has made it

> impossible for men to live together without usurping each other's place, deceiving, betraying and destroying each other. From now on, we must be on guard against being seen for what we are; for where two men have common interests, a hundred may be opposed to them all. Such is the unhappy source of violence, and all the honours compelled by a state of things in which everyman who pretends to work for the fortune or reputation of others, is trying only to lift his above theirs, at their expense. (Rousseau quoted in Colletti 1972: 160–61)

It is in this sense that Rousseau underlines the fact that "man is born enemy by birth and becomes a rascal by duty." And his rascality cannot be either tamed or fully regulated by the state. The respect for the state and its laws is based upon the supposition that they serve common good. Thus,

> most of the people in a political system obey the law because they are deceived into thinking it represents some common good greater than many tempting private goods. In fact, the regime and its laws almost always exist for the sake of some private goods—some class alliance or of some individuals. Those who are privately benefited may or may not be aware of the deceptiveness of the claim of the regime to exist for the sake of the common good. (Pangle 1976: 1068)

This is enough to suggest that even the rule of law may turn out, as St. Augustine pointed out long ago, to represent nothing more than band of robbers, if it does not serve the cause of justice. And there is the "rascal-ity" of man that Rousseau refers to because of the prevalence of a strong tendency of individuals to gain privileged access to and control over societal resources. This tendency has encouraged tremendously the phenomenon of self-aggrandizement, *pleonexia*, as Aristotle calls it. It is true that people have been granted the gifts of liberty, equality and fraternity, as the French Revolution declared so vociferously. If the gifts of liberty and equality are to strengthen the claim of separate individuals against any organized powerful individual or institution, then the gift of fraternity is supposed to join the separate individuals in a common life as is evident from the rallying cry of the French Revolution.

These gifts become necessary because self-defining subjects need a niche where they can be themselves and practise their little godhood without being cramped and warped by their avaricious fellowmen or the overpowering social environment. Freedom and equality are supposed to provide this niche. Thus, while freedom is essential for sustaining individuality and individual welfare in the age of modern, self-defining subjectivity, its exercise creates conditions that tend to restrict the exercise of individual freedom and infringe equality. If the exercise of freedom is left unrestrained, it affects equality adversely, disrupts pre-existing consensus without creating a new, abiding consensus, destroys harmony and creates the possibility of the disruption of order.

Thus, there exists between freedom and equality a relationship of animosity and hostility; if liberty is unrestrained, equality suffers and if equality is promoted, freedom tends to be circumscribed. Consequently, each of them has tended to tread the path of self-aggrandizement with the result that fraternity has gradually been drained of its substance. In Martin Buber's words:

> The abstractions freedom and equality were held together there through the more concrete fraternity, for only if men feel themselves to be brothers can they partake of a genuine freedom from one another and a genuine equality with one another. But fraternity has been deprived of its original meaning, the relationship between children of God, and consequently of any real content. As a result, each of the two remaining watchwords was able to establish itself against the other, and by so doing, to wander farther and farther from its truth. Arrogant and presumptuous, each sucked into itself, ever more thoroughly, elements foreign to it, elements of passion for power and greed for possession. (Quoted in Oliver 1968: 116–17)

The expectation that the leaders of the French Revolution had from these abstractions, which they supposed to be the birth-right of every individual, was to enable the individual to regain his wholeness, which he had lost when the medieval civilization passed away. However, what the modern self-defining subjectivity could achieve was to postpone the regaining of the wholeness; instead, it reinforced man's status as a broken totality and went a long way to scar and bruise his psyche. The self-defining subject was left only with his dry and calculative, expedient rationality. It enabled him to undertake cost and benefit analysis of his proposed actions with a view to ensuring his subsistence and, if possible, improve his economic condition for a comfortable life. This has to be achieved in an inhospitable, if not completely alien world, which must be treated as a potential instrument for the realization of man's purposes. He was forced to live with others, to be sure; however, he put himself emotionally apart from them. He is linked with them only in a functional relationship. This is indicative of the evisceration of sociability. This is equally matched by the hollowness of the claim of greater welfare that has been claimed to be possible by the rising levels of consumption of goods and services that are continuously disgorged by the industrial machine. As Fred Hirsch observes:

> [I]ncrease in resources (and thereby in the availability of goods) does nothing to increase welfare since wants increase correspondingly. The

extent to which existing demands are satisfied may never increase because wants increase commensurately with resources. So economic advance appears as one of those hoax races that leaves the participants in the same place. (1977: 60)

If economic development creates a situation in which what the wealthy have today can no longer be delivered to the rest of the people tomorrow, freedom too is mauled in the mad rush of the people to get ahead in the race of life. This is due mainly to the fact that the satisfaction of individual wants, itself alters the situation that faces others who also seek to satisfy similar wants. This provides a fresh impetus to those who seek to raise the level of their living but fail to do so because of the stiff competition, especially by those who are better endowed both by nature and by their stature in society. As this competition grows intense, the addition to material goods becomes instrumental in eviscerating morality. To quote Hirsch again:

For addition to the material goods that can be expanded for all will, in itself, increase the scramble for those goods and facilities that cannot be expanded. Taking part in this scramble is fully rational for any individual in his actions, since in these actions he never confronts the distinction between what is available as a result of getting ahead of others and what is available from a general advance shared by all. The individual who wants to see better has to stand on tiptoe. (Ibid.)

The individual has necessarily to engage in the game of beggar your neighbour. This in itself endangers freedom. What adds to it is the fact that when everybody engages in improving his worldly lot, the situational context of competition is considerably altered. This limits the exercise of freedom by every individual. If "the point of freedom is that what I live in (signifies) conditions that are only partly the fruit of my decisions, to that extent I am not integrally free" (Taylor 1979: 106).

The cumulative result of these changes, which have been associated with the rise of the self-defining subject, has been the transmutation of traditional norms of behaviour. This transmutation has been greatly promoted by the assumption that economic affairs are of primary importance in man's life. As this assumption grew in strength and became widely accepted, economic system gradually evolved to occupy the centre-stage in man's existence. As economic affairs grew in importance in man's life, the social order itself went through a radical change. This change is well captured in the pregnant phrase introduced by Sir Henry Maine. As he noted, the social order transmuted "from status to contract" (1894). This underscores the emergence of a market mode social order and underlines its corollary, that is, the extension of choice at the individual level, exercised through market exchange process. It is true that the functioning of the market has often invited increased intervention by the state for regulating the functioning of the market process to ensure fair exchange. However, these interventions have aimed primarily at creating "the conditions in which individualistic calculations can continue to operate in a socially benign way" (Hirsch 1977: 121). With individual choice getting an upper hand in society, an entirely new approach to the problem of internalising socially benign norms came to the fore. Earlier, religion used to play this role. However, the modern way of life, including the compulsions of economic life and relations, kept religion firmly outside the active considerations of man's calculations. The economic sphere has relied on what Hirsch calls "ad hoc" incentives for people with privately oriented norms so that they can direct their self-regarding actions in a socially desirable way (Ibid.: 140). This is expected to be achieved through taxes, incentives and subsidies.

With the burgeoning market economy and the increased intervention by the state in economic life and relations, isolated individuals needed some protection against not only the market and the state but also against their covetous fellow beings, who are always on the lookout for augmenting their wealth and influence. Recognizing this, liberal philosophy grants to individuals certain inalienable rights as protection against any kind of non-legal encroachment on their person or domain. However, differences in economic strength of different social groups have differential impact on their political enfranchisement that has followed their economic advance. For the economically well-off groups, political enfranchisement was the function of their economic status. However, the working class, the poor and the handicapped ethnic groups acquired political rights ahead of economic advance. This is undoubtedly the recognition of economic reality; however, this has had some serious ramifications for the political system. These ramifications can be summarily put as an insistence on the need to move away from "equal start" to "equal outcome."

The reason for this lies in the mismatch between political rights and economic status of enfranchised groups. To quote Hirsch:

> The continuing relative economic disadvantages of the individuals and groups concerned have limited the extent to which the formal political rights have translated into full political power, which rests also on economic power. Pressures have grown for economic opportunity to be more equally evenly spread by means of political action, that is, the demand for "equal economic opportunity" and this pressure has expanded through its own force to impel political action for a more equitable economic outcome. (Ibid.: 162)

The growing demand on the political system to complete the transition from "equal start" to "equal outcome" has left it gasping in the heat of the increasing social conflict. The virulence of conflict points to a situation where social values that were capable of restraining the aggressiveness of self-regarding action and that tempered it with a sense of social obligation, no matter how weak and changeable, have decidedly gone into eclipse. Thus, the modern society has been quite effective in destroying those values and orientations that nurtured the sense of social obligation. And "a system that depends for its success on a heritage that it undermines cannot be sustained on the record of its bountiful fruits" (Ibid.: 12). The overall result of the erosion of values that kept self-regarding action under leash is increased social conflict. It is this situation that MacIntyre describes as the "civil war carried on by other means" (1984: 253). And this civil war is clearly the outcome of what Hanna Arendt calls "overwhelming of the political by the social demands."

The reasons why this civil war cannot be stopped are not far to seek. The importance of the ever-escalating levels of the standard of living has taken deeper roots in the individual psyche. This is due mainly to the fact the promissory note that everybody's needs would be satisfied, has been effective in winning people to new thought-ways and work-ways after the rosy picture of blissful life after the life on this earth became very dim and doubtful. While the individual psyche is now fully attuned to the need to satisfy the material needs of his existence, the promise of redistribution of wealth has lagged far behind; even if it has been effected to some extent, it has not kept pace with the rising demand for equalization of life condi-tions. Political participation and human rights have proved ineffective in improving the lot of those who have not been able to cross the barriers raised by the unequal distribution of talents and assets. The unrestrained exercise of natural liberty tends to reproduce the original inequalities. Even partial redistribution of wealth fails to mitigate the inequity of the social order. Thus the search for equality, which Tocqueville declares to be "the permanent social revolution" stirs up the deprived and the depressed social groups to demand equal outcome in addition to equal start.

In addition, the eclipse of the traditional significance of differences among partial communities has left nothing for them but the need to pursue self-interest as a means to relate them with the whole of the social universe. Moreover, modernization, as the concomitant of economic growth adds to the differentiation of social, economic and political roles and inexorably bring with them differences of values, culture and modes of life as well as of reality perception. Groups based on these differentiations, in turn, demand certain measures of autonomous life. Modernization has not only encouraged these differences, but also created a paradoxical situation in the sense that while it has promoted greater homogenization, it has also transformed differentiations into reciprocal resistance and not infrequently active opposition among different and differently located groups.

Two factors are helpful in explaining this paradox. First, the revolu-tion of the subjectivity of the self-defining subject has been instrumental in radically changing our attitude towards society. Society is no longer justified on grounds of what it is or what it expresses; it is now justified by what it does or is capable of doing with respect to the fulfilment of the needs of its members, their desires and their purposes. This utilitarian perspective has given birth to, as Taylor argues, the utilitarian man whose loyalty is contingent upon the satisfaction gained by what it actually does or can do to help the individual to satisfy his wants. And "the very notion of satisfaction is now not so firmly anchored, once we see that it is inter-woven with 'expectations' and belief about what is appropriate and just" (Taylor 1979: 113). With the sharpening of individualistic perspectives, the world becomes what Sennet calls "a peculiar mirror of self":

It exists to fulfil the self; there are no human objectives with a reality all their own. The peculiarity, and the destructiveness, of the narcissistic vision is that the more the environment of the human being is judged in terms of its congruence with or subservience to self-needs, the less fulfilling it becomes. For the very reason that the expectations of fulfilment become so vast and amorphous, the possibilities of fulfilment are diminished. (1977: 177)

It is no wonder, then, that some of the richest societies in our day are most affected with dissatisfaction. It is against this background that the second factor assumes critical importance. It points to the fact that greater homogeneity induced by modernization shakes men loose from their traditional moorings, to be sure. However, it can neither replace traditional partial communities as foci of identity nor can it provide an overarching perspective that can link partial communities with each other and all of them with some idea of the whole in a bond of unity or at least, of belonging together in that whole. Moreover, modern societies function with a large part of their traditional outlook intact. One of the important elements of this outlook is the salience of the traditional referents of identity formation. As long as a single unifying perspective that can suppress, if not erase, socio-cultural differences among partial communities and hold them together remains viable and vital, traditional referents of identity formation remain muted and inactive. When, however, this unifying perspective gets eroded, different elements of traditional referents of identity formation are utilized to form groups for political mobilization and action. This is indicative of the extent to which a particular partial community has become alienated from the society it happens to be a part of.

The commitment in modern times to ideologies that promise greater homogenization aims at deprecating social differences. This occurs in a situation in which they provide the rallying points for identity assertion and political action in the absence of other viable alternative. When a vacuum of unifying ideology develops, ethnic or national differences fill the gap and become the foci of identity assertion, which forms the basis of political action for pressing particularized demands concerning access to societal resources. In a situation where socio-cultural diversity happens to be a harsh fact, the idea of nation soon degenerates into separate nationalities and ethnic groups. This affords yet another focal point for using traditional referents of identity formation for political gains. Thus, the traditional referents of identity formation become the instrument of sharpening differences and of increasing the salience of partial communities. This is especially true of societies, which have set upon the course of modernization and have initiated the process of faster homogenization.

This creates a paradox: while homogenization breeds alienation, the panacea that is prescribed for fighting and overcoming alienation is still more doses of modernization. This is especially true of democratic political systems where greater participation is relied upon to remove or, at least, neutralise the cause of minority or ethnic alienation. However, it only aggravates the problem as homogenization has gone a long way in undermining the solidarity of communities that formerly were unified despite internal differences of status and assets. Also, it becomes instrumental in subverting the characteristics by which people belonging to partial communities formerly identified themselves as members of a particular community, while no substitute is being put in its place that could hold different partial communities together. As such,

> [T]he increasing alienation in a society, which has eroded its traditional foci of allegiance makes it harder and harder to achieve the basic consensus, to bring everyone to "general will," which is essential for...democracy. As traditional limits fade and the grounds for accepting them (weaken), society tends to fragment; political groups become increasingly truculent in their demands, as they see less reason to compromise with the system. (Taylor 1979: 113)

Pluralism, multiculturalism and antagonistic differences—all these are the by-products of this paradox. It is this paradox that confronts modern societies. As a result, they become a fertile breeding ground where partial communities are transmuted into antagonistic groups. These groups, then, constitute a multiple of hostile political camps that afford a free play to contrary socio-economic forces. The very constitution of antagonistic groups is indicative of the decline of social consensus. This, in turn, is symptomatic of the erosion of common sense, which is increasingly in evidence because politicization of partial communities has created a situation in which people share less of common understanding of things with one another. With the decline of what is common, there is a less of a community between human beings. As such, civil war by other means is inevitable and cannot be stopped no matter how much material prosperity is generated and made available to traditionally depressed and dispossessed sections of the population. It is true that this civil war often poses the threat of disintegration of even settled political systems. The possibility of disintegration of any political system can never be ruled out, since disintegrative forces are a part of all systems; however, it achieves success only in a few cases. It is the absence of any countervailing force of union, a shared conception of the common good that makes destructive forces so powerfully visible and seriously threatening. This is the case today, because

> liberal principles no longer seem to possess a core of their own; it has been lost in the process by which the present crisis of pluralism unfolded. There is little possibility of reassertion of unifying dogma, because it has been the inexorable logic of liberal orientation itself that has led to the present disintegration. Liberal pluralism cannot stand apart to impose coherence on the very incoherence it has brought forth. (Walsh 1997: 15)

This incoherence is the result of separate individuals making decisions that aim at increasing their own welfare regardless of whether they hurt or help others. The only foundation of liberal order, that is, democracy, is the aggregation of private valuations which rules out a shared worldview because being liberal means that we do not have to share worldview. In the lack of a shareable commonality pervading the whole society, the basis for the formation of groups is provided by compatibility of interests. This compatibility provides the vantage point from which people suffering from a sense of deprivation can perceive their environment and come together for mounting political action, if their interest seems to be in jeopardy. However, when groups form, they become divisive and encourage friction. Thus, one may admire pluralism for its vaunted capacity to prevent the concentration of power in a few hands; however, it is nonetheless deleterious for the political system as a whole.

It was Thomas Hobbes who first contemplated the abyss of pluralism. He saw inherent in it not only the endless friction and disagreement endemic to politics but also the cataclysm that catches up with and overwhelms the political system and when it is invaded by men who would prefer to live without any order rather than compromise on the order of their vision. It is the unabashed promotion of private visions that is the springboard of group rights. It is the official recognition of the legitimacy of such promotions that represents a concession to the claim that it is the location of the individual in a social group that gives meaning and direction to the individual's life. It is also expected that the regaining of the sense of community, lost in the wake of the rise of the individual as the self-defining subject is possible only upon the exercise of group rights.

Thus, it is the failure of the individual human rights in overcoming and finally putting an end to exclusionary practices in society that has provoked the demand for group rights. But the trouble is that today,

> previously excluded groups are no longer willing to be silenced or marginalized or to be defined as "deviant" simply because they differ in race, culture, gender, ability or sexual orientation from the so-called normal citizen. They demand a more inclusive conception of citizenship, which recognizes (rather than stigmatizes) their identities, their differences. (Banting and Kymlica 2006: 327)

It is exactly this situation that led the makers of the Indian Constitution to realize the need to make constitutional provisions for bringing exclusionary practices to an end. This recognition prompted them to grant group rights in addition to the grant of certain human rights to individuals. Group rights have been granted to several socio-economic interests in India. Thus, the Indian Constitution combines in itself both individual rights and group rights. This prompts Bhikhu Parekh to celebrate the Indian political system as "an association of individuals and a community of communities, recognizing both the individual and communities as bearers of rights" (quoted in Parekh 2010: Chapter 6). That this co-mingling of individual and group rights creates both theoretical and pragmatic muddles, completely escapes Parekh and those who take pride in thinking like him. The first question we must ask and expect a satisfactory answer is in what sense a group can be said to be the bearer of rights. To be a bearer of rights, one must be attributed with the office of agency and must be capable of discharging the responsibilities that agency implies. Can it be said that a collective entity, which today does not display any characteristic of an organic society since almost all groups represent only an aggregation of separate individuals, and chooses a course of action for realizing group purposes and fulfils an obligation? To insist that a collective entity does all this is to indulge into the use of metaphors, that is, to take recourse to anthropomorphism.

The problem with group rights is what Anthony de Jasay refers to as the Russian Doll problem. As we unscrew the doll, we find a smaller one inside it that can, in turn, be unscrewed to reveal another doll till we come to the last one (Jasay 1997: 224). Groups are like Russian dolls; no matter how we define a group, it can still be differentiated in numerous ways. Usually groups have within them subgroups of different descriptions; these subgroups will and usually do differ in numerous ways, notably in terms of wealth, power and status as well as in terms of the level of economic development. These differences are, however, ignored on the untenable ground that they are knit firmly together because some notion of common good brings them together and keep them together. It is not true that ethnic minorities do not have subgroups within their fold; they are usually marked by internal differentiation. As such, they may have within their fold subgroups differentiated by class, education, wealth and so on. And since the formation of a group involves the perception of the environment from the same vantage point, any of these grounds may constitute the basis of group formation if a subgroup becomes acutely aware of being meted out injustice in the distribution of societal resources.

This awareness creates a political exigency that propels the affected group to channel its demand into the political system for access to resources by evoking any of the traditional referents of identity formation. To make any one of these referents of identity formation the basis of group rights is to refuse to acknowledge the reality and relevance of other grounds of identity formation. This is not the only theoretical *faux pas* that anthropomorphism commits in respect of group rights when a particular group identity is supposed to subsume other grounds of group formation. It commits another *faux pas* when the fact is ignored that a collective entity does not itself act; a particular self-appointed organ not only usually decides and acts on behalf of each of the members of the group, but also tends to self-perpetuate itself. As Jasay notes, instead of exercising its rights,

> they are exercised indiscriminately on behalf of every member by some decision-making organ, often self-appointed and self-perpetuating, which lends the group the character or at least the outward appearance of a "unit of

agency." Its decision commits to a uniform course of action. Some may like
it, others not. They are nonetheless forced to go along with it. (Ibid.: 226)

The extent to which it really happens leads to the conclusion that
group rights and liberties override the rights and liberties of dissenters
or unwilling followers. Moreover, it is the individual who exercises rights
even when a particular right has been granted to a group. Kymlicka rightly
questions right claims on behalf of communities when he points to the
woolliness of the notion. As he observes, "groups have no moral claim
to well-being independently of their members—groups just aren't the
right sort of beings to have moral status" (1989: 242).[2] Moreover, group
rights are exercised by individuals as members of a group, which happens
to be differentiated on the basis of unequal endowments of natural and
acquired talents and assets. No doubt, group rights confer benefits, to be
sure; however, such benefits accrue to different members of the group
in indeterminable proportions. This should alert us to the fact that the
benefits of group rights are not equally reaped by all the members of the
group. It results, as Marc Gallanter notes, in the clustering of benefits that
leads to and reinforces cumulative inequality (2002). This is particularly
true of the Indian experiment in securing social justice to deprived and
dispossessed groups.

This phenomenon casts a thick shadow of doubt on the appropriateness
of the notion of group rights. Also, group rights tend to preserve social
divisions; they are eminently designed to preserve and perhaps accentuate
the separate identity of partial groups. The reason for this is that group
rights go a long way to protect and foster their key distinguishing characteristics. Thus, making group rights the basis of securing social justice
unwittingly panders by reinforcing separate "cultural identity" to the very
group differences that are sought to be tamed and hopefully, abolished by
talking rights at them. As such, what Epstein says makes a lot of sense.

> Statements about groups of individuals must be translated into statements
> about individuals.... No independent rights of the group attach to the
> corporate forms.... [A]t all points the rights of groups depend on the rights
> of their members. No group has a right, which is more than the summation
> of its rights. (1985: ix, 13)

Moreover, the grant of group rights to one group stimulates other groups that have not been so favoured to politically organize, channel their demand into the political arena and press for the satisfaction of their demands, which they consider legitimate. Thus, there takes place a copious flow of demand for the grant of group rights on the part of socio-economic interests who feel themselves ignored in the distribution of benefits by the state. Three things happen because of the channelling of such demands in the political arena. One, all kinds of groups ranging from wandering tribes to homosexuals come forward to claim certain rights, even if they do not qualify as a group. Two, there seems to be a confusion between liberties and rights when all kinds of rights are claimed to be legitimate. Halfway between liberty and right there is a long list of hybrid claims that has been lengthening of late. They now include right to education, to work, to have sufficient material resources or assured access to them and so on. Their resemblance to genuine rights is hollow, for no lone has accepted or comes forward to accept or no one is being put under the obligation of performing and providing the needed service. That is why Feinberg describes them as "manifesto rights" (1980: 130–43).

And last, these "manifesto rights" are recognised as legitimate rights only because of political calculations for and/or retaining political power. However, the search for someone who obliges stops generally at the door of the government who, in the absence of any other, must bear the cost of providing the services promised under a granted group right. This brings into operation what Jasay calls "transmission principle," that is, the shifting of the burden of providing a particular service to the taxpayer. What needs to be kept in mind in this connection is that non-unanimous politics is, perhaps without any exception, redistributive. This also applies to the benefits granted under a group right. The taxes of some go to supplement the resource of others. In this process, the taxpayer is refrained from doing what he would like to do and forced to do what he has perhaps never contemplated to do. Moreover, the redistributive process is seldom transparent.

The very lack of transparency is evident from the fact individuals are unaware that they are paying for some benefit that accrues to others; however, in ignorance of the cost to themselves, they do not begrudge because of the fear of being penalized by the state. This throws a bad light on democracy, which is claimed all around to be an open system of governance. What makes the matter still worse is that the cost of providing benefits entailed by a particular group right severs the link between costs, material and moral and the benefits they usually yield. This is tantamount to what is generally known as consequentialism in the sense that the selection of a particular course of action is based more on calculation of political returns that are expected from the grant of a particular group right than any definite idea of the proper relationship between ends and means.

It should be apparent by now that the question of group rights raises not only some uncomfortable theoretical questions, but also creates some pragmatic muddles as is evident from the Indian experience. Moreover, the claim that the formation or emergence of a group for political action is the precursor of the revival and/or restoration of community in the traditional sense of the term is dubious. It is dubious in view of the fact that what we witness today is not the reinforcement of the bonds of belonging or what Plato calls *philia politike,* love for fellow-beings, but the politicization of traditional referents of identity formation. Thus, the glue that keeps a group together today, at least, for some length of time, is nothing more than the phenomenon of expediency, not primordial or emotional bonding, which gets increasingly frayed under the press of homogenization.

The conclusion that neither individual rights nor, for that matter, group rights are capable of reviving *philia politike* becomes inescapable. This is so because these rights are not only rooted in the ethics of deontology but also because groups today do not signify meaningful differentiation in the traditional sense of the term; their traditional signification has almost withered away under the stress of homogenisation that epitomises an emotional desert. Hegel saw the modern dilemma and sought to resolve it by introducing the idea of *sittlichkeit*, a moral community. However, this idea is not at all acceptable to the modern mind. Tocqueville too tried to grapple with this problem in quite a different manner. He felt that the panacea of the modern problem of the loss of the sense of community could be tackled if the central importance of a democratic polity of vigorous constituent local communities in a decentralized structure of power is recognized. However, he was aware of the very strong pull of the demand for equality, which tended to take modern society towards uniformity and submission under an omnipotent government. The combination of these two factors is strong enough to act as a strong deterrent to the evolution of a successful decentralized democracy.

It is clear, then, that the solution of the modern dilemma lies elsewhere, particularly in M. K. Gandhi's thinking. We cannot rely on individual rights because they eviscerate sociality and we cannot put our faith in group rights as the effective instrument of restoring the lost sense of sociality because they only prove to be the weapon to be used by groups for gaining political benefits and tend to freeze differences rather than erase them. As such, Gandhi seems to be one of the most important visionaries in our own age who has understood the life-corroding character of human existence, which takes its meaning from the satisfaction of material needs at the expense of the spiritual pursuit. As Gandhi insists, it is this exclusive concern for what he calls "bodily comfort" that is at the root of dilemma that faces mankind today. He, therefore, underlines the need for illuminating and modifying the reality we confront by inner illumination made possible by attuning the soul to the ground of being. This inner illumination provides the foundation for building real community. This is so for the reason that love of man is possible only through the love of God. And the love of man is most likely to flourish at the local community level where face-to-face interaction among persons takes place. As such, the most appropriate organization for promoting love of man is the decentralized political order, the locus of self-government.

Notes

1. This is well illustrated by Homer (2008) in *Odyssey* when he recounts the episode of the killing of the sacred cows of the Sun God, Helios, by the sailors of the Odysseus' boat moored in the Island of Helios even after they were warned of the evil consequences of their action.

   The loss of the sense of the sacred is, no doubt, due to the rise of passions as the primary impulse in man's life. This becomes instrumental in relegating reason to an instrumental role. Then the question of how to keep passions, some of which are turbulent and destructive, under leash assumes importance. Recognizing passions to be the dominant trait of human personality and recognizing, too, the inadequacy of moralizing philosophy and religious precepts, the search for the regulating principle came to centre around, first, on entrusting the state with the responsibility of keeping passions under control and later, subordinating them to one master passion. This passion was identified as self-interest, in the sense of the grand passion for augmenting fortune and the desire for bettering one's material condition, in a word, avarice, as Adam Smith puts it. See, Hirschman (1987).

When avarice becomes the propelling force in man's life, he becomes an "externalized creature," an object. This is the result of the self-interest crowding out man's inner being. See Wood (1972: 111). It is in self-interest, then, that the fleeting, fluid self gains a firm anchor, which lends it a particular character and constitutes the driving force of human action. It is in this sense that John Dewey's dictum "I possess, therefore I am" expresses a truer characterization of man in modern times than the Cartesian "I think, therefore, I am."

2. Cf. Dworkin, "A recognizable unit of agency must be equipped with sufficient power, functional unity and legitimacy to stand for, commit, 'represent' the collective entity in question" (1992: 211–12).

References

Banting, Keith, and Kymlicka, Will. 2006. *Multiculturalism and the Welfare State: Recognition and Redistribution in Contemporary Democracies*. Oxford: Oxford University Press.

Colletti, Lucio. 1972. *From Rousseau to Lenin: Studies in Ideology and Society*. New York: Monthly Book Review Press.

Cooper, John M. 1975. *Reason and Human Good in Aristotle*. Cambridge, MA: Harvard University Press.

Dworkin, R. 1992. "Liberal Community," in *Communitarians and Individualism*. Eds. S. Avineri and A. Shalit. Oxford: Oxford University Press.

Epstein, R. A. 1985. *Takings: Property and Power of Eminent Domain*. Cambridge, MA: Harvard University Press.

Feinberg, J. 1980. *Rights, Justice and Bounds of Justice*. Princeton, NJ: Princeton University Press.

Gallanter, Marc. 2002. *Competing Equality: Law and the Backward Classes in India*. Delhi: Oxford University Press.

Hirsch, Fred. 1977. *Social Limits to Growth*. London: Routledge & Kegan Paul.

Hirschman, Albert O. 1987. *The Passions and the Interests: Political Arguments for Capitalism before its Triumph*. Princeton: Princeton University Press.

Hobbes, Thomas. 1991. *Man and Citizen*. Ed. Bernard Gert. Indianapolis, IN: Hacket.

Homer. 2008. *Odyssey*. Trans. Thomas Hobbes. *The Iliad and the Odyssey*, Clarendon Edition, by Eric Nelson. Oxford: Oxford University Press.

Jaeger, Werner. 1930. *Paideia*, 3 vols. New York: Oxford University Press.

Jasay, Anthony de. 1997. *Against Politics: On Government, Anarchy and Order*. London: Routledge.

Kymlicka, Will. 1989. *Liberalism, Community and Culture*. Oxford: Clarendon Press.

MacIntyre, Alasdaire. 1984. *After Virtue*, 2nd edition. Notre Dame: Notre Dame University Press.

Maine, Sir Henry. 1894. *Ancient Law*. London: Murray.

Oliver, Roy. 1968. *The Wanderer and the Way: The Hebrew Tradition in the Writings of Martin Buber*. Ithaca: Cornell University Press.

Pangle, Thomas L. 1976, September. "The Political Psychology of Religion in Plato's Law," *The American Political Science Review*, 70(3).

Parekh, Bhikhu. 2010. *Gandhi: A Brief Insight*. New York: Sterling Publishing Co.

Sandoz, Ellis. 1981. *The Voegelinian Revolution: A Biological Introduction*. Baton Rouge: Louisiana State University Press.

Sennet, Robert. 1977. "Destructive Gemeinschaft," in *Beyond Crisis*. Ed. N. Birnbaum. London: Oxford University Press.

Taylor, Charles. 1979. *Hegel and Modern Society*. Cambridge: Cambridge University Press.

Tocqueville, Alexis de. 1956. *Democracy in America*. Ed. D. Phillips Bradley. New York: Vintage Books.

Unger, Roberto M. 1975. *Knowledge and Politics*. New York: The free Press.

Voegelin, Eric. 1952. *The New Science of Politics: A New Interpretation*. Chicago: University of Chicago Press.

Walsh, David. 1997. *The Growth of the Liberal Soul*. Columbia: University of Missouri Press.

Wood, Ellen M. 1972. *Mind and Politics: An Approach to the Meaning of Liberal and Socialist Individualism*. Berkeley: University of California Press.

8

Back to the Roots

In the mere consideration of the world as it is...there arises in me the wish—no, not the mere desire, but the absolute demand—for a better world. I cast a glance on present relations of men towards each other and towards nature; on the feebleness of their powers, on the strength of their desires and passions. A voice within me proclaims with irresistible conviction—it is impossible that it can remain thus; it must become other and better.

—Johann Gottlieb Fichte

The very talk of going back to the roots suggests that there is something grievously wrong with things as they are. If this perception is valid, then three questions need to be answered. First question involves the elucidation of what these things are and what is wrong with them. If our enquiry leads us to conclude that things are not really as they should be, then the question whether they can be put right by relying on the elements integral to the perspective on man and his world that has made the things what they are, assumes importance. And if they cannot be so mended, then the question, "what must then be done?" must be confronted and satisfactorily answered.

In respect of the question, "what must be done," it is apparent, as the title of this chapter suggests that the only satisfactory answer is to go back to the roots, as interpreted by Mohandas Karamchand Gandhi. Two questions—what the going back to the roots involves and why this going back is unavoidably necessary—need to be explored. It is these questions that this chapter seeks to answer.

The onset of the modern age represents almost a complete break from the older patterns of specifying who man is and what relations he has or should have with the external world, both society and nature. Traditionally, a two-tiered view of good life held sway. Elaborating this two-tiered view, Charles Taylor observes:

> Traditional moral views consider good life to consist primarily in some
> higher activity distinct from the fulfillment of ordinary life needs involved

with the production and reproduction of life. Meeting these ordinary needs was, of course, unavoidable and good but was simply infrastructural to a distinct activity that gave life its higher significance. On one version, this was defined as contemplation, on another influential version, the life of the citizen. On either version, lives which lacked the favoured activity, and were entirely absorbed in meeting life-needs, were truncated and deprived. (Taylor 1981: 112)

The need for pursuing a higher life purpose in either of the versions means, as Gandhi underlines, that man must rise above the level of the beast since it is man's destiny to become more than the brute. As man is the maker of his destiny (Pyarelal 1958: II, 20–21), he must strive to become perfect. But complete perfection, as Gandhi notes, is possible only after the dissolution of the body since man is limited by the bonds of his fate (Tendulkar 1951–54: V, 392–93). Thus, complete perfection is out of reach. However, man has still to try to elevate himself, lift himself up from the brute state because he is "a special creation of God precisely to the extent that he is distinct from the rest of his creation" (Gandhi 1969: VI, 110). Perfection in lifetime, therefore, means a continuous ceaseless striving towards knowing one's nature. "In eating, sleeping and in the performance of other physical functions, man is not different from the brute. What distinguishes him from the brute is his ceaseless striving to rise above the brute on the moral plane" (110–11).

It is the ceaseless striving to rise above the brute that constitutes a higher life purpose, since it represents a determined effort to put in chain the brute in man. This brute in man is nothing else than what we know as the natural man, natural because he gives exclusive preference to the appeasement of his animal appetites. These animal appetites constitute ordinary life-needs representing the central importance of the acquisition of wealth, power and prestige. In all traditional societies, the fulfilment of ordinary life needs was considered important insofar as their fulfilment was essential for survival and for the creation of culture and civilization. However, they were not supposed to be autonomous; their fulfilment was necessary but only under the suzerainty of the pursuit of higher life purposes.

Contemplation that Plato talks about and the life of the citizen that Aristotle views as *sine qua non* for a salubrious political order, both are surrogates of a higher life purpose. They are, however, beyond the reach of a person who considers the attunement of his soul to the divine ground of being either frivolous or is unable to breach the limits carved by the primacy of the single-minded pursuit of self-interest. Thus, all societies that valued the pursuit of higher life purposes for making human existence noble and exalted subordinated the satisfaction of ordinary life-needs to the pursuit of higher life purpose and had a mooring in the idea of divine entity. Without such a mooring, restraining the depredations of passions that clamour for a free play is not possible. Once the fear of or respect for the sacred, the transcendental entity loses its relevance, passions become unfettered and play havoc in man's existence.

With the fear of or respect for the sacred gone, the pursuit of a higher life purpose suffers neglect, even rejection. The rejection of higher life purpose has several adverse consequences for man and his world. First, the rejection of the transcendental entity results in the emergence of man as a self-defining subject who discovers his purposes in himself. As Taylor points out, the rejection of the divine paves the way for the emergence of humans as beings who discover their purposes in themselves. "Nature" becomes internalized in the modern period. On this view, the free subject becomes someone who follows an internal purpose and who owes no a priori allegiance to a pre-existing order but only to structures that one has created by one's consent. Even the ancient conceptions of freedom of the citizen, which was essentially defined as a certain relation to the whole— the polis or republic—go into eclipse and we find atomist conceptions of freedom developing where persons are seen to enjoy "natural liberty" in a state of nature (Taylor 1981: 112).

To be free in this sense is to be disengaged from the external world and to be disengaged is to drain the external world of its significance. When the external world is drained of its significance, both society and nature become available for exploitation as potential means for realizing human purposes (Taylor 1983). This signifies a radical separation between the inner realm of mind or consciousness and the external realm of matter. The enlightenment perspective treated the external world as a realm of merely contingent correlations utterly devoid of human meaning and subject only to purely causal laws and modes of explanations. The categories of purpose and value and all associated modes of teleological understanding, tended either to be rejected as illusory projections on to an indifferent universe or else to be treated as applicable to the "inner" realm of human experience.

The claim of autonomy, both from divine connection and the surrounding social order in a situation where the need for fulfilling ordinary life-need has been released from the bondage of the pursuit of higher life purposes, makes man ego-centric in the sense that the individual becomes the centre of experience. Autonomy in this sense connotes man's ability to define his life purposes and to choose appropriate ways and means of realizing them. Appropriateness of the means of realizing self-determined purposes does not signify, in any way, conformity of means chosen to the idea of what is right; it is determined, on the contrary, by the benefit it promises to yield. Thus, while selection of means for a given end involves instrumental, calculative reasoning, the end also is treated as something, which need not be judged at the bar of reason, understood in non-instrumental sense. This at once makes it clear that whatever ends one plans to pursue need not depend either on the prevailing prior consensus in society or on agreement among individuals. Every individual has his own end to pursue without taking into account whether the action he proposes to take has benign or malignant consequences for others.

Once autonomy in the sense described above comes to be coveted and provides the essential ingredients of human existence, the sense of what Heraclitus calls *xynon* (a shareable commonality) that lies buried in the interior of every individual is deadened. While *xynon* remains an active or an actively acknowledged element in social life and relations, man remains awake, aware of his essential relatedness with his maker and his destiny. "Only one cosmos...exists for the 'waking' alone, while the 'sleepers' each have their own private world, a world of dreams" (Heraclitus, quoted in Jaeger 1939: I, 180). Propelled by personal world of dreams, the individual wakes up only when he thinks of his egoistic self and proceeds to satisfy its demands. Such a self is immersed in materiality and has to confront competition from other selves similarly propelled.

The goal of this competition is to acquire more and more goods and services with a view to satisfying the demands of his world of dream. Once the individual lets himself be reduced to the status of "sleepers," the pursuit of self-interest assumes a central place in his life. This reduces both society and nature to the status of potential means for the realization of individual purposes. In addition, reason is transformed into calculative, practical reasoning; with it, concerns for truth, meaning and value are eroded. Also, as more and more of the needs are fulfilled, demands for ever greater qualities of goods and services escalate, but their satisfaction becomes more and more difficult. As expectations from the external world grow, dissatisfaction and disillusion also go on increasing. As a consequence, human existence gets denuded of all meanings. This, in turn, leads to alienation.

The phenomenon of alienation is one of the prominent characteristics of the modern age. It is not only true of the individual being who has, in the process of satisfying his ordinary life-needs, lost his wholeness. He has become, as Iris Murdoch notes, a "broken totality" not only because he has snapped his relationship with the divine ground of reality, but also because his reliance on instrumental rationality dries up the font of his emotions and sentiments. This makes it utterly difficult for moral sentiments to survive, much less flourish. The alienation within the psyche of the individual finds its expression in man's disengagement from the external world, both society and nature. This is symptomatic of the disruption of the field of energy that surrounds the cosmos; this also means the rejection of the idea that the creation has a purpose. This puts paid to the ancient idea of the cosmos as an organic system. In the traditional thinking, the cosmos symbolized a metabolism signifying a structure of inter-dependence that sustained itself on mutually supportive and sustaining process of exchange of gifts and benefits.[1] This process of exchange transformed the cosmos into a primordial community comprising *martya*, *amartya*, *prithiwi* and *dyau* or as Plato puts it, man, god, society and the world.

The revolution of modern self-defining subjectively broke the bonds of this primordial community and left man isolated in this wide and inhospitable world. Man lacked tangible resources, except his potentialities slumbering undeveloped in his breast. However, two boons were granted to the lone man isolated from his fellow-beings. But he was, in lieu, burdened with the responsibility of rebuilding, with the help of these two boons, the community he had lost in the process of responding to the demands of his animal nature. These boons, as the slogan of the French Revolution testifies, are freedom and equality. The boon of freedom was meant to make man not only free from all encumbrances that a society imposes on him; it was also to enable him to give a desirable shape to the pattern of his living according to what he thinks is appropriate for him. Moreover, this was to be achieved by fulfilling his material needs alone. In addition, what is more important, it is claimed that it is in the process of need fulfilment that the self-making of man becomes possible. In the process of self-making, man acquires certain modes of thinking and working.

The exercise of freedom, in a situation where inequality in the distribution of talents and assets constitutes the hallmark of a social order, proves vacuous. In order, therefore, to make freedom effective, removal of inequality or at least its reduction becomes necessary. Equality of opportunity as a means of promoting equality, however, proves insufficient. This engenders social movements that demand a shift from equality of opportunity to equality of outcome meaning equality of life conditions. However, such a shift becomes difficult for both practical and political reasons. As a result, society is caught in what Alexis de Tocqueville calls "permanent social revolution." And the trouble is that no resolution of this revolution can be found nor there is any respite from it. Social unrest and political turmoil become an integral part of the social order.

The putting together of freedom and equality with a view to promoting and securing material well-being of man is expected to ensure fraternity or, to borrow a term from Plato, *philia politike* (love among men in a community). However, as will be clear shortly, this expectation remains unfulfilled. Several deleterious consequences for man and his relationship with the external world follow from this. First, the earlier hierarchical ordering of the biological and the moral has been displaced by their fusion in the sense that the fulfilment of man's biological needs is said to be necessary in man's moral and spiritual development. This has accentuated the opposition between man's sensibility and the external world. This opposition translates itself in the exploitation, manipulation/transformation, of nature as the necessary condition for fulfilling the promise of everybody's hope of a better life. Moreover, since economic development constitutes the basis for the overall development of man, exploitation of nature is rationalized and camouflaged by the bewitching idea of the self-making of man. However, it leads to "endlessness of needs;" that is, needs become endless in two important senses: One, they are detached from higher life purposes and become their own end and two, they proliferate endlessly. When needs become endless, the emergence of industrial civilization becomes unavoidable, especially when powerful technological means of exploitation becomes available. At the heart of this civilization stands the mighty industrial machine geared to producing more and more of goods and services for the consumption of man who is unable to exercise any control on his galloping hunger for goods and services.

It is this industrial civilization that Gandhi characterizes as Satanic precisely because it makes bodily welfare, the springboard of man's motivation and action. When the economic system is geared to producing more and more of goods and services for satisfying man's ever proliferating needs, religion and morality are pushed back to the fringe of man's consciousness. Two factors account for this. First, as John Locke suggests, man has no time to say hallelujah because he has to devote himself fully to the earning of loaves and fishes. However, the reason goes much deeper. It needs to be emphasized that indifference either to morality or to religion is grounded in the modern outlook that considers them irrelevant. Second, it promotes what John S. Mill calls self-regarding action; it signifies that when individuals act, they take note of their own good whether or not it is beneficial for others. This eclipses morality.

The withering away of the concern for others makes James Dewey to substitute the Cartesian "I think, therefore I am" by "I possess, therefore I am" as a better characterization of man as he is today. The emphasis on increasing one's worldly possession makes every individual a competitor for getting access to scarce societal resources. The competition of each against all signifies, first, that it is one's own welfare that must receive priority and second, that such welfare consists in not only getting ahead of others in the race for material wellbeing, but also in creating a situation in which others may not find it possible to compete successfully. If self-interest occupies the centre of life activity, inequality becomes the primary characteristic of social order. And inequality is sustained by exploitation and domination. It is against this background that we can appreciate Gandhi's stricture of industrial civilization insofar as it promotes Mammon worship and "enables the strong to amass wealth at the expense of the weak…" (Gandhi 1954: 158).[2]

This tendency towards amassing wealth at the expense of the weak not only makes the principle of "might is right" the animating force in society; it also detracts from individual dignity, kills self-reliance and blocks the growth of individuals to their full human stature. In a situation where the growth of the individual to full human stature is viewed to be fully dependent on access to scarce societal resources, the prevalence of inequality of possession must be viewed as loathsome and therefore, deplorable. It is not surprising then that there is such a great accent on achieving equality of life conditions. As a result, the demand for ensuring the equality of conditions pervades the political order. Thus, modern democracies have come to be characterized by what Tocqueville calls "permanent social revolution." The reason for this is that the spread of democratic ideals has fostered a widespread passion for equalization of power, property and status within the spheres of state and civil society.

It is true that the passionate struggle for equalization has reached dizzying heights. However, groups fighting for equality find it difficult to gain it on their own. This forces these groups to take the help of the state to secure equality. Thus, these groups are forced willy-nilly to be content with the goal of state-secured equality. The dependence on the state allows the government to intrude more and more in different areas of the people's life. The more the state institutions get involved in providing public services, the less civil society can cope without state intervention and direction and so the need for state intervention constantly grows. The state functions as a kind of tutelary power, which "perpetuates in the social body a type of administrative drowsiness which the heads of the administration are inclined to call good order and public tranquillity" (Tocqueville 1996: I, 158).

The immense increase in the power of the state, confirmed by the intrusion of the government in different areas of the people's life is tolerated, however, in the belief that it is for the good of the individual and society. However, as Gandhi observes:

> I look upon an increase of the power of the state with the greatest fear, because although while apparently doing good by minimizing exploitation, it does the greatest harm to mankind by destroying individuality which lies at the root of all progress. (Gandhi 1959: LIX, 319)

Apart from making the state extremely powerful, it has also enfeebled freedom itself. The exercise of freedom in a situation characterized by extreme inequality of talent and assets tends to reproduce and reinforce inequality. However, when equality is restricted, the cry for equalization of life conditions goes up. And since equality constitutes one of the central values that a modern society lives by, its curtailment cannot be allowed. Thus, the unrestrained exercise of individual freedom, when inequality of possession, happens to be the characteristic feature of society, produces inequalities in social and economic resources so great as to bring about serious violation of political equality and hence of the democratic process (Dahl 1985: 60). When this happens, the state is again forced to intervene in order to promote and safeguard equality.

It is interesting to note that freedom is supposed to be the driving force of progress. The need to improve one's lot in the world propels men to overcome their propensity to insolence. "The desire for honour, power or wealth stimulates the individual to strive after rank among his fellowmen—whom he can neither bear to interfere with himself, nor yet let alone," becomes the universal trait. This, however, results in discord. However, Kant views discord as something that awakens in man all his latent power. Undoubtedly, discord is an unsocial quality; however, insofar as it awakens man's latent powers, the "first steps are taken from rudeness of barbarism to the culture of civilization." As Kant underlines:

> Thanks be then to Nature for this unsociableness, for this envious jealousy and vanity, for this unsuitable desire for possession, or even, of power. Without them all the excellent capacities implanted in mankind would slumber eternally undeveloped. Man wished concord, but Nature knows better what is good for his species and she will have discord. (Kant, quoted in Colletti 1972: 172)

For two vital reasons, however, the wish for concord must be satisfied, if not fully then even partially. First, civil society characterized by inequality and discord not only confirms but also reinforces the unsocial character of private interests; it also fails to generate norms and values of citizenship meaning the need for self-transcendence to contribute meaningfully to collective good. Man in such a civil society turns out to be a highly confused and parochial being.

Second, discord, if pervasive, tends to disrupt public order and detracts from the legitimacy of the state, if discord is allowed to linger on. In a situation of prolonged discord, neither freedom nor equality is safe from the depredation of aggressive pursuit of self-interest. What such a situation signifies is that modern societies are bedevilled by unremitting conflict between freedom and equality. Unrestrained exercise of freedom produces inequality; if it is restrained, creativity and innovation suffer. This dilemma has pushed both freedom and equality to seek ways and means to establish their supremacy against the other. Their tussle for power and unchallenged ascendancy has, however, left fraternity without any substance. As Martin Buber observes:

> The abstractions freedom and equality were held together there through the more concrete fraternity, for only if men feel themselves to be brothers can they partake of a genuine freedom from one another and a genuine equality with one another. But fraternity has been deprived of its original meaning, the relationship between children of God, and consequently of any real content. As a result, each of the two remaining watchwords was able to establish itself against the other, and by so doing, to wander farther and farther from its truth. Arrogant and presumptuous, each sucked into itself ever more thoroughly, elements foreign to it, elements of passion or power and greed for possession. (Buber, quoted in Oliver 1968: 116–17)

The opposition between freedom and equality is the natural outcome of the aggressive pursuit of self-interest, which puts equality in jeopardy. When equality becomes restrictive of freedom, the cry for safeguarding freedom goes up. This opposition is a natural consequence of a mode of living that, as Gandhi never tired of pointing out, celebrates bodily comfort. The celebration of bodily comfort deadens the soul-force with the result that man loses discrimination in respect of judging what needs he should satisfy and what he should reject. Loss of discrimination is also symptomatic of the loss of morality in the sense that self-regarding action extinguishes concerns for others and for the common good. Moreover, the very meaning of what constitutes common good undergoes sea change. Aristotle was quite clear about the fact that the good of the whole cannot be treated as the aggregation of the good of separate individuals as is the practice today. This transmutation of the notion of the common good has made the pursuit of self-interest all the more important as the prime factor in the promotion of the individual good. And the sum-total of the good of separate individuals is erroneously treated today as the common good.

With the pursuit of self-interest assuming a central place in man's existence, man becomes what *Chhandogya Upanishad* calls *arthasamgrahi* (one who amasses wealth) and turns out to be *kamachar* (driven by appetites) or as Plato calls "the slave of many mad masters." To become the slave of passions and appetites is tantamount to losing auto-control. With the erosion of auto-control, man's interior becomes a veritable battleground of riotous appetites. The individual proceeds to appease his appetites because to do the bidding of appetites is supposed to promote the good of the individual. However, in doing so, the individual must be said to live lustfully; as a result, he becomes dead, entombed in the passion and frenzy of his body, dead to the call of his own "inner voice" warning him against the malignant consequences of his willing surrender to his passions. Willing surrender to passions is indicative of the fact that the individual does not know which appetite to satisfy and which he must not.

In the absence of the knowledge of what is the greatest good and lacking the basis for choosing reliably among multitudinous apparent goods, it becomes very difficult to achieve completeness of existence or integration of being. He is, therefore, forced to welcome them all and try to settle in what manner and to what extent all the goods that he seeks might fit together. Apart from the loss of the completeness of existence, the individual also finds himself, because of the intense competition, on the one hand and the operation of both physical and social limits to growth, on the other, unable to satisfy his own increasing and proliferating needs. If he tries to overcome these limits, he is prone to invite the wrath of the state. In the meantime, inequality of possession that cannot be totally vanquished leaves a vast room for exploitation and oppression.

All these ill effects are no doubt due to man's propensity to turn his back on his soul and commit himself to bodily comfort. It is the search for bodily comfort that accounts for the enslavement of man to his passion or many mad masters. In order to gain equanimity, that is pacification of conflicts within his interior and to live peacefully with the world outside, the individual must find ways and means to escape his enslavement to riotous passions. It must be kept in mind that when the soul of the individual gets diseased, this disease spreads outside and afflicts society. And when society gets diseased, it becomes very difficult for those, who want to recover the health of their soul or who seek to remain unaffected by society's disease, to escape the pollution of their soul. This does mean that virtuous people live in hell if society is simply a potential means for the realization of individual purposes articulated in material terms.

However, can we say that even those who have sold their soul for seven days of earthly existence are enjoying the bliss of terrestrial paradise?

It must be pointed out that the common man enjoys the pleasures of the world with the help of his possession as long as he is safe from the envious greed of the powerful. Liberal societies seek to protect the individual and escape this eventuality by relying on three factors. First, a heavy reliance is placed on human rights as the bulwark for protecting the individual from encroachment on his person and property from any authority external to him. One component of this bulwark is, of course, freedom, which the individual can exercise not only for determining his life proposes but also for selecting ways and means of realizing them. Protection of individual liberty is based on the assumption that this is the best way for human beings to flourish. Two factors vitiate this supposition. First, the only foundation to liberal political order must be the aggregation of the private valuations of the individuals who compose it. There can be nothing approaching a shared worldview because being liberal means precisely that we do not have to share a worldview. If there is no such thing as a shared worldview, it follows that a consensus on the meaning of human flourishing may also be lacking. As a result, the idea of human flourishing may differ and differ sharply from person to person.

Second, lack of consensus does not preclude the prevalence of a generalized notion of what human flourishing may mean for all. As already pointed out, it is widely held that human flourishing, whatever it may mean to different individuals, can be ensured only through continuous rise of the standard of living. However, this requires access of individuals to societal resources. However, demands for access to societal resources soon degenerate into that of privileged access. This is due not least to the open-ended nature of man's needs, on the one hand, and the de-linking of freedom from any moral value, on the other. These two factors make for unrestrained exercise of freedom.

Thus, when individual liberty seems to be in danger of violation, the government intervenes to promote and protect it—especially, the liberty of opportunity. In addition, reliance is also placed on other institutions of society not only for facilitating the exercise of freedom by individuals, but also as a device of controlling and curbing the tendency towards self-aggrandizement. All these devices aim at keeping the people on the path of virtue. Moreover, if these devices prove ineffective, one can always take recourse to exhortation to encourage people to cultivate virtues so that personal life and social relations may remain salubrious and support public order.

Ineffectiveness of these devices results in widespread dissatisfaction and alienation born of disillusionment with the political system. Long ago, Adam Smith made avarice the springboard of economic prosperity and public peace. Smith transformed what was earlier considered a vice into a virtue. And what is interesting to note is that the state has been carved out of private vices and is made responsible for keeping them within tolerable limits. However, restricting avarice or failure in equitable distribution of societal resources promotes alienation. The instability of liberal political systems is in no small measure due, to this alienation. Can this be cured by recourse to institutional reforms? What needs to be emphasized in that, the remedy cannot lie in simply institutional, social or political reforms. It is generally believed that social reforms can rid the society of its ills and ensure human perfection or something very close to it. The instability is, however, not purely institutional or conceptual. They will not, however, lead towards the transformation of man and, through it, that of politics. Nor will the reforms of laws and institutions lead to socio-political improvement, unless the spiritual dimension is brought back in man's existence. It must be emphasized that it is the neglect of the spiritual or moral dimension that is the source of instability. As Gandhi puts it, "it is an inward change.... It is the transformation of the heart...." And it "is a radical change more in inward spirit than in the outward form. If the first is changed, the second will take care of itself. If the first remains unchanged, the second, no matter how radically changed, will be like a whited sepulcher...." (Gandhi 1969: VI, 14).

But how is the change in the inward spirit accomplished? It is not that the liberal worldview does not underline the need to cultivate spirituality with a view to facilitating man's proper development. However, its talk of spirituality does not allow the soul to tune to the divine ground of reality. The liberal outlook presupposes and prefers the growth of the soul, to be sure; however, the structures that it has created are meant to as such promote the fulfilment of ordinary like needs; they are quite incapable of promoting and sustaining the growth of the soul in the spiritual sense. The spiritual growth that it refers to has no meaning apart from the attunement of the soul to the transcendent reality by which the process of growth is ordered.

The elaboration of the process through which the growth of the soul is assured contains enough intimation of its direction to evoke a responsive unfolding of the soul. Once the movement of moral enlargement occurs, the process begins to sustain itself as the existential illumination of the good, draws the soul ever more profoundly towards itself. It is this dynamic interaction between the unfolding of the soul and the magnetic attraction of the good that has a vital impact on the texture of reality. Reality becomes illumined from within the perspective of participation through the growth of the soul that changes the reality involved.

It is this change, that is change in the inner being of man or "change in the inward spirit," that Gandhi insists upon. And since this change involves the self-conscious, active recognition of a transcendent entity, Gandhi insists on the need for the soul to be attuned to the divine ground of reality. For Gandhi, this transcendental reality is God. For him, God is not something like the Platonic form, which does not enter anything nor does it allow anything to enter into it; he is completely realizable because he is also immanent in man's being. This is what the Vedic literature has been teaching and this teaching has become an integral part of Hindu culture. A definite and "living recognition of the presence of the mighty spirit residing within" is necessary for the transformation of the heart, the fountainhead of "a radical change in inward spirit" that Gandhi talks about.

Rooted firmly in the ancient Indian thought, Gandhi believes the possibility of ultimate realization of the absolute transcendent entity. For him, the consummation of man's strive is his total identification with God. This is what he calls self-realization. "Coming face to face with God" or "coming nearer to one's own maker" constitutes the supreme ideal for Gandhi. "Man's ultimate aim is then realization of God, and all his activities, social, political [and] religious, have to be guided by the ultimate aim of the vision of God" (Ibid.: I, 107). "Coming face to face with God" does not mean a complete turnaround from the phenomenal world and its concerns. It simply means that devotion to God must animate the being of the individual and constitute the regulating force of all his action. As Gandhi says:

> I am an Advaitist and yet I can support Dvaitism (dualism). The world is changing every minute, and is therefore unreal, it has not permanent

existence. But though it is constantly changing, it has something about it which persists and it is therefore to that extent real. (Gandhi 1959: XXXV, 1)

If this world is real, then, its concerns too are real and therefore, worthy of man's attention. The world is real not because it is out there; a large part of what is out there is subject to change and decay and one cannot cling to what decays and dies. As such, one has to focus his attention on that which endows it with the quality of substance and permanence. Following the teaching of *Isopanishad*, Gandhi considers the world to be resident of the Absolute (*Ishavasya idam sarvam...*). But this knowledge is not enough to allow the growth of the soul; one must actively engage in keeping this world worthy of God's residence. To keep the world worthy of God's residence is, on the one hand, to firmly believe in the oneness of life and on the other, to engage in the service of God's creation.

We cannot treat them as something that can be grabbed by force or by agreement. They are faculties that remain dormant as long as man remains immersed in the phenomenal world, with eyes turned away from his maker. They have to be awakened and developed through self-realization. Self-realization, for Gandhi, does not mean the realization of one's hidden potentialities with a view to transforming/manipulating the external world for satisfying one's material needs, as Immanuel Kant understands it. Self-realization in Gandhi's sense means the growth of the soul, as the seat as well as the sensorium of the divine, so that one can develop a sense of identity with God's creation. It is the belief in God that engenders the belief in the oneness of life. This, in turn, finds its expression in the attitude of treating others on a footing of equality. This does away with the idea of superiority and infirmity. In Gandhi's words:

> I believe in the rock-bottom doctrine of Advaita my interpretation of Advaita excludes totally any idea of superiority at any stage whatever. I believe implicitly that all men are born equal. All...have the same soul as any other. And it is because I believe in this inherent equality of all men that I fight the doctrine of superiority, which many of our rulers arrogate to themselves. (Gandhi 1954: 107)

The belief in God prevents man from arrogating to himself a superior position and from treating others as inferior. It also produces in him a sense of relatedness with other determinate beings; this provides the ground for identification with fellow men. To relate oneself to the indeterminate, that is, the absolute, the God, and to feel related with the determinate as the result of one's attunement to the divine ground of beings, constitutes the basis for an extended self. The significance of the extended self lies in the fact that a person does not feel any difference between himself and others. To become an extended self is to feel compassion, the quality of being sympathetically affected by the suffering of others. To identify with others is then to identity oneself with the suffering of others (Gandhi 1946) and since this world is full of suffering, self-realization must include the alleviation of the sufferings of others. This is necessary because self-development that Gandhi talks of must be attained in the world of here and now in the midst of one's fellow men. And to run away to some isolated cloister or to a cave in the Himalayas is utter selfishness. It also violates the principle of the oneness of the world. Thus, for Gandhi, it is the love for God that engenders love for fellow men and it is this love that prompts one to undertake the task of alleviating the suffering of others.

There is yet another weighty reason for Gandhi's insistence that the pursuit of self-realization must be carried out in society. If the objective of self-realization is to serve God, how can we serve him when we do not know him? Gandhi's reply is very clear. "We may not know God, but we know his creation. Service of His creation is the service of the God." (1959: LXII, 253). Thus, man's total commitment to the quest for the transcendent entity, which constitutes the source not only for man's identity with the external world but also for his morality, is what Gandhi underlines. Gandhi is aware of the fact that "the ultimate aim of the vision of God is that indefinable something which we all feel but which we do not know," can become concrete when we commit ourselves to the pursuit of truth and non-violence. For Gandhi, truth is God and it is the sovereign principle, which includes numerous other principles. "It is the absolute truth, the Eternal Principle that is God.... I worship God as truth only" (Gandhi 1969: VI, 40).

To discover truth completely is to realize one's self and one's real destiny. However, the realization of the absolute truth is not always possible. Therefore, Gandhi says, "But as long as I have not realized this Absolute Truth, so long must I hold by the relative truth as I have conceived it. The relative truth must, meanwhile, be my beacon, my shield and buckler" (1969: VI, 95). But to hold on to relative truth is to be confronted with many versions of reality and to negotiate these several versions of reality may involve incompatibility of perspective leading perhaps to conflict. But active conflict must be avoided since it may involve violence and violence refuses to acknowledge the integrity of other persons. Two things therefore become necessary. In the first place, in order to safeguard the essential integrity of others, one must commit to the observance of non-violence. In the second place, if the conflict of opinion is not resolved, one must, eschewing violence, practise Satyagraha. *Ahimsa* is a necessary step towards seeking and finding truth inasmuch as it directs our attention from an external enemy to an internal one and enables us to conquer the latter to reform the former. It is in this sense that Gandhi underlines the fact that *Satya* and *Ahimsa* "are two sides of a coin" with the latter constituting the means of the end, that is truth. This leads Gandhi to declare, "If we take care of the means, we are bound to reach the end sooner or later" (1959: XLV, 39).

For Gandhi, then, commitment to truth as God is what makes a person noble in the sense that he develops, through his spiritual quest, the capacity to rise above his self-interest and relate to others in a way that does not allow the link between the good of one person and the good of all persons to snap. This relationship is not restricted to the realm of thought; it takes a concrete form when the search for truth is translated into the service of God's creation, especially that segment of his creation, which is suffering because of poverty and penury. Such a translation means engaging in action; for Gandhi, action, however, must be associated with detachment. Self-realization, as Gandhi understands it, means self-elevation for realizing one's higher self or more precisely, the real self. This is possible when a person overcomes attachment to the world and its concerns. As such, without the sense of detachment, "action leads to bondage unless it is performed in a spirit of sacrifice" (Gandhi 1968: 13). Moreover, it is detachment or selfless action that proves instrumental is preserving the social order. In this sense, action signifies *Yajna*, that, according to Gandhi, means exerting oneself for the benefit of others, in a word, service.

Thus, when Gandhi underlines the need for detachment not only as an aid to self-realization but also as a means of preserving the social order, he strikes at the very root of liberal worldview and by the same token, highlights the immense importance of the past that liberal worldview jettisons as a dead weight. When Gandhi hints at the importance of the past, he does not mean its revival as it was before or restoring its institutional arrangements; what he means is to take inspiration and cues from their underlying principles and use them in giving a concrete shape to the present. As such, Gandhi does not imply the restoration of the institutional practices or the restoration of the past; what he hints at is to use the cue from the past to open the horizon of the future. It is in keeping with this that he goes back to the traditional idea of who the man is. Similarly, he also spurns the liberal conception of the relationship between the individual and society and equates this relationship to that of the drop in the ocean. To quote Gandhi:

> The ocean is composed of drops of water; each drop is an entity and yet it is a part of the whole; "the one and the many." In this ocean of life, we are little drops. My doctrine means that I must identify myself with life, with everything that lives, that I must share the majesty of life in the presence of God. The sum-total of life is God. (1969: VI, 109)

The majesty of life is not safeguarded by the egoistic individual who thinks himself separated from others and uses them as potential means for realizing his own proposes. By doing so, he disrupts the flow of life, which pervades not only this phenomenal world but also the world beyond, the world that we cannot see. The preservation of the flow of life and therefore, its majesty is what safeguards cosmic metabolism, the exchange of energy among different beings of the cosmos. It is this exchange of energy that helps the primordial community of men, gods, the earth and the heaven to continue unbroken. This cosmic metabolism is disrupted when a man acquires more than he needs to live.[2] Gandhi, too, emphasizes the need to preserve the cosmic metabolism and refuses to have what others do not or cannot have. This means the practice of detachment and resistance of the temptation to engage in self-interested action that takes away from public good. Gandhi treats taking away from public good as stealing. As he says, "whoever enjoys the fruits of the earth, without serving the people and without having first given them their share is a thief" (Gandhi 1968: 13–14).

Detachment leading to non-possession is, for Gandhi, an abstraction as well as undesirable. It is undesirable because it is bound to put a break on people's talent for doing whatever they are capable of doing efficiently and skilfully. To insist on detachment is to then rob a person of the reward he expects by using his talent. As such, there should not be any curb on the use of talent for getting requisite reward. The only curb Gandhi insists on is the voluntary acceptance of the idea of using whatever one makes or earns for promoting public good, after one has kept enough to satisfy one's minimum needs of living. This is what he calls the principle of trusteeship, which is based on the principle that one who has given up, enjoys. *(Ten tyakten bhunjitha, Isopanishad)*. The idea of trusteeship is grounded in Gandhi's recognition of the fact that one cannot completely eradicate inequality. As he says:

> For even after existing inequalities of wealth have been removed, the problem of recurring inequalities resulting from the varying capacities and talents of different individuals will remain. Unless outstanding talent is fostered and held in trust, to be used in the interest of society, it will again give rise to privileged class, no matter what name or garbs. As the only answer to the problem of securing inequalities arising from "residuary ownership," the doctrine of trusteeship has a perennial value and use. (Pyarelal 1958: II, 626)

The need for trusteeship does not mean the license for everyone to increase his possessions for satisfying his need. One must, Gandhi insists, practise restraint in both acquisition and the use of wealth for satisfying needs. Gandhi does not believe that multiplication of wants and machinery contrived to supply them is taking the world a single step ahead. It is for this reason that he condemns modern civilization as satanic (Gandhi 1927), because it caters to the appeasement of the demand of the body at the expense of the soul. Thus, Gandhi insists on voluntary minimization of wants in order to escape the depredations that modern civilization has wrought. Minimization of wants is essential not only for the growth of the soul but also for avoiding ecological degradation as well as for installing the economy of justice. Moreover, it will go a long way in making villages self-sufficient.

Gandhi's emphasis on the self-sufficiency of the village is due not only for saving the earth from the depredations of man's greed. It is also for the crucial role it plays in the growth of the soul as a basis for what Plato calls *philia politike* (love among men in a community). Moreover, village self-sufficiency is an essential factor in self-rule at the lowest level of the political community as a whole. Thus, Gandhi sees a linkage between self-control and self-rule and, for him, this link is very vital. Significance of this link can be appreciated by the fact that it regulates the exercise of freedom. The proper exercise of freedom requires the awareness of such exercise by others. As such, unrestrained exercise of freedom tends to disrupt order and the disruption of order invites constriction of the exercise of liberty. Once society has been drained of its significance because of the rise of self-defining subjects, it devolves upon the government to apply constraints. This leads to a situation where the government becomes very powerful and makes encroachments on individual liberty.

It is, therefore, necessary for the individual to develop the capacity of self-government because it is only through this that he can safeguard his autonomy. And self-government is only of value if human beings attempt to govern themselves in order to reach their full human stature; unless human beings are essentially governing beings, there can be no case for self-governing societies. For Gandhi, then, self-government is essential since it helps people to develop the capacity to resist authority when it is abused. "Self-government means continues effort to be independent of government control, whether it is foreign government or whether it is national. Self-government will be a sorry affair if people look up to it for regulation of every detail of life" (Young India 1925).

The Gandhian way, then, underlines the need of returning to the traditional concept of who man is; this means that it is the spiritual aspect of man's existence that must constitute the governing principle of his worldly life. All life activities must be subordinated to and governed by the spiritual aspect of man's existence. Once man's soul is attuned to the divine ground of brings, he becomes swarat in the sense that Chhandogya Upanishad uses it. To become swarat is to establish a benign relationship with the external world, both society and nature. This relationship must, then, be translated into the service of the God's creation which, in turn, necessities, minimization of wants for installing the economy of justice. All this joins together to make the case for a fully decentralized political order. This order rests on village self-sufficiency and dynamic democracy at the lowest level of the political order. It is only through this that micro-variability with micro-viability can be retained; however, micro-variability is vacuous in the absence of micro-viability. This can be ensured only by making local communities autonomous, self-sufficient and self-reliant. This is what the Gandhian way underscores.

Notes

1. Men have ownership over only that much as would fill their belly; he who thinks as his own what is more than that is a thief and deserves punishment. *Bhagwat Purana*, Ch. 6, See also *Taittiriya Brahman* 2.8.1.
2. See *Taittiriya Brahman* 2.81.1 where it is underlined that the preservation of the cosmic order depends on ensuring the continuity of the process of exchange between man, gods and other beings. It is this process that maintains and sustains the cosmic metabolism.

References

Colletti, Lucio. 1972. *From Roussean to Lenin: Studies in Ideology and Society*. New York: Monthly Review Press.

Dahl, Robert A. 1985. *Preface to Economic Democracy*. Cambridge: Polity Press

Gandhi, M. K. 1927. *Young India*. 17 March.

———. 1946. *Harijan*. 21 July.

———. 1954. *Sarvodaya*. Ed. Bharatan Kumarappa. Ahmedabad: Navajivan Publishing House.

———. 1959. *Collected Works of Mahatma Gandhi* (CWMG), 100 vols. Delhi: The Publications Division, Government of India.

———. 1968. *Discourses on the Gita*. Ahmedabad: Navajivan Publishing House.

———. 1969. *The Selected Works of Mahatma Gandhi* (SWMG), 6 vols. Ed. Sriman Narayan. Ahmedabad: Navajivan Publishing House.

Jaeger. 1939. *Paideia*. New York: Oxford University Press.

Oliver, Roy. 1968. *The Wanderer and the Way: The Hebrew Tradition in the Writings of Martin Barber*. Ithaca: Cornell University Press.

Payarelal. 1958. *Mahatma Gandhi: The Last Phase*, 2 vols. Ahmedabad: Navajivan Publishing House.

Taylor, Charles. 1981, July. "Growth, Legitimacy, and Modern Identity," *Praxis International*, 1(2).

———. 1983. *Social Theory as Practice*. Delhi: Oxford University Press.

Tendulkar, D. G. 1951–54. *Mahatma: Life of Mohandas Karamchand Gandhi*, VI vols. Bombay: V. K. Jhaveri and D. G. Tendulkar.

Tocqueville Alexis de. 1996. *Democracy in America*. 2 vols. New York: Harper and Row.

9

Philosophical Background of Gandhi's Thinking

The distinctive aspect of Gandhi's thinking and doing is to throw powerful challenge to the regnant mode of thinking and doing. It is this challenge that tested and finally vanquished the might of the British Empire that lasted almost a century. While it ruled India as an imperial power, it diverged sharply from its traditional pattern of abstaining from interfering in indigenous social order and set Indian society on a course that collided violently with the age-old traditional pattern of social order. The collision that took place fully uprooted the roots of social and cultural patterns of thinking and doing. The termination of the British rule in India and the end of colonial rule elsewhere has by no means meant the overthrow of the mould of thought-ways and work-ways that made imperialism possible. They are still flourishing all over the world and are responsible for what is known as modern *problematique*.

The challenge that Gandhi posed to the regnant mode of thought-ways and work-ways has proved inefficacious, although it successfully drove the British rulers out of the country. Yet it has not fully exhausted itself. It is still powerful and vital, picked up repeatedly by those who find the regnant mode of thinking and doing an ever-present threat to the well-being of mankind and therefore, wish to create a better world by advocating ideas that could mould the mind of the people to rebel against and replace the dominant modes of thinking and doing. Gandhi had been a pioneer in this respect. Someone, who not only advocated refreshingly new ideas, at least in the age in which he was born and did his life's work, but also guided, actively and intelligently, the people of India to gain freedom from the grip of the British imperialism, as the first step towards refashioning society in accordance with their own long cultural tradition.

The voice of rebellion that Gandhi raised against the mighty British Empire and all that it implied raises two questions. One of these questions is: What there is in Gandhi's thinking that attracts these people, persuades them of its curative power in healing the world suffering from the disease of what Thucydides calls *kinesis* and enthuse them to fight for its realization even when it means a great deal of suffering? Alternatively, it can also be asked: What is distinctive about Gandhi's perspective on man and his world and in what deeper ground of ideas is this perspective anchored? Satisfactory answers to these two questions are *sine qua non* for clearly apprehending the nature of the philosophical background of Gandhi's thinking. However, this chapter deals primarily with the second question because the answer to the first question is contained in it.

Before the answer to the second question can be detailed out, two ancillary points need to be quickly disposed of. The first point relates to the need of excavating Gandhi's perspective for exposing its foundational vision it animated and invigorated whatever Gandhi thought and did. It could be argued that there already exists a large body of writings discussing, analyzing and critiquing Gandhi's thinking and doing. Therefore, it is not necessary at all to undertake any fresh exploration either for exposing the foundational vision of his thinking or for examining it in any detail. It is true that an enormous amount of comments and critiques already exists that throw ample light on what Gandhi thought and did. And the accounts presented in these comments and critiques are by no means amateurish or wayward. They highlight some of the very important aspects of Gandhi's life work.

However, these comments and critiques either present a historical account of Gandhi's life and work, whether fully or partially or examine discursively thinking and doing of Gandhi or take up particular aspects of Gandhi's thinking and doing and examine them in some detail. Rarely has the foundational structure of Gandhi's thinking been subjected to close scrutiny. However, the fact remains that without such a scrutiny, the superstructure of Gandhi's ideas and actions do not make themselves quite transparent. This foundational structure is basically a philosophical vision, which projects a particular perspective on man and his world and articulates "who man is." It needs to be emphasized that, as Voegelin puts it: "Unless we have an idea of man, we have no frame of reference for the designation of human phenomenon as relevant or irrelevant. Man is engaged in the creation of social order physically, biologically, psychologically, intellectually and spiritually" (Voegelin 1998: 161).

The idea of man cannot be empirically derived because of the untold variation in the characteristics of man, on the one hand and, as Heschel underlines, the idea of man is not scientific but creative, on the other (1965). The point that needs to be made is that no sophisticated scientific analysis can ever catch the idea of who man is because of the wide variations one notices in the characteristics—physical, cultural, intellectual and spiritual—of man in time and space. Moreover, the idea of who man is has varied sharply because of socio-cultural differences in units of civilization. Whatever the idea of man may be it constitutes the principal defining category of what man, in reality, becomes in different cultural settings.

This means that the idea of man is formative of the substance of man. Given the importance of the idea of man, what should also be emphasized is that the entire institutional apparatus and the pattern of interpersonal and group relations either reflect the underlying idea of man or are, in an essential sense, supportive of it. It is in view of this that a philosophical perspective becomes necessary to project on the idea of "who man is." It is this philosophical perspective that establishes the relationship between physical, biological, intellectual and other activities and their interrelationship influences the establishment of the social order. It is this philosophical perspective that seems to be lacking in most of the historical, discursive and critical writings on and about Gandhi. Without exploring the foundational vision, discussion of Gandhi's thinking either in historical or discursive mode offers only a disjointed image of Gandhi. The result is that the essential nature of what Gandhi stood for and fought for escapes our view.

The second point concerns the fact that it was Gandhi who stood alone among other leaders of note and not only courageously challenged the powerful currents and variations of the regnant mode of thinking but also offered an alternative and perhaps a better and salubrious alternative to it. At the root of this alternative was a very powerful attempt to recover and restore the vision of man that had animated for long the cultural tradition of India.[1] It was this vision of man that, for Gandhi, was the most appropriate instrument of shaping the pattern of his everyday existence and created his world; it also constituted the ground for evolving the institutional arrangement that would serve as an appropriate instrument of guiding and controlling inter-personal and inter-group relations.

The question that arises in this connection is: what were the factors that made a deep impact on Gandhi and his intellectual and spiritual make-up. It is needless to say that we will fail in our effort to apprehend these influences fully if we focused and explored only Gandhi's thought-ways and work-ways. The exploration of his thinking and doing can tell us only the direction Gandhi is moving, not the reason why he chose that direction. We have, therefore, to go beyond his thinking and doing in order to apprehend different sources of the influences that gave a definite shape to Gandhi's thinking and doing.

This "beyond" is defined by the interplay of three different forces that act on any thinker. We can think of other forces; however, all of them are included in these three major forces. These forces are: a body of ideas that has evolved over the ages and is available for any person to pick for his own purpose, the times in which a thinker lives, and his own intellectual make-up, his beliefs and commitments. Insofar as the body of ideas is concerned, it is composed of different streams of thinking that have taken shape and influenced mankind throughout human history. However, not all of the extant ideas are relevant or useful for a particular thinker; he has his own scale of values and index of priorities that influence his decision for choosing a particular stream of thinking. His choice of what is relevant for his purpose is determined by what is called *homo politicus* pre-selectivity. This refers to the fact that embedded within the interior of every person is a scale of valuation that yields an appropriate criterion of what to choose and what to borrow from the extant body of ideas for his own purpose. And guided by *homo politicus* pre-selectivity, he chooses to embrace that stream of thinking that considers the attuning of the man's soul to the divine ground of being as the necessary condition for ordering his interior as a means of ensuring order in society.

The second source of influence that impinges on what Gandhi thought and did was the times he lived in. This is necessarily so because one cannot easily escape the main tendencies of the age in which one lives and acts insofar as these tendencies go very deep into the making of what one is. Two important features of this time need to be noted. Gandhi lived and worked in a period of history marked, on the one hand, by the revitalization of Indian National Congress as the spearhead of the freedom movement under Gandhi's able leadership. On the other hand, this period saw the termination of the British rule and the birth of an independent, resurgent India making a fresh tryst with destiny for a better dignified and economically prosperous individual and collective existence. It was also a period that saw a concerted attack on the dignity and self-respect of

Indians. Gandhi personally had to be exposed to indignities and humiliations at the hands of the white rulers. He saw the naked play of racial superiority pressing down the people over whom they ruled calling them niggers. But what, for Gandhi, was most disturbing was the conscious effort by the English rulers to sweep Indians away from their traditional cultural moorings and cast them in Western moulds of thinking and doing, so that they may all become Indian Sahibs.

However, more important, Gandhi saw English rule as simply a medium through which something sinister, something quite terribly and inimical to the well-being of man was working out its design for the unopposed march of Mammon. This design had its origin in man's rebellion against God and the assertion by him of his freedom from all divine connections. It was this design that made the value of bodily comfort the central focus of human existence and enterprise and impelled men to engage in the strategy of "beggaring your neighbour." Springing out of the womb of liberalism, the design of the secular man resulted in the unsettling of the peace of mankind, the upsetting of order everywhere and in the marked tendency of individuals who choose to ignore the claim of the soul and engage in seeking evermore bodily comfort at the cost of spiritual pursuit. And the cultivation of bodily comforts has lifted all controls, whether personal or social, over desires. The inevitable result of this has obviously been the phenomenon of the endlessness of needs, on the one hand, and the transmutation of needs into wants, on the other. Needs have become endless in two vital senses: one, needs have de-linked themselves from any higher purpose and have become self-legitimating and two, they proliferate endlessly. This has become possible because of the denial of the divine ground of reality. Consequently, *prajnana* or *sophia* has been displaced by instrumental rationality; this has been, in turn, a boon companion of objectification, that is, treating everything as objects. The alliance has proved fateful in the sense that it has paved the way for the exploitation of society and nature as potential means of the realization of individual purposes. And the efforts to satisfy the proliferating needs of individuals have encouraged the promotion of technologically induced and sustained economic growth. This has culminated in the rise of what Gandhi calls "satanic civilization."

The flourishing of satanic civilization is consequent upon the progressive realization of the liberal vision of man and his world. The distinctive contribution of this vision is the systematic demolition of the system that not only permitted but also legitimized the rule over men by one person or a few persons. Undoubtedly, this has been the most enduring contribution of the liberal vision since it put paid to the rule of one person over another, no matter if that person happens to be the most learned, wise and able. This has proved instrumental in making each of the members of a polity, not any rulers or conquerors, the centre of order. And it is this that made possible for democracy to take root, grow and become a universal aspiration. Democracy signifies a political arrangement that works to assure every one of freedom, equality and self-determination. It also becomes a powerful instrument for levelling social and economic inequalities and gaping differences that have marked all societies.

Most important of all, when it tied itself up with the urgency of fast economic growth, it also promised to all a life of plenty, liberation of everyone from the miseries of destitution, poverty and exploitation. Along with all this, inherent in the promise of the liberal democracy has been the vaunted claim of rescuing man from his bondage to such external forces as society, tradition, customs, conventions, etc. The autonomous man, free from the constraints of ignorance, superstition, economic want and political illiteracy, is supposed to manage his affairs as well of the whole society in partnership with other autonomous selves sagaciously and efficiently. Thus, the autonomous self is not removed from the dense network of social relations; he is an integral part of this network but, paradoxically, he is supposed to retain and, if possible, extend his freedom. And his freedom finds its most salient expression in his autonomy of defining his purposes and mounting efforts to realize them. Thus, at the hard core of liberal democracy stands the self-sovereign self (not in the sense of the *Chhandogya Upanishad*) as the arbiter of his own destiny and the builder of the social order. The liberal vision of democracy installs self-defining subject who relies on his own powers, both natural and acquired, to refashion the conditions of his own living.

Given all these numerous achievements, what the liberal vision of man and his world has made possible is the private valuation that constitutes the animating force of man's thinking and action. Private valuation is concerned primarily with the search of material well-being, which finds its fullest expression in the fulfilment of ordinary life-needs after the higher purpose of life was jettisoned when man wilfully snapped his relationship with the divine ground of reality. The resultant eclipse of the pursuit of a higher life purpose has resulted in the merger of id with ego, as Freud notes, neutralizing, in the process, the super-ego. It is this merger of the id and the ego that constitutes, in a very profound sense, the foundational structure of the liberal vision of man and his world. This merger refers to the fact that the centre of order now rests on man as *homo economicus*, "the economic man," which formerly used to be located in the psyche as the site and sensorium of divine. Thus, order has now found a new home in the soul, not only now besieged by appetites but as its captive. The primary goal of the economic man is the satisfaction of appetites and the satisfaction of appetites does not require the assistance of what Plato calls *sophia* or what is known in the classical Indian thinking as *prajnana*, wisdom; what is appropriate for the satisfaction of desires is prudence that installs calculative reasoning as the dominant mode of rationality. To seek to appease appetites in a situation of scarcity is to adopt a strategy of pushing others out of one's way for going ahead. Such a strategy erodes morality and disrupts interdependence, cooperation and harmony (Hirsch 1977).

What is also interesting to note here is that the primacy of the fulfilment of ordinary life-needs enters into the re-conceptualization of order at both the cosmic and the human level. The source of order in nature was previously seen to inhere in divine substratum of reality. However, this conception of order has been rejected in favour of one that sees order emerging when different elements of nature mesh well without friction or clash. When translated into human terms, it meant that since everybody is always in quest of happiness, order in society must be seen to lie in the pursuit of happiness by one individual compatibly with all others. Thus, the concept of order, which formerly took its inspiration from its divine connection, is now expressed in only mechanical terms. As Taylor puts it:

> [I]nstead of seeing nature as expressing a meaningful order one, which has to be accounted for in terms of ideas, we see it as a set of interlocking elements whose relations can be explained in terms of efficient causation. The order (as against disorder) in things does not consist in their embodying ideas, but rather in their meshing without conflict and distortion. (1970: 75)

Happiness in modern times depends on the amount of information about the external world one has. However, access to information is governed by two very potent resources, wealth and power. Given the fact that these two resources happen to be unequally distributed, access to information too is not equally open to all. Add to it is the fact that one needs the wisdom or insight to see where the compatibility between the pursuit of happiness by one individual and a similar pursuit by others lies. It is very difficult to judge what needs or does not need to be done. When no one is in possession of information about where the limits of compatibility lie, it is not possible for the individual to do otherwise than whatever promises to ensure happiness for him. It is this fact that makes it clear that the only foundations of liberal order must be the aggregation of private valuations of the individuals who compose it (Walsh 1997: 16).

Such an order is, however, very fragile because when passions arise, reason flies through the window of the mind. What takes over is, to use an Aristotelian term, *pleonexia*, the tendency to claim even for those things, which one's merit does not qualify. Everybody is engaged in protecting what he has and getting more than what he needs; as a result, compatibility between the good of one individual and the good of all individuals becomes problematic; it becomes hard to achieve. It does not need to be pointed out that the pursuit of self-interest is, in this perspective, both natural and rational. And when moved by passion to achieve what he wants,

> the individual fails to confront in his own action the distinction between what is available as a result of getting ahead of others and what is available from a general advance shared by all. The individual who wants to see better has to stand on tip-toe. In the game of beggar your neighbour, that is what each individual must try to do, even though not all can." (Hirsch 1977: 19)

This situation paves the way for a general scramble for grabbing whatever one can get, which paves the way for what Macintyre calls civil war by other means (1984: 253).

The outbreak of "civil war by other means" is symptomatic of the collapse of shared worldview and the mushrooming of private worlds in which everyone clings to his own private world without caring for what happens to other private worlds. The breakdown of what Heraclitus calls *Xynon*, a shareable commonality, underlines strongly the fact that being liberal means precisely that we do not have to share a world-view. And interestingly enough, as Pierre Manent underlines, liberal democracy is rooted in differences, even separation. The natural result of the break-down of *xynon* is the rise of pluralism and multiculturalism. It refers to a situation in which there is less and less of understanding of things with one another. It also invites our attention to the fact that the breakdown of common understanding eclipses the spiritual understanding that it is through the love of God that love of fellow-beings is possible.

The reason for this is not far to seek. It should be pointed out that in the understanding of the classical political science about reason there is the assumption that it is grounded in a common *nous* or divinity of spirit for all men. Every man is ordered, through participation in that *nous* and in orientation towards that *nous*. That order in the relation between them constitutes the order of society as it does with regard to order in man's interior. As such, the common *nous* as the basis of common reason is the substance that makes society as ordered as possible. The substance that makes society ordered is what Aristotle calls *homonoia*. It is this divinity of spirit that is present in every one of us, which is constitutive of man and forms the foundation as well of dignity of man and the obligation to have respect for other men. However, when the basis of common reason is surrendered, there is, Nietzsche insists, no particular reason to love anybody. And when men cease to love each other, the breakdown of what Plato calls *philia politike* (erosion of love among members in a political community) takes place.

The substantive aspect of the consequences of the breakdown of *philia politike* is best expressed in an Egyptian poem, entitled "Dispute of a man, who wants to commit suicide, with his soul," going back to fifteenth century bc This man describes the disordered social world in which he lives. We quote the first three stanzas of what he says:

> To whom can I speak today?
> One's fellows are evil,
> The friends of today do not love.
> To whom can I speak today?
> Faces have disappeared
> Everyman has a face downcast towards his fellows.
> To whom can I speak today?
> There is no contented of hearts
> The man with whom one went no longer exists. (Vogelin 2004)

This is the description of society where *xynon* has completely eroded and society has fallen in disarray. Disorder of society hurts everybody.

Therefore, the dissolution of society follows when destruction, disappearance of contentment, the phenomenon of alienation and more make their presence acutely felt. However, public disquietude that often results from disorder of society is kept at the minimum because of the hope of making good in economic terms. We should not lose sight of the fact that central to liberal political philosophy has always been the philosophy of economic growth. Relative quietude in societies yoked to liberal political philosophy is purchased in considerable measure through a growing economy. However, growth always includes decline and instability (Walsh 1995: 21). The cycle of growth and decline is what, according to Robert L. Heilbroner, causes the cycle of boom and crash in the capitalist economic system. Decline and instability translates themselves into real human dislocation and suffering. Yet the fact remains that the government can neither muster self-discipline nor can it educate its citizens into the virtue of confronting and coping with economic uncertainty (Walsh 1995: 24). In the meantime, aspirations soar up without the real possibility of being satisfied. Frustration in getting what one needs and wants creates widespread resentment, finding its expression in blaming the government for their own incapacity.

The cumulative effect of the syndrome of factors rooted in liberal political order is destined to alternate between license and discipline, coherence and incoherence and finds no satisfactory way out of this alternation. The result is the grievous loss of normalcy. The one resource available to and usually adopted by the powers that be is to go on changing the external environment of man in the hope that the psychic disorders of man will somehow be overcome to allow society to recover from its own disorder and move ahead even if at the speed of a tortoise. The manifestation of this process of the frequent changes in the external environment takes the shape of institutional, social and political reforms. It is usually forgotten that it is the neglect of the spiritual or moral dimension that is the source of instability. As such, the remedy does not lie in institutional, social or political reforms. We can understand why Gandhi says that what we must be concerned with "is a radical change more in inward spirit than in the outer form. If the first is changed, the second will take care of itself. If the first remains unchanged, the second, no matter how radically changed, will be a like a whited sepulcher" (Gandhi 1959: LV, 62).[1]

If normalcy in individual and social life and relations has to be won, the spiritual aspect of mans' existence must be given primacy as it enjoyed formerly. Gandhi's spiritual orientation and his personal experience with the liberal political order impelled him to take on the task of reconstructing a new order. However, reconstruction worth the name must take its departure from the existing reality, which a thinker confronts. Three different aspects of project of reconstruction can be identified here. First, as Aristotle pointed out long ago, it is the sense of the practical or the real that must constitute the starting point from which all theoretical reflection must begin. The goal of this reflection is to move from the practical world to go to a point where an understanding of its place in relation to the wider context of human life becomes quite illuminated. This is necessary for understanding the actual forces that have gone into the making of the extant reality. Second, if the reflection of the lived world or the practical world is perceived by the thinker that something is terribly wrong with it, then it is natural that he should become disenchanted with it.

Disenchantment with the practical world is symbolic of the undoing of the evocative ideas that lie at the root of the prevailing order that has so far guided and regulated thought-ways and work-ways of man. Expression of this disenchantment by a thinker constitutes an act of creating chaos if not in reality, then, in the world of ideas. And lastly, a new world is created out of the fragments that this chaos has wrought. Out of this chaos, then, the thinker must create a new world, a world that is expected to provide succour to the people afflicted with the troubles that the existing order has brought forth and has failed to lighten or remove. The world that Gandhi creates is the result of his meditation on the substance of cosmic order; this meditation yields a design of order, which, when embraced, becomes the ground of order in the interior of man. The order in man's interior is then transformed into social order.

The emotional core from which the intellectual journey of creating a new world or a new order must begin is the manifold of desires that constitute a necessary attribute of man. In the process of creating a new order, there rises from a shapeless chaos of conflicting desires a little world of order, a cosmic analogy, a cosmion. The function of this cosmion is the creation of a shelter in which man may give to his life a semblance of meaning. In addition to creating a meaningful world out of the chaos and disorder caused by manifold, conflicting desires, it also makes the

fragmentary life united and whole by making it a part of a more comprehensive social unit as well as the world beyond this world, with a view to
overcoming the limitations, individuals in isolation suffer from.

The individual forced to live an isolated existence seeks achievements
for himself and in doing so, his life becomes devoid of meaning, except
the accumulation and possession of material objects. This makes his life
full of discontentment. It is to escape from this existential disorder that
it becomes imperative to link individual achievement by making it a part
of a group purpose. It does not need to be emphasized that even if the
constructed or "imagined" order is the analogue of the cosmic order, it
suffers from limitations. The "little world of order," the cosmion, is not
the complete copy and replica of the divine cosmos; it is only a faint and
humanly created imaginative analogue of the cosmic order. That is to say,
it is only imagined, not empirically real. It can be empirically real only
when man realizes that order emanates from a divine source, from God
to individual and to the larger socio-political order. Thus, there is a flow
that connects man to God and the mortal to the immortal. The successful
working of the cosmion depends on the constancy of this flow. When this
flow is disrupted, disorder follows. Thus to make the imaginatively given
order empirically real, man has to attune his soul to the divine ground of
reality and make conscious efforts to make this world complete by making
his own life whole and complete.

Thus, for Gandhi, the foundation of a new order is God, which appears
to him in two important modes, truth and non-violence. "One may
banish the word 'God' but one has no power to banish the Thing itself"
(Gandhi 1959: II, 62). This "Thing" represents, for Gandhi, the *raison de
etre* of the universe and constitutes the norm of being, which regulates
the course of events and thought. Anchoring oneself in God enables man
to attain the virtue of *samatva* (sameness), the basis of like-mindedness
as well as of *philia politike*. When the soul of man is attuned to the divine
ground of reality, self-discipline or self-rule becomes, possible. It is also
the pathway to self-realization. "For realizing the self, the first essential
thing is to cultivate a strong moral sense" (Gandhi 1969: VI, 102–3). Apart
from the performance of certain *vratas* and following certain regulatory
principles (*niyamas*), service of the people and the country also constitutes an integral part of morality. Surrender to God helps cultivate the
adhyatmam-adhidaivam perspective and enables one to appreciate the

value of community, that is, a structure for human beings to dwell more intimately with each other.

This is possible only when the most intimate community, that is, the primary unit of any political system, the village in the case of Gandhi, becomes self-reliant and self-governing. It is also necessary to recognize the need of minimizing wants not only for keeping within the limits of available resources but also for controlling unruly desires.

It needs to be kept in mind that "earth provides enough to satisfy everyone's needs but not every man's greed." However, to control desires and minimize needs depends on the cultivation of the capacity to resist and block desires. This is possible only when man becomes self-governing by hitching the wagon of one's life to the ultimate reality. And the practice of self-rule in the political sense must begin at the level of the community, a community that is largely dependent on its own resources and enjoys true democracy when everyone participates in the act of ruling. It is at the community level that man learns to rule and be ruled. Unless humans are essentially self-governing beings, there can be no case for self-governing societies. It is this vision of Gandhi that manifests itself in the conception of an oceanic circle, which is grounded in Gandhi's conception of swaraj. Gandhi conceives swaraj as a parallelogram one end of which stands for political independence, the other, economic swaraj with morality as the third end and social harmony the fourth (Gandhi 1959: LXIV, 191–182).

Gandhi's square of swaraj projects a holistic view of society, a society characterized by economic equality, the insurance of the satisfaction of the basic minimum requirements, interaction among persons based on *ahimsa* and the sovereignty of the people based on pure moral authority. A society organized on these principles is in Gandhi's view an example of *Ramarajya*. It is Gandhi's contention that without the support of pure moral authority, a political authority, even while it is constitutional and representative democracy, has to rely on violence in order to support its authority. Gandhi does not reject democracy; what he rejects is the idea of democracy that draws its legitimacy not from what Maritain calls democracy of persons, but of individuals. Gandhi would prefer the democracy of persons in which decisions are made not based on the whims of the rulers or on power contests among socio-economic interests, not even on the basis of a constitution that, at best, represents powerful interests at a particular moment. It is a system in which decisions are based on truth and justice. In such a democratic political order, the ruler is not a master but a guardian and servant.

True democracy, in Gandhi's view, subsists on genuine public opinion, which becomes difficult if there is a great distance between where public opinion is created and where the seat of authority is located. The larger the democratic political order, the more numerous would be the intermediaries that link public opinion at the grass-roots level with the distant seat of government. This creates distortions and misinterpretations based on misapprehension. Gandhi therefore emphasizes that dynamic democracy can grow only out of meaningful relationships and spontaneous organization that spring among people, when they come together at the local level to solve their basic problems by cooperation among themselves.

"In such a community, achievement of self-sufficiency and security by neighbourly cooperation engenders a strong sense of local strength and the individual's sense of responsibility and solidarity to the community and concerns for its welfare are at their highest" (Pyarelal 1958: II, 581). Thus, what Gandhi suggests is a democracy whose roots lie in hundreds of village republics. This will ensure micro-variability as well as micro-vitality.

> The village republic will represent a structure composed of a network and in this structure composed of innumerable villages, there will be ever-widening, never ascending circles. Life will not be a pyramid with the apex sustained by the bottom. But it will be an oceanic circle whose centre will be the individual always ready to perish for the village, the latter ready to perish for the circle of villages, till at last the whole becomes one life composed of individuals, never aggressive in their arrogance but ever humble, sharing the majesty of the oceanic circle of which they are integral units. Therefore the *outermost* circumference will not wield the power to crush the inner circle but will give strength to all within and derive its own strength from it…no one…(will) be the first and none the last. (Pyarelal 1958: II, 580–81)

Note

1. Several commentators have pointed out that Gandhi borrowed some of his seminal ideas from, for example, Thoreau and Tolstoy. What must be made clear is that Gandhi would not have "borrowed" these ideas if they did not mesh in with his own ideas. Recently, a

commentator, Akeel Bilgrami, to be specific, has gone to the extent to say that Gandhi's attack on scientific rationality, that is elevated as a defining principle of modernity, has had a very long and recognizable tradition going back to the seventeenth century in the heart of the West, which anticipated in detail and with thoroughly honourable, intent, those lamentable developments around the notion of scientific rationality. (Bilgrami 2006: 24). He further argues that the polemical and instructional pamphlets of figures such as Winstanby, John Lilburne, Richard Overtone and others raised the voice of enlightenment and reason, saw divinity in everything we behold and called for some environmentalism. Gandhi borrowed his concern for environment from this tradition of thinking. Bilgrami, needless to say, is quite ignorant of the classical and pre-classical thinking of India. If he were not ignorant, he should have referred at least to Prithwi Sukta of *Atharvaveda* and the first *shloka* of *Isopanishad.* Cf. Thoreau: "Undoubtedly if we were to reform this outward life truly and thoroughly, we should find no duty of the inner omitted.... But a moral reform must take first and the necessity of the other will be superseded..." (Thoreau 1975).

References

Bilgrami, Akeel. 2006. "Gandhi, Newton and the Enlightenment," *Social Scientists,* 34(5–6) (May–June).

Gandhi, M. K. 1959. *Collected Works of Mahatma Gandhi,* 100 vols. Delhi: The Publication Division, Ministry of Information and Broadcasting Government of India.

———. 1969. *Selected Works of Mahatma Gandhi,* 6 vols. Ed. Shriman Narayan. Ahmedabad: Navajivan Press.

Heschel, Abraham. 1965. *Who Man Is?* Stanford: Stanford University Press.

Hirsch, Fred. 1977. *Social Limits to Growth.* London: Routledge and Kegan Paul.

MacIntyre, Alasdair. 1984. *After Virtue.* Notre Dame: University of Notre Dame Press.

Pyarelal. 1958. *Mahatma Gandhi: The last Phase,* 2 vols. Ahmedabad: Navjivan Publishing House.

Taylor, Charles. 1970. *Hegel and Modern Society.* Cambridge: Cambridge University Press.

Thoreau, H. D. 1975. *The Selected Works of Thoreau,* revised and with a new Introduction by Walter Harding. Boston: Houghton and Mifflin Co.

Voegelin, E. 1998. *Collected Works of Eric Voegelin. Vol. 27. The Nature of the Law and Related Legal Writings.* Columbia: University Missouri Press.

Walsh, David. 1997. *The Growth of the Liberal Soul.* Columbia: University of Missouri Press.

10

Gandhi's Critique of Democracy

If democracies are still able to escape grave dangers, it is by turning themselves decisively in the direction of an essentially different type—democracy of the persons discovered in its real significance. And this presupposes, truly speaking, something quite different from a simple weakening or a simple extenuation of the errors of democracy of the individual; it means an internal transformation, a complete turn about toward spirit.

—Jacques Maritain, *Scholasticism and Politics*

I

It is ironical that democracy, as a political institutional arrangement, which Plato condemned as a degenerate form, is now considered to be the ideal one. The emergence of modern democracy as a coveted form of political institutional arrangement became possible only when Christianity-inspired civilization breathed its last in the seventeenth century. Benjamin Franklin announced, in the eighteenth century, the rise of a new Sun, the Sun of democracy. This Sun has now climbed very high in the sky; it radiates its rays all around the world to gladden the hearts of millions of people. Alexis de Tocqueville too referred, in 1835, to the advent of democracy as the universal and irresistible force. And Federico Mayor, the Director-General of the UNESCO, noted in 1996 that for the entire world, democracy has become the focus of the people's hopes for a brighter future and aspirations for a life of freedom and dignity. Democracy has become so popular and mighty that even despots and dictators claim their regimes to be democratic.

Despite these encomiums and adulation, democracy also invites sharp and not infrequently, virulent criticisms in two important respects. First, democracy, as it is practised, raises the question about its real meaning.

Tocqueville, for example, points to the confusion in the use of such terms as democracy and democratic government; this tends to work to the advantage of demagogues and despots. Similarly, Bertrand Jouvenal complained in 1945 that discussions about democracy, arguments for and against it are intellectually worthless, because they do not convey the real significance of democracy. Add to it the voice of George Orwell who noted that, not only no agreed definition of democracy exists but also that such a definition is resisted from all sides. This is so for the fear that the claim to democracy by non-democratic regimes might be challenged successfully.

Second, the way democracy works in practice does not do any good to those who happen to be located at lower echelons of society. It favours those who enjoy the privileges of wealth, power and prestige. Moreover, it gives prominence to power game that drives morality out from the arena of politics. This is a clear indication of the yawning gap between what democracy promises and what it delivers in its divergent manifestations in different political systems. It is this gap that attracts the criticisms of the students of democracy. What is also very clear is that while critics celebrate the idea of democracy, they denounce or, at least, look unfavourably at its performance.

Their love for and dedication to the idea of democracy makes them blind to the conditions that have given birth to democracy in modern times and influence its functioning. Modern democracy was born along with the rise of the self-defining subject. The self-defining subject decides for himself his life purposes, the purposes that he derives from his own nature, independent of any external authority, whether it is tradition, social conventions or any authority beyond him. Having defined his life purposes, he also chooses the means of realizing them.

There exist two versions of liberal tradition about the way the individual should go about realizing his self-defined purposes as well as the relationship between the individual and democratic political system. The Lockean-Benthamite tradition, the classical version of democracy, emphasizes the power of the individual to satisfy his ordinary life-needs, while its radical, Rousseuvian version, emphasizes equality and participation. Both these versions have now merged to produce the type of democracy that we encounter today. In both these versions, spirituality and morality, find themselves pushed to the outer limits of human consciousness. It is because of this that certain distortions have crept in the working of democracy.

A major factor that causes distortion relates to the necessity of the government to intervene with a view to promoting and protecting individual liberty, especially the liberty of opportunity. Scarcity of resources happens to be a harsh fact that man has to confront in his effort to realize his material needs. Coupled with it is the fact that everyone needs to have access to different resources. This induces acute competition among individuals located in different facets of the factual order. The growing competition for access to these resources often creates situations of conflict. The need to maintain normal political life and relations makes it necessary for politics to intervene. However, politics today is nothing more than a process of reciprocal resistance.

It is this characteristic of politics that engenders and constitutes the fundamental features of politics in modern times. It is, therefore, not surprising that the search for freedom and equality, especially by depressed and deprived socio-economic groups, does not prove efficacious. This search by different socio-economic groups, however, encounters resistance and opposition from those who are blessed by fortune. And since the state is committed to liberal values of freedom and equality, it has, therefore, to assure that these groups are not prevented from enjoying the fruits of freedom and equality. This has allowed the state to enter different areas of the people's life. Allowing the government to assume a large degree of control on the course of the people's life.

This, in turn, has produced another distortion. This distortion is responsible for the transformation of citizens into passive subjects. As passive subjects, they invest their trust in the benevolent power of the state and welcome its intervention because without it, realization of their life purposes will prove difficult. In the name of securing freedom and equality for those who are the victims of social inequities, the state assumes the power as the regulator of social life. Thus, the state today represents, as Tocqueville notes, a titular power, a type of "state despotism," which is popularly elected.

It is true that it is, unlike older versions of despotism, not absolute; however, it is always engaged in refining the tools of control. The long struggle for ridding the world from the menace of despotism has ushered in a new variety of despotism; it signifies that the ideal of freedom from despotism has been replaced, bit-by-bit, by the goal of state secured freedom and equality. Thus, the vaunted claim of independence by self-defining subjects has slowly but certainly been modified into a kind of slavery which is gilded.

Yet another major distortion can be identified as the proneness of democracy to become a victim of its own success, to the extent that, for long time, non-democratic movements and regimes have been declaring themselves a democracy. This has prevented it from developing its own substantive conceptual justification except in such malleable terms as freedom, equality and justice. However, the subservience of these values to material well-being has robbed them of their true significance. Consequently, they have come, as Martin Buber notes, to face each other as antagonists. This is so for the reason that the inherent opposition between the value of freedom and that of equality has led them on the course of self-aggrandizement pitting them against each other.

It is this opposition and the resulting self-aggrandizement that has led to the loss of what Heraclitus calls *xynon,* a shareable commonality, a commonality that fills men with a sharpened sense of a common destiny and common endeavour. The primacy of material well-being has also meant the eclipse of moral sensibility. This is well reflected in the Rousseuvian understanding that the fulfilment of biological needs constitutes the highest moral aspiration when the needs have already been reduced to mere appetites. It is no wonder that Rousseau calls to our attention the fact men are born as rogues by birth and become villain by duty. That is why human individuals do not hesitate to become rich at the cost of their neighbours, a fact, that Gandhi also mentioned.

All these factors have combined to make democratic regimes crisis prone. Alternating between license and discipline, coherence and incoherence, democratic politics seems to be lacking an existential core. This means that democratic politics is unable to become decisive. The incapacity to take effective action in the public policy domain allows profound moral conflicts rend democratic societies. A paralysis of action everywhere arises from the "interminable" and "incommensurable" disputes that cleave democratic societies into a multiplicity of hostile camps. Commonsense is decreasing and being eroded because we share less of common understanding of things with one another. With the decline in what is common, there is a lack of commonality between human beings. Pluralism, multiculturalism and difference are the watchwords. Democratic politics does come to resemble Alasdaire MacIntyre's notorious description of it as "civil war carried on by other means."

As the "civil war carried on by other means" pervades the polity, the need to protect and promote the sphere of individual liberty grows more pressing. This in itself is enough of a ground for the government to intervene to prevent violations of individual freedom. The protection of the sphere of individual liberty that is inviolate either from private or public invasion is based on the assumption that this is the best way for human beings to flourish. However, if the concept of human flourishing has became empty, as it has in modern times, of what value is liberty that is supposed to protect it? If we take happiness or satisfaction as the over-riding political goal, then the line between public and private must be redrawn quite differently. Constitutional limitations become much less significant if we are aiming at a society of "contended slaves."

The distortions that have infected democratic functioning today are, no doubt, well known and well discussed. However, it is expected that they can be taken care of by innovative theorizing matched by institutional reforms. However, neither of these has proved sufficient to stop the endemic unravelling tendencies of democracy. This inability is not purely institutional or conceptual. As such, the remedy cannot be institutional, social or political reforms or the development of arguments of impenetrable brilliance. This is so for the reason that it is the neglect of the spiritual or moral dimension that is the source of the troubles of democracy.

II

The troubles of democracy can be attributed mainly to the rise, after the collapse of the medieval civilization infused with Christian ethos, of the self-defining subject. The rise of the self-defining subject laid the foundation of modern democracy and the industrial civilization. Man in modern times asserts his independence from any transcendental authority, insists on self-determination and relies on his innate powers to make and remake the condition of his own living. However, man's living today requires the fulfilment of his ordinary life-needs involved with the acquisition of wealth, power and prestige.

It is precisely this factor that that has led both to the rise of the industrialization and the rise of democracy as the appropriate mode of organizing political life and relations. The linking of man's life purposes to his desires has been instrumental in making subjectivity the pivot of man's existence. The public face of this subjectivity is, on the one hand, the proliferation of needs leading to the rise of the industrial civilization, and on the other, democracy as the symbol of the primacy of individual freedom. Thus, man's subjectivity gave rise to formal democracy as a necessary means of making collective choices. His proliferating needs made it imperative to initiate, sustain and accelerate technologically induced and sustained economic growth.

It is the conjunction of these three forces—man's subjectivity, the growth of industrial civilization and the pre-eminence of formal democracy in ordering man's political life and relations—that have been instrumental in infecting democracy with the distortions described earlier. Mahatma Gandhi does not reject democracy; what he rejects is democracy that gets afflicted by adverse consequences flowing from the conjunction between the modern ideas of man and emanating from it, industrial civilization and formal democracy. Gandhi firmly believes that these adverse consequences are caused by and reflected in what he calls industrial civilization. We can better apprehend and appreciate Gandhi's critique of democracy when it is etched out against the background of his understanding and condemnation of the industrial civilization. The thought-ways and work-ways that we associate today with man have been shaped by the modern idea of man as it has worked out in industrial society. This has, in turn, introduced distortions in the working of democracy.

Thus, to comprehend and appreciate why Gandhi rejects modern, formal democracy—a political institutional arrangement of great value and prestige today by all means—we have to go back to his idea of who man is, what kind of world he lives in and would like it to become. It is here, in this context that the thesis propounding *purushartha* as the key to a deeper understanding of Gandhi's philosophy falls apart. It needs to be pointed out that prior to *purushartha* is the *Purusha*, the Absolute, who is conjoined to actions taken within the framework of *purushartha*. Insofar as *purusha*, the human individual, is concerned, he is characterized as one who is entitled or authorized to act by virtue of accepting the *Purusha* as the overlord.

And what he is entitled or authorized to do is explicated by the substantive meaning of the term *Purusha*. Literally, *Purusha* means the one who resides in the city, the *Brahmapur*, signifying all beings in the world. As we learn from the *Chhandogya Upanishad, a* person who surrenders to and accepts the suzerainty of the indwelling *Purusha,* becomes *swarat,* self-sovereign; he becomes a person who has pleasure in *Atman*, delight in *Atman*, union in *Atman,* joy in *Atman*. He becomes self-sovereign; he becomes free to act as he wishes in the entire world. It is in this sense that the *Brihadaranyak Upnishad* talks of a person as the spark of the divine. *Yathagni kshudra visphullinga vyucharanti.* Such a *purusha*, when he acts, acts well and by acting well he can be called a *purusha* insofar as he does what he is entitled by *dharma* to do: *yamadhikritya purushah pravartate.*

As such, it is necessary to grasp Gandhi's idea of "who man is" if we are to appreciate why he rejects modern democracy. After all, the foundational vision of the industrial civilization, too, rests on some substantive idea of who man is. Unless we have an idea of man, we have no frame of reference for the designation of human phenomenon as relevant or irrelevant. For man participates in the creation of social order physically, biologically, psychologically, intellectually and spiritually. However, the stark fact is that man today has spurned the divine, the font of spiritual nourishment in the true sense of the term. The abandonment of the idea of the spiritually attuned and awakened individual is, for Gandhi, the root cause of the rise of what he calls the satanic civilization. Man's life purposes are determined mainly, evenly exclusively, by his ever-proliferating material needs. These needs have become the real and dynamic moving force of industrial civilization.

It is, therefore, not surprising that Gandhi's indictment of modern (industrial) civilization begins with what he thinks is its corrupt influence on man. As he says, "People living in it make bodily welfare the object of life…. This is considered an emblem of civilization and this is also a matter to promote bodily happiness" (Gandhi 1938: 35). Accent on the promotion of bodily happiness brings into operation three undesirable consequences. First, it brings about the externalization of man; he has become, in essence, a receptacle of interests (Wood 1972: 111). As an externalized creature, man becomes the reflexive creature of external, largely material, objects, which attract or repel him. As *Kathopanishad* II.1.2 saw it clearly long ago, Swayambhoo (the self-born) created the senses, to be sure; however, they were damaged in the process of being created. As a result, they can see only the things outside, not the divine within. And when the senses look, they see a multiplicity of objects and get entrapped in them. As such, man indulges in material pleasures and the more he indulges, the more entrapped he becomes in the external world and the more unbridled his passions become.

This is unmistakably the symptom of discontent, which, in turn, leads to more appropriation of societal resources. The desire to amass wealth in a situation, where resources are necessarily limited, leads to violence at both the individual and the collective levels. Amassing of wealth by one individual means preventing the less fortunate others from having access to resources that they direly need but cannot have. Such a situation is symptomatic of the central importance of self-interest that rules out other regarding action. Since the criterion for judging which appetites must be satisfied, which must be suppressed and for ascertaining where to stop in satisfying wants, life becomes a ceaseless struggle of trying to acquire more and more resources for oneself. This would not be a problem if resources were abundant and every desire could be satisfied without sacrificing others or coming into conflict with other individuals. Since this is not the case, this initiates a process of what Gandhi calls "life-corroding competition" leading inexorably to exploitation, inequality and domination. This becomes instrumental in creating a situation in which, as Rousseau puts it, "every man finds his profit in the misfortunes of their neighbours." This may not always lead to physical violence; but it does have more severe consequences than physical hurt. It brings into being a social order in which inequality, oppression, discrimination and deprivation prevail with disastrous implications for human dignity. Gandhi would ask us to reflect with Rousseau: "…what must be the state of things when all men are forced to caress and destroy one another at the same time; and when they are born enemies by duty, and knaves by interest" (quoted in Roy 1985: 40). The prevalence of exploitation, oppression and injustice in such a social order becomes the dominant pattern of social interaction pattern of social interaction.

Millions remain poor. Gandhi notes, while some become rich (1969: IV, 469). It is this situation that *Chhandogya Upanishad* characterizes as *kamachar* (a life involving a ceaseless effort to satisfying material desires) or as Plato calls "the slave of many mad masters." More importantly, as an externalized creature, man ignores or downright denies the existence of the indwelling divine; consequently, his individuality turns out to be pure egoism, acquisitive and possessive egoism. His relationship with the external world becomes purely instrumental. His world is, then, one of potential means, which he understands with a view to control. As a result, cut off from the nourishing source of the divine, man also becomes devoid of morality.

Second, the rise of man as *kamachar* not only kills his real self but also makes him impervious to external control. To be a *kamachar* means, in effect, that man must give in to "multiplication of wants and machinery contrived to supply them." As man's need proliferates, technologically induced and sustained economic growth becomes a *sine qua non* for the maintenance of an elegant life style in society. However, three things happen to spoil this pleasant dream. One, it promotes a complex industrial system of production and exchange that reduces man to the mere cog of the industrial machine. It robs him of his power of self-determination.

Two, as need proliferates, competition for access to necessary goods and services accentuates. With this, there occurs a breakdown of the linkage between the good of one individual and the good of all individuals. The inevitable result of this breakdown is another breakdown, the breakdown of what Plato calls *philia politike*, that is, the loss of fellow feeling among the members of a political community. And three, as civilization grows complex, man loses control over decisions that have a vital bearing on his everyday life. As such, the industrial society emasculates man and opens the path for exploitation and dominance as well as for the unleashing of violence and the loss of morality.

Lastly, as society grows complex, the government becomes big; the hypertrophy of the state becomes an established fact. As material needs of the people proliferate, the economy also expands. The expanding economy makes it incumbent on the government to intervene both for controlling the distortions of the market and for sustaining and extending the process of economic growth. The inability of most of the people to partake in the opened up opportunities makes it necessary for the government to intervene and insure freedom and equality to especially depressed and deprived sections of society. As their dependence on the government increases, the government intrudes in different aspects of the people's life. The state acquires more and more power over the people's life. As the state gets involved in providing public services on a progressively larger scale, the civil society is less able to cope with the everyday problems of life without state intervention and direction.

This, as Tocqueville describes, is tantamount to state despotism, which is popularly elected. In this garb, the government assumes more and more power as well as auto-legitimacy. The increase in state power means the retreat of the individual who, in his isolation, becomes more vulnerable to manipulation, exploitation and dominance by the state as well as others. That is why Gandhi looks upon "an increase of the power of the state with the greatest fear because, although while apparently doing good by minimizing exploitation, it does the greatest harm to mankind by destroying individuality which lies at the root of all progress" (Gandhi 1969: IV, 61–62). The hypertrophy of the state transforms citizens into subjects who invest their trust in the benevolent power and busy themselves with their humdrum, everyday life.

All the three consequences flowing form the promotion of bodily happiness conspire to make man a slave. The enslavement of man by "temptation of money and of luxuries money can buy" handicaps man in developing his individual personality. This hampers the advance of man and "diseases man's mind and heart, (and) imprisons him in clothing, housing and factory" (Gandhi 1959: LIX, 319). The diseased mind of man not only alienates him from his own essential nature, which he has derived from his grounded-ness in the divine, but also from his fellow beings and the world. What is also important is the fact that the disease of the soul spreads out and makes the society diseased. When society becomes diseased, it becomes very difficult for a person to get out of the pervading sickness or what Plato calls *nosos* and recover his soul, the surrogate of his essential nature. Thus, a vicious circle is created in which man gets entrapped and cannot get out of easily.

The search for bodily happiness induces acute competition for access to societal resources. This competition transforms politics into a process of reciprocal resistance in which rival socio-economic interests vie for articulation, rise and control and seek to outbid each other. As a result, politics becomes a process of determining who gets what, when and how adding to the acuteness of competition for comparative advantage in a situation of scarcity. Politics has, then, to intervene to bring the contestants to the negotiation table for a settled compromise for partial satisfaction. Every settled compromise leaves the residue of dissatisfaction, which again flares up and calls for political intervention. It is a continuous process that characterizes the modern political system. This necessarily radiates a sense of being unsettled. The role of politics is, then, to ensure civil stability without blocking change. As such, politics constitutes "an activity expressive of society's need for constant readjustment" (Gandhi 1969: IV, 71–72).

In this framework society emerges as merely constituted by a myriad of socio-economic interests vying for the control of societal resources. It is quite clear in this perspective that society has been conceived of as something caught in a flux, a continuous process of change, which does not recognize anything of permanent value. Nor does it manifest any a *priori* defined purpose or goal that transcends particular interests and animates social life and relations. In other words, it is without any final cause; it is something that is open-ended. In its open-endedness, politics is not influenced by any set principle but by the changing power equations making might into right. This underscores the fact that society lacks any substantive vision, a vision that identifies certain core values that society must seek to realize in collective life and relations. In the lack of such a vision, except that of the necessity of having bodily happiness that makes subjectivity the cornerstone of social and political life, the political order must depend for its effectiveness on appropriations of societal resources and legality of the procedures of making collective choices.

It is the nexus between the idea of man in modern times, industrial civilization and modern democracy that accounts for the distortions of democracy today. These distortions impel Gandhi to reject the Western type of democracy because it is an embodiment of, to use Wolin's characterization, "the law of violence and the enthronement of violence as if it were the eternal law" (1960: 11). Gandhi's indictment of democracy concerns the degeneration of democratic ideal into democratic ideology and its institutional manifestations. Given the distortions that modern civilization has wrought in man's life, Gandhi has no hesitation in condemning it as Satanic and the present system of government as its best exponent (Gandhi 1959: LXVIII, 390).

Installed as a providential check on human cupidity and to put under leash the self-aggrandizing tendency of the greed-besotted man, the state, especially in democratic political systems, often become a potent weapon in the hands of the strong to subjugate, exploit and oppress the weak. Thus, democracy as a form of government that should aim at freeing man from political and social enslavement and from economic exploitation, paves the way for gilding their slavery. Democratic governments become diseased under the *Upas* tree of modern civilization that introduces in social life "life-corroding competition;" it makes power the central organizing principle of politics. Political institutions fail to preserve their impersonal, universal character and are reduced to being instruments of subservient powerful interests.

The degeneration of the government as an umpire into either an interested player or a meek and pliable watchdog is inherent in politics that recognizes the centrality of self-interest. The irony is that despite this, the government is harnessed avowedly for the benefit of public weal. Or else, democratic politics transforms the ruler into the servant of his passion and power, as Meinecke puts it. It is this ironical situation that impels Gandhi to condemn the "Mother of Parliament" as "a sterile and a prostitute" (Gandhi 1959: XXXIII, Appendix, 468). Like Rousseau, Gandhi also considers the legislature as charged with the responsibility of representing the general will. This, for Gandhi, means that there pre-exists a conception of what is good for all that transcends particular wills and that the people know it well. However, the Parliament has not yet done, of its own accord, a single good thing. Moreover, it does not conduct its business with finality. "What it does today may be undone tomorrow." The members of the Parliament, too, give in to pressures and are often reduced to being mere "rubber stamps."

If the Parliament is ineffective, the Prime Minister and the people's representatives peddle specific, particular interests rather than serve the public interest (Gandhi 1969: IV, 113). Speaking generally, the Prime Minister "is more concerned about his power. His energy is concentrated upon securing the success of his party" and "his care is not always that the Parliament shall do right." If the Parliament does not prove an appropriate vehicle of promoting public good, the electoral process too proves to be not an effective instrument of expressing real public opinion. In a society where large-scale illiteracy prevails, the voters cannot be expected to express informed rational choice about issues and candidates. In such a case, "people would follow a powerful orator or a man who gives them parties, receptions, etc. As are the people so is their Parliament" (Ibid.: 113).

Above all, the choice of the electoral system itself deprives people of their true role in a democracy. Instead of participating directly in the process of collective decision-making, the people are reduced to the status of those who participate in the selection of persons who are going to rule over them. Moreover, supposedly, only the most popular, not the wisest people are usually chosen to fight elections. Add to it the fact that people vote not for what contributes to the good of society but either for partisan reasons or for promoting their own interest. The consequence of the electoral system that fails to reflect the true *vox populi* is that such representatives are elected who do not care much for the good of the people. They frequently fail to protect the interests of those who have voted for them and have helped them to acquire power. They are usually concerned with the good of the dominant economic interests in the constituency. That is why Gandhi observes, "The members of the Parliament are hypocritical and selfish" (Gandhi 1969: IV, 31). The people chose the representatives but their first loyalty is to the political party on whose label they entered the electoral fray because the so-called discipline binds them to the party. Moreover, most of them take little interest even in debates on matters that are of vital importance for the people of the country. As he says, "When the greatest questions are debated, members are seen to stretch themselves and doze" (Ibid.). Even while the working of the Parliament demonstrates so many anomalies, the power of attraction of this "costly toy" prevents the people from paying any attention to its deficiencies.

If the Parliament is an unfit instrument of either representing the people or of promoting and safeguarding their interest the executive is still more so. Gandhi is emphatic when he says, "The true democracy cannot be worked by twenty persons sitting at the centre" (Ibid.). Moreover, if a few among these 20 persons are dishonest or indifferent to the good of the people, democracy can play havoc with the life of the people or the fate of the country. Democracy that is neutral or indifferent to morality can only breed violence. And as long as democracy lacks the support of moral authority, the political system will be afflicted by the prevalence of pervasive violence; without non-violence, true democracy will ever remain a distant dream. Gandhi does not reject democracy; what he rejects is what Manicas calls "the victory of democratic ideology against democracy." The democracy based on Gandhi's idea can be realized only be individuals, each of whom is law unto himself but walks under the shadow of God and continually keeps on purifying his heart (Gandhi 1948).

References

Gandhi, M. K. 1948. *Harijan.* 28 January.

———. 1959. *Collected works of Mahatma Gandhi*, 100 vols. Delhi: The Publications Division, Ministry of Information and Broadcasting, Government of India.

———. 1969. *Selected Works of Mahatma Gandhi*, 6 vols. Ed. Shriman Narayan. Ahmedabad: Navajivan Publishing House.

Roy, Ramashray. 1985. *Self and Society: A Study in Gandhian Thought.* New Delhi: SAGE Publications.

Wolin, Sheldon. 1960. *Politics and Vision: Continuity and Innovation in Western Political Thought.* Boston: Little, Brown and Co.

Wood, Ellen Meiksin. 1972. *Mind and Politics: An Approach to the Meaning of Liberal and Socialist Individualism.* Berkeley: University of California Press.

11

Local Democracy: Jefferson and Gandhi

For while the rubble, with their thumb-worn creeds,
Their large professions and little deeds,
Mingle in selfish strife, lo! Freedom weeps.
Wrong rules the land and waiting justice sleeps.

—From Life of Abraham Lincoln by Joseph Gilbert (1998)

I

To rise against tyranny is to generate revolutionary spirit that impels and sustains the people who rise in rebellion to face all hazards and dangers to life and property with a view to winning freedom. As Condorcet had remarked long ago, "the term 'revolutionary' can only be applied to revolution whose aim is freedom." It can be argued that the war of liberation, if successful in its drive, too sets a people free. However, as Arendt notes, "...liberation may be the condition of freedom but by no means leads automatically to it; that the notion of liberty implied in liberation can only be negative..." (1965: 29). Liberation is, in a sense, a political phenomenon since it liberates a people from the shackles of political bondage. In contrast, freedom is more than a political phenomenon; it implies unfettered capacity of the people to give a particular pattern and direction to their existence in the phenomenal world.

Wars and revolutions are the grist of history. All through the ages, wars have been fought and revolutions mounted in the name of freedom and justice. It is true that most wars have, throughout history, as their real objectives, expansion, dominion and exploitation, usually camouflaged by such respectable terms as freedom and justice. Drives towards expansion have resulted in colonization, which in turn, has crystallized in the structure of exploitation and oppression. If the drive towards expansion

has invited retaliatory wars, its concrete manifestation has been colonization; its malign ramifications have provoked revolutions for pulling
down tyrannical rule with a view to obtaining freedom from it. Thus, the
occurrence of a war of liberation or revolution constitutes a phenomenon
that runs through the course of history. History testifies to the fact that
"...no cause is left but the most ancient of all, the one in fact, from the
beginning of our history has determined the very existence of politics,
the cause of freedom versus tyranny" (Arendt 1965: 11).

To rise against tyranny is to generate revolutionary spirit that impels and
sustains the people who rise in rebellion to face all hazards and dangers
to life and property with a view to winning freedom. As Condorcet had
remarked long ago, "the term 'revolutionary' can only be applied to revolution whose aim is freedom." It can be argued that the war of liberation
too sets a people free. However, as Arendt notes, "...liberation may be
the condition of freedom but by no means leads automatically to it; that
the notion of liberty implied in liberation can only be negative..." (Ibid.:
29). Liberation is, in a sense, political phenomenon since it liberates a
people from the shackles of political bondage. In contrast, freedom is
more than a political phenomenon; it implies unfettered capacity of the
people to give a particular pattern and direction to their existence in the
phenomenal world.

It is the quest of freedom that inspired the American and the French
people to launch a bloody and violent revolution against what they considered to be tyranny. What inspired and sustained them in their struggle
against tyranny was the revolutionary spirit that the quest for freedom
engendered. The revolution, when successful, does not end with terminat-
ing the tyrannical rule it so valiantly fought. In a very significant sense,
revolution is nothing more than a transitory stage; what it does is to wipe
the slate clean and erase even the faint impressions recorded in the past.
However, if freedom has to be secured against all attacks and encroachments, the slate has to be filled anew with distinct and bold characters.
The wiping clean of the slate simply means the end of one body politic
before a new one could be installed.

The installation of a new body politic is as essential as it is vital
to terminate the pre-existent one. However, where does one look for
guidelines that could give proper direction to the labours of founding a
new body politic? As Alexis de Tocqueville observed just a few decades

after the American Revolution, "I go back from age to age up to the remotest antiquity, but I find no parallel to what is occurring before my eyes; as the past has ceased to throw its light upon the future, the mind of men wanders in obscurity" (1956).

The past thus has no relevance for reconstructing the present, which has freed itself from its grip. What is distinctive about revolution, especially in modern times, is that they are "inextricably bound up with the notion that the course of history suddenly begins anew, that an entirely a new story, a history never known or told before, is about to unfold..." (Arendt 1965: 28). It is this state that Tocqueville characterizes as wandering in obscurity. The plot of the story may be shrouded in obscurity; however, its moral is never in doubt, not ever ambiguous in significance, nor ever uncertain in its value.

This moral is, of course, freedom and the plot of the new story, therefore, must be woven around this moral. Thus, freedom, its preservation and promotion, must then, provide the guidelines for evolving the institutional framework of the new, preferred body politic. And freedom means self-determination, it cannot be circumscribed or limited to the State as the symbol of the collectivization of individual wills. This is so for the reason that the political system does not and cannot have a separate existence form the members who constitute it. As Dov Ronen points out, at the core of the quest of self-determination is "not a national or group aspiration, but the aspiration of the individual human being to the vague notions of 'freedom' and the 'good life' (1979: 8).

Thus, self-determination or freedom in its extra-political sense, symbolizes the aspiration of individuals to rule one's self and not to be ruled by others and to be free from what they perceive as others, "as a positive human condition, for the good life, self-fulfilment and the like" (Ibid.: 7). Thus self-determination is never a group aspiration, although "it manifests through identities associated with various groups, various aggregates, because individual self-determination as an institutionalized socio-political entity is inconceivable" (Ibid.: 53). It is clear, then, that even while the individual must out of necessity be identified with some particular group, he is the ultimate beneficiary of self-determination.

Thus, freedom as a guide to the founding of a new body politic must aim at securing, promoting and preserving freedom of the individual *qua* individual. However, whenever a new body politic has to be founded after a successful revolution, whether fully bloody or not, it is the State that gets preference over the freedom of the individual. This preference proves ultimately, to say the least, so injurious to individual freedom that it needs to be discarded in favour of another political arrangement that ensures individual freedom without, of course, endangering or curtailing from the common good. The preference given to the state ends up with centralization of authority and power. This, however, dwarfs man and makes him dependent on the state. It robs man of his capacity to manage his own affairs based on self-reliance and imposes on him what Tocqueville calls "perpetual childhood."

With the increasing pace of centralization of authority and power, local communities find slipping their control on and direction of their everyday affairs. Moreover, politicization of national life and relation along with the centralized strategy of economic development is also instrumental in denuding political activities at local community levels of their real substance. Political participation becomes formal. Politics at local levels revolves around petty concerns of everyday life and breeds envy, jealousy and reciprocal resistance between different socio-economic groups. These groups come into being, continue for some time, break only to re-form again in different manners. Thus, politics at the local level is characterized not only by pervasive factionalism but also by the tenuousness of different groups. Such politics is not an apt instrument for transforming the individual into a citizen.

It is against this background that we need to examine why democracy is prevented from making its appearance at the grass-roots level. We also propose to examine an alternative system of political institutional framework that can assure the individual the needed freedom to shape the pattern of his own existence. The appearances of freedom at the grass-roots level can alone help people to organize and guide political life and relations in local communities and thus regain their vigour and vitality. We organize our discussion around the seminal ideas of Thomas Jefferson and Mahatma Gandhi who had definite views about how and why full democracy should be instituted at local community levels.

II

The success of the American Revolution, in a sense, created a kind of "state of nature" that had to be ended by constituting a new political order. An order aimed at organizing freedom into a definite institutional format so that a judicious balance between individual happiness and collective good could be firmly established. This meant the installation of a political institutional arrangement that would allow the exercise of freedom without strangulating common good. This question, as James Madison saw it, resolved itself into two dimensions of the collective existence of free people.

As he noted, "It is of great importance in a republic not only to guard against the oppression of its rulers, but to guard one part of society against the injustice of other parts" (*The Federalist*: No. 51). More specifically, these two problems referred, on the one hand, to the need to protect and safeguard individual freedom for which the American people had fought hard against the British colonial masters and on the other, to prevent the formation of a permanent majority based either on singularity of passion or similarity of interests.

The constitutional convention that met at Philadelphia in 1787 was charged with the responsibility of organizing freedom in a shape that would prove a durable base for a "more perfect union." Two important guidelines were to guide its deliberations. One of these guidelines required the convention only to amend the Articles of Confederation in the light of the experience gained during the war of independence; it was not to substitute it for an entirely new instrument of government. The second guideline was contained in the Preamble of the Declaration of Independence of the United States (4 July 1776), which, as Arendt argues, provided the sole source of authority for framing the Constitution, not as an act of constituting government, but as the law of the land (1967: 193).

The Declaration of Independence is symptomatic of the claim of man in modern times to make freedom the organizing principle of not only his own existence but also of the political existence of the community of men. Thus, the Declaration underscores the idea that all men are created equal as well as that they are all endowed by their creator with inalienable rights. Among these rights, the rights of life, liberty and happiness stand out as very significant. It further notes that it is to secure these rights that governments are instituted among men. The instituted government derives its powers from the consent of the people; it enjoys their allegiance as long as it remains respectful of the people's rights.

It also underlines:

> [W]henever any form of government becomes destructive of these ends,
> it is the Right of the People to alter or to abolish it and to institute new
> Government, laying its foundation on such principles and organizing its
> powers in such form, as to them shall seem most likely to affect their safety
> and Happiness. (*The Federalist*: 619)

The Declaration also recognizes the right of the people to rebellion; but this right is to be exercised only when their fundamental rights are subjected to "a long train of abuses and usurpations pursuing invariably the same object that evinces a design to reduce them under absolute Despotism" (Ibid.).

The constitutional convention, instead of improving the instrument of confederation, forged a new instrument, which scuttled the confederation and installed a federation. The new constitution was seen to be quite "energetic" so much so that a radical departure in the direction of a unified national government was made. As Richard Henry Lee was to comment: "the proposed government was not federal in principles at all but it was calculated to make the states one consolidated government" (*The Federalist*: Introduction, xiii).

This radical departure was prompted by two very important considerations. The first factor was, of course, the experience of the confederation itself. It underlined the difficulties in mobilizing resources and coordinating action during the war years. The experience was so bad that Alexander Hamilton pronounced the Articles of Confederation as an imbecility. As he observed, a full display of the principal defects of the confederation would show that, "the evil we experience do not proceed from minute or partial imperfections, but from fundamental errors in the structure which cannot be amended otherwise than by an alternation in the first principles and the main pillars of the fabric" (Ibid.: No. 15).

If the imperfections of the articles of Confederation were not enough, certain inherent destructive possibilities blighted its existence. As James Madison noted, interest or passion is the animating force in human existence. Man's perspective on life and world is shaped by the need to acquire property; its acquisition is influenced by "the diversity in the faculties of men, from which the right of property originates," and inequality in the distribution of property results. Inequality of possession influences "the division of society into different interests and parties." It is this division that is conducive to the formation of factions.

This would not be pernicious in itself except for the fact that each faction "united and actuated by some common impulse of passion or interest" works to ensure its pre-eminence which proves to be "adverse to the rights of other citizens or to the permanent and aggregate interest of the community" (*The Federalist:* No. 10). Each faction is attached to leaders who engage in

> ambitiously contending for pre-eminence and power; or to persons of other descriptions whose fortunes have been interesting to the human passions, have, in turn, divided mankind into parties, inflamed them with mutual animosity and rendered them much more disposed to vex and oppress each other than to cooperate for their common good. (Ibid.: No. 10)

This creates a situation where

> most frivolous and fanciful distinctions have been sufficient to kindle their unfriendly passions and excite their most violent conflicts. This applies especially to smaller neighboring states. If "men are ambitious, vindictive, and rapacious," so are the states. As the examples of Greece and Italy show, small republics were constantly agitated and at the rapid succession of revolutions by which they were kept in a state of perpetual vibration between the extremes of tyranny and anarchy. If they exhibited occasional calms, these only serve as short-lived contrasts to the furious storms that are to succeed. (*The Federalist:* No. 9)

And as John Jay was to stress, the small states would "neither love nor trust one another, but on the contrary, would be prey to discord, jealousy and mutual injuries; in short, that they would place us exactly in the situations in which some nations doubtless wish to see us, viz., formidable only to each other" (Ibid.: No. 5). Thus "love of power or the desire of pre-eminence and dominion—the jealousy of power or the desire of equality and safety" (Ibid.: No. 6) pitches one state against another. Moreover, territorial disputes have at all times been found one of the most fertile sources of hostility amongst nations (Ibid.: No. 7).

As such, multiplicity of small states does not augur well for internal peace, harmony and safety from external aggression. These small states, when combined with popular government, that is pure democracy, prove disastrous. If Hamilton found the splitting of a large territorial unit into an "infinity of little, jealous, clashing, tumultuous commonwealths, the wretched nurseries of unceasing discord and miserable objects of universal pity or contempt," (Ibid.: No. 9) Madison declared democracies to be the "spectacles of turbulence and contention." Moreover, these states have ever been found "incompatible with personal security or the rights of property and have in general been as short in their lives as they have been violent in their deaths" (Ibid.: No. 10). This is due to the malignant nexus between liberty, interest and opinion.

Liberty is *sine qua non* for the functioning of a popular government; however, as Madison pointed out, it "is to faction what air is to fire." It fans the fire of hunger for more and more possession and divides the society into antagonistic economic interests. Add to it also the fact that interest plays a significant role in the formation of opinion. Thus, the interplay between liberty, interest and opinion creates a situation in which multiplicity of interests and a diversity of opinions become not only the characteristic features of society but also the cause for its fragmentation into highly contentious groups. These groups, then, vie among themselves for dominance and superiority. Such a situation is symptomatic of self-regarding perspective and action that swamp public spirit and go a long way to deaden it.

This eventuality is quite congenial to a majority faction, to "sacrifice to its ruling passion or interest both the public good and private rights of citizens" (Ibid.: No. 10). This is particularly true of a pure democracy signifying a society consisting of "a smaller number of citizens, who assemble and administer the government in person." It is easy for a majority faction to form in such a society, animated by common passion or interest. Then there would be nothing to check the inducement to sacrifice the weaker party or an obnoxious individual. And if the inducement is compelling, neither religious nor moral motives can be relied upon to checking the majority action from sacrificing public good or private rights of other citizens.

The formation of a majority faction or party, animated by common passion or interest is just one possibility. There is yet another possibility, the possibility of factions with different passions or interests of uniting or coalescing to form a durable majority. Both these possibilities have greater chances of realization in pure democracies. This again may pose a threat to the smooth functioning of the popular government. But this is not the only probable threat; there is also the danger of private interests eclipsing the realization of common good. Every individual has his own passion or interest, which moulds the way he thinks and acts. When speaking in public place, he is most likely to give, whenever he speaks in public, expression to his views that reflect his interest or passion.

There is the additional fact that momentary passions and interests have often more control over human conduct than general or remote considerations of policy, utility or justice (Ibid.: No. 6). This is also true of groups of men or parties when common passion or interest bring them together for political action. It can be argued that one can rely on an enlightened statesmen's wise counsel for protecting the republic from contrary pulls and pushes of partisan politics. However, they are not always available, nor it is certain that their wise counsel would be heeded when passion of partisan politics invades man's better judgement.

Thus opinions of persons and groups, even of legislators, for that matter, are usually expressions of self-interest, often biased. They not improbably express the views of those whose integrity has been corrupted. The result is that self-regarding opinions have "divided mankind into parties, inflamed them with mutual animosity and rendered them much more disposed to vex and oppress than to cooperate" (Ibid: No. 10). The division of society into rival factions and parties is likely to give rise to two different situations: either a dominant majority or a badly splintered space of public opinion. In the case of the former, the majority would most likely use its power to benefit itself at the cost of both individual rights and public good. If the space of public opinion is badly splintered, it would lead either to recurrent crises of deadlock in the making of public choices or intrigues, manipulation and horse-trading by "ambitious, vindictive and rapacious" politicians (Ibid: No. 6).

All this creates the confusion of a multitude, making it necessary to guard against this confusion. For this, it is necessary to renounce popular government, that is, pure democracy, because public opinion, as the aggregate of self-regarding individual opinions is biased, is likely to prevail over public spirit. It is in this sense that rules based upon public opinion amount to tyranny and pure democracy turns out to be a newfangled form of despotism (Arendt 1965: 226).

Given the turbulence of popular government and its instability, the way for the violation of individual rights and eclipsing of public good is paved. It is against this background that Madison observes that "it is of great importance in a republic not only to guard the society against the oppression of its rulers, but also to guard one part of the society against the injustice of other parts," to save "the rights of individuals or of the minority...from interested combinations of the majority" (*The Federalist:* No. 51). Solution to the confusion of the multitude is, in fact, available.

This solution, of course, lies in a representative and not a democratic government. This means a democratic republic usually characterized by the regular distribution of power into distinct departments; the introduction of legislative balance and checks; the institution of courts composed of judges holding their office during good behaviour; the representation of the people in the legislature by deputies of their own election. To these must be added the enlargement of the orbit within which a political system would revolve. Thus, the case of popular government or pure democracy, where "a small number of citizens...assemble and administer the government in person," was lost, a new constitution favouring democratic republic was adopted.

The option of representative democracy was thus the result of the imbecility of the Articles of Confederation as well as a particular understanding of the nature of *homo politicus*. It was preferred because it was "much more a technical device for governments among large populations; limitation to a small and chosen body of citizens was to serve as the great purifier of both interest and opinion, to guard against confusion of a multitude" (Arendt 1965: 227). Madison considered it prudent to

> refine and enlarge public views by passing them through the medium of a chosen body of citizens whose wisdom may best discern the true interest of their country and whose patriotism and love of justice will be least likely to sacrifice it to temporary or partial considerations." (*The Federalist:* No. 10)

In short, the responsibility of the purification of opinion must be relegated to a small body of men who may not themselves be wise but whose common interest is public wisdom. Institutions that are integral to democratic republic "tend to the amelioration of popular systems of government." Moreover, they offer as "the expedient for extending the sphere of popular governments and reconciling the advantage of monarchy with those of republicanism" (Ibid.: No. 9).

Thus, as Madison declared:

> [N]o other form would be reconcilable with the genius of the people of America; with the fundamental principles of the Revolution; or with that honourable determination which animates every votary of freedom, to rest all our political experiments on the capacity of the mankind for self-government." (Ibid.: No. 39)

Thus, a democratic republic was born with the purpose of assuming "among the powers of the earth, the separate and equal station to which the Laws of Nature and of Nature's God entitle them... [Declaration of Independence]." And the American revolution escaped the fate of "a multitude of Commonwealths, Crimes and Calamities...till at last the exhausted Provinces [would]) sink into slavery under the yoke of some Conqueror" (John Dickinson in a letter to William Pitt, 1765).

III

The Constitution that was adopted did, of course, prevent the American Revolution from splintering into a multitude of commonwealths, crimes and calamities. However, it did so by paying a heavy cost, the cost of what Manicas calls "the victory of democratic ideology over democracy" (1988: 137). As he points out, the victory of Hamiltonian Federalists meant the jettisoning of an alternative political arrangement in keeping with the democratic ideal, signifying a radically decentralized and layered arrangement of building blocks of the political system. In this arrangement, the constitutive units were to yield increasingly specific powers as territory and scope were enlarged (Ibid.: 152).

The jettisoning of a fully decentralized political system is sufficient evidence of the distrust of the Federalists of a democratic political system. What further reinforces this conclusion is the omission of the bill of rights from the newly drafted constitution. The constitution prescribes a limited government to prevent the government to acquire more and more power. As the government acquires more power, the possibility of its abuse enhances. It is, therefore, necessary to protect the individual against the powerful state. The denial of democracy and the installation of a representative democracy have led to a situation where "power and freedom have parted company..."

(Arendt 1965: 137). While freedom lies with the private life of the citizen, power resides in the public realm. It is precisely for this reason that freedom of the citizen needs to be protected against the powerful government.[1]

This protection could perhaps be ensured if the constitution grants the citizen certain rights detailed in the Bill of Rights. These civil rights have to be safeguarded through constitutional guarantees. The Bill of Rights is, therefore, incorporated in the constitution that installs a limited government. These rights are "never intended to spell out the new revolutionary powers of the people, but, on the contrary, [are] felt to be necessary in order to limit the powers of government" (Ibid.: 143). However, despite some limitations on governmental powers, the American Constitution included no Bill of Rights and on no score was it so generally condemned.

This prompted Jefferson to indicate to Madison that civil rights are "what the people are entitled to against every government on earth, general or particular and what no just government should refuse or rest on inference" (Jefferson 1787b). It was thus on the insistence of Jefferson that the first session of the Congress adopted the first 10 amendments incorporating the Bill of Rights in the Constitution. Thus, it is to the Jeffersonian Republicans rather than to Hamiltonian Federalists that the American people owe credit for having the Charter of Individual Rights.

Was the exclusion of the Bill of Rights an oversight or was it an indicator of some sharp divide in the views among prominent leaders about the nature of government and the place in it of civil rights? Sharp differences of views existed between Hamilton and Jefferson; they represented two poles of opinion even while linked together by a common thread of the importance of constitutional government, but being looked at from different perspectives. That they expressed two radically different perspectives on the government indicates something more than an oversight. As Grey and Hofstadter note, Hamilton and Jefferson represented "two powerful, though, to some extent, antagonistic forces in American life." If Hamilton leaned "toward closer union and a stronger national government," Jefferson preferred "a broader, freer democracy" (Grey and Hofstadter 1993: 52).

At the root of this difference of perspectives between them, lay a deeper and fundamental difference. While Hamilton feared anarchy and thought in terms of order, Jefferson considered freedom much more important. He argued, "every man and every body of men on earth possess the right of self-government" (Ibid.: 53). It is not, therefore, surprising that when

Hamilton was inclined towards a stronger national government, Jefferson, while recognizing the value of a strong national government, saw its need only in foreign relations. He feared that a strong government might prove oppressive in other areas of the people's life. Believing as he did in the worth of individual liberty, Jefferson promised in his inaugural presidential address a wise and frugal government that would "preserve order among the inhabitants" but would "leave them otherwise free to regulate their own pursuits of industry and improvement" (Ibid.: 55; see also Boorstin 1981).

It is true that the views of Hamiltonian federalists won the day. However, the voice of Jefferson uttering what must have been in those days a political sacrilege, that is, favouring a decentralized political system, is still vigorous and it still agitates the conscience of all thinking men. In Jefferson's case, this voice did not burst upon the political scene all at once. It went through three distinct phases of evolution and got full articulation, mostly through letters, only after his retirement from active politics.

The first stage of the evolution is linked to his belief in the mutability of constitutions. He did not consider the constitution a permanent, unchangeable document, guiding and regulating political life and relationships for all times to come. He criticized those who looked at "constitutions with sanctimonious reverence and deem(ed) them like the ark of the covenant, too sacred to be touched" (Jefferson 1816). Jefferson was outraged at the injustice that only his generation should have in their power "to begin the world over again;" for him, it was plain "vanity and presumptuous to (govern) beyond the grave." He asserted that "nothing is unchangeable, but the inherent rights of rebellion and revolution" (Jefferson 1824).

For him, rebellion or revolution becomes necessary because governments tend in time to become corrupt. He believed that no government stays for long on the path of virtue; eventually, it is tempted to test the power it has been endowed with, by God or men. In testing its power, it frequently dips its fingers in the muck of oppression and the warmth of blood and robs the people it rules over of their tranquillity, resources, even their power to think and act. It is only the occasional outbreak of rebellion or revolution that can keep the government on the path of virtue.

When the news of Shay's rebellion in Massachusetts reached Jefferson, he was confirmed in his belief that people would not tolerate infringement of their rights or encroachment upon their interest. The very fact that people had taken it upon themselves to rise and act against the injustice done to them by the government, was enough for him to have his faith confirmed in the ability of the people to safeguard their liberty, rights and interests. He thus put his faith in the phenomenon of recurrent revolution for keeping the tree of liberty alive and green, for "the tree of liberty must be refreshed, from time to time, with the blood of patriots and tyrants. It is its natural manure" (Jefferson 1787a). However, he could not sustain this belief for long in view of the brutality and atrocities committed during the French Revolution.

The catastrophe of the French Revolution that frustrated all attempts to provide a secure space to freedom, made it necessary for him to revise his views. He moved away from "his earlier identification of action with rebellion and tearing down to an identification founding anew and building up" (Arendt 1965: 234). He argued that, no, one generation had the right to dictate to future generations the kind of constitution they would like to live under and that each generation must choose for itself the government it prefers. As such, every 30 years or so, each generation must be constitutionally allowed to elect its own constitutional convention armed with the authority to modify, adapt or change the constitution as circumstance demanded.

Jefferson's intention in proposing this measure was not simply to allow each generation to choose for itself the kind of constitution it considered appropriate for itself. More importantly, it was a step towards finding ways and means for the opinion of the whole people to be "fairly, fully and peacefully expressed, discussed and decided by the common reason of society" (Jefferson 1816). What it signifies is not only the jettisoning of violence as a means of keeping alive the revolutionary spirit so evident during the revolution. It was also meant to instil into the American people the value of peaceful ways of making and changing governments.

What Jefferson proposed was, in essence, a "recurring revolution" but without violence. It meant, in effect, a remedy against "the endless cycle of oppression, rebellion, reformation," a remedy worse than the disease. It would have

> either thrown the whole body politic out of gear periodically or, more likely, have debased the act of foundation to a mere routine performance, in which case even the memory of what he most ardently wished to save—"to

the end of time, if anything human can so long endure—would have been lost." (Arendt 1965: 235)

Its impracticality must, therefore, have dawned upon Jefferson. Hence, he developed the idea of a decentralized polity.

Jefferson's central concern was the protection of individual rights from encroachment, from either the government or some section of society itself. However, can individual rights protect the individual or a minority community against tyranny from the government or society? Madison had equated all institutional safeguards against infringement of these rights to what he called "parchment barriers" (see Rakove 1991: 98–143). He was sceptical about these rights being fully secured. He recognized that one could enumerate individual rights that are worth protecting; he, however, doubted whether any formal declaration, however, carefully stated or comprehensive, could counteract the real forces threatening their security in the republican polity (Ibid.: 130).

For Madison, the regulation of economic life and relations form the principal task of modern legislation; it, however, involves the spirit of party and faction in the necessary and ordering operations of government. He observed: "What are so many of the most important acts of legislation, but so many judicial determinations concerning the rights of large bodies of citizens: and what are the different classes of legislators, but advocates and parties to the cause they determine" (Ibid.: 131)? Thus, for Madison, all decisions about economic policy involve questions of private rights, of justice and therefore, of rights (Roy 2002: 157). Issues of public policies encourage coalescence of factions and parties. And since these are contentious issues, they incite manipulation, which, in essence, represents brute force insofar as all such legislative actions are embedded in passion and interests (Ibid.: 158).

Jefferson, too, was convinced that "in every government on earth some trace of human weakness, some germ of corruption and degeneracy, which cunning will discover and wickedness insensibly open, cultivate and improve" (quoted in Boorstin 1981: 178). He also believed that rulers tend to turn into wolves and destroy the herd of the sheep. As such, "the time to guard against corruption and tyranny is before they shall have gotten hold of us. It is better to keep the wolf out of the fold, than to trust to drawing his teeth and claws after he shall have entered" (Ibid.: 179). The tendency of the rulers to turn into wolves constitutes the source of tyranny arising out of society or government. Can representative democracy and its institutional framework safeguard individual freedom? Republican politics is the politics of representation, but it proves wanting in some crucial respects. For example, most of the lawmakers seek office only to gratify their ambition and personal interest. Those who are not swayed by either ambition or interest are often either inexperienced or weak to resist the influence of leaders with certain designs of their own electors. (Roy 2002: 157). Even the limitation of legislative power does not help the cause of freedom. The reason is that the civil society proves inadequate or incapable in responding to the pressure of change. As such, legislators take upon themselves the responsibility of making "proper" responses to it. And most often, these responses are influenced by fickle public opinion rather than by any enlightened judgement.

Additionally, there is also the problem of the significance of the term "representative." If the representative is merely an agent of his electors, which section of these electors influences his legislative role performance? The electors are numerous; they are heterogeneous in interest or opinion; and they are divided in competing camps. Moreover, if the representatives are bound by the instructions of their electors, they have "a choice of regarding themselves either glorified messenger boys or hired experts who, like lawyers, are specialists in representing the interest of their clients" (Arendt 1965: 237). If, on the other hand, the representative is supposed to be the ruler, even if only for a limited time, then, there is, of course, no representation in the strict sense of the term. "All power resides in the people" is true only for the day of the election. This, in essence, resurrects the age-old distinction between the ruler and the ruled. This distinction that the Revolution had set to abolish has, then, "reasserted itself again. Once more the people are not admitted to the public realm; once more the business of government has become the privilege of the few." With the distinction between the ruler and the ruled reasserting itself, the well-being of the people has come to depend on those who "alone may exercise (their) virtuous disposition" (Jefferson 1771). And if they either fail or prove unable to do so, the way is paved for "elective despotism."

Tocqueville too had referred to this phenomenon, which he characterized as "a new type of state despotism which is popularly elected." This creates a situation, which ends up in "lethargy, the forerunner of death to the public liberty," or "the preservation of the spirit of resistance" to whatever government they have elected, since the only power they retain is "the reserve power of revolution" (Jefferson 1787a). And if once people become inattentive to public affairs "you and I, Congress and Assemblies, Judges and Governors, shall all become wolves" (Jefferson 1782).

It is true that there still exist townships and town councils; in political matters, this is traditionally known as schools of the people's school. These institutions provided to the citizens spaces where they could assemble, discuss and decide matters of common interest fully and freely. They taught the people the art of ruling and being ruled. They constituted an integral part of common political life. And if it is, as Keane notes, in and through political life that "men's true individuality can be cultivated within an ensemble of responsibilities (sharing in tasks and of deliberation and executing public decisions and so on)...that encourage them to see what is good for themselves and desirable for others, in general" (1984: 116), then, these townships and councils did mould the political life and relations of the people at local communities.

Thus, townships and councils did not represent simply a physical location; they represented "the organization of the people as it arises out of acting and speaking together and its true space lies between people living together for this purpose, no matter where they happen to be" (Arendt 1958: 177). Thus, the possibility of enlightened opinion becomes real only where men communicate freely with one another and have the right to make their views public. And it is the confrontation of opposite views that conduces the people to exert their reason coolly and freely. Despite their utility as the school of the people in political matters, they were, however, not incorporated into either the state or the federal constitution. Lewis Mumford later pointed out that this failure was "one of the tragic oversights of post-revolutionary political developments." Consequently, the importance of townships and councils dwindled and the schools of the people in political matters withered away.

In short, then, while the Revolution gave freedom to the people, it failed to provide the space where freedom could have made its appearance and it could be exercised. Only the representatives of the people, not the people themselves, had the opportunity to engage in those activities of "expressing, discussing and deciding, which, in a positive sense, are the activities of freedom" (Arendt 1965: 235). Jefferson, therefore, called for providing these organs of true democracy and asked to "divide the counties into wards" (Jefferson 1824). He recommended the introduction of what he called "elementary republics" as a means of securing and guaranteeing the exercise of freedom by individuals, the freedom which was their inalienable birth right. Jefferson was convinced that if the plan of elementary republics was executed, it would deliver representative democracy of its shortcomings and would shed off most of its blemishes. "Could I once see this, I should consider it as the dawn of the salvation of the republic..." (Ibid.: 249).

IV

Jefferson's scheme of elementary republics operating in wards of different counties enjoying self-rule does provide a counter-weight to the strong tendency towards centralization of governmental authority and power. But, it can be asked, would it prove an adequate and effective countervailing force or would the wards enjoy full democracy in which individual freedom would be fully exercised? Of course, the exercise of individual freedom must be compatible with the exercise of freedom by others, so that the rights of others are not encroached. Given this limitation, however, what the exercise of freedom signifies in this context is a proper mixture of freedom and responsibility so that it conduces to the reconciliation of the good of one individual with the good of all individuals.

It is true that Jefferson's scheme of elementary republics provides scope to the members of local communities for exercising their freedom in managing local affairs. However, this freedom, as we shall see shortly, is neither full-fledged nor sufficiently powerful to counteract the centralizing tendency that grows more vigorous as a result of the growing complexity of economic life and relations. In order to appreciate why this is so, a set of three issues needs to be explored for determining the nature of their impingement on both the adequacy and effectiveness of elementary republics. These issues are: (a) the status of local self-governing institutions in the over all framework of representative democracy, (b) the primacy of self-interest in shaping public issues and (c) the possibility of enlightened common reason emerging out of the contention of private interests.

Insofar as the first issue is concerned, it can be asserted that elementary republic, if instituted, would represent islands in the vast ocean of representative democracy. This is evident from the fact that if the wards would enjoy some sort of self-government that allows citizens to participate in the making of public decisions, the rest of the country would be ruled not by citizens but their chosen representatives. Thus, two different systems of government would co-exist whose relationship would not be quite harmonious and restful. The reason is that there would flow just one-way influence emanating from the apex of the system and going down to the wards. Consider the fact that wards would have no presence either in state or national legislatures, except through the representatives elected from constituencies much larger than themselves. They would not, therefore, be in a position to directly influence decisions that have direct or indirect bearing upon their own affairs.

Wards would not, sociologically speaking, constitute self-sufficient units of political organization, even if they were granted self-rule. They would form, economically, politically and administratively, an integral part of larger politico-administrative entities. As parts of larger territorial entities, they would be exposed to influences that originate not in the wards themselves but in their immediate and distant environment. Changes occurring elsewhere would have their impact on wards, calling for an appropriate response that would help them sustain their existence. Large parts of these changes have their origin in the technologically induced and sustained economic growth process.

This demolishes barriers between different economies, breaks their self-sufficiency, disturbs their internal coherence and sets in motion a process of homogenization by linking them up with national, even international economy; this linkage tolerates no deviance and suffers no autonomy. Whether elementary republics would have enough internal resources to cope with the forces of change is a question whose affirmative answer becomes an important desideratum of their capacity for self-governance. The significance of this question lies in the fact that while economy constitutes today the prime mover of man's thought-ways and work-ways, it is beyond the capacity of local communities, whether natural or artificially created, to manage or control it.

This constitutes a significant factor in the successful working of democracy at the grass roots, which is self-evident in view of the fact that most aspects of collective existence in modern times are influenced by the economic motive and economic activities undertaken in response to it. Lack of control over economic life and relations would in itself become an important factor not only in restricting the scope of the authority and power of local bodies, but would also weaken their strength in coping with the forces impinging on them from outside. Add to it the fact that the sheer weight of state and national governments would further limit this capacity to manage changes.

The second issue relates to man and his primary concern in life today. Earlier, two components—the pursuit of a higher life purpose such as self-knowledge, better citizenship, etc.—defined the good life. However, with the rejection of higher life purposes in the seventeenth century, primary importance was given to the pursuit of ordinary life-needs involved with production and reproduction. Pursuit of happiness, then, came to be identified with "augmentation of fortune." This signified appeasement of desires as far as possible. For this, acquisition of wealth, power and prestige became necessary. This further enhanced the importance of economic activities. As a result, interest came to occupy the centre of man's existence.

Pursuit of interest requires freedom; however, freedom cannot by itself yield a criterion of action; it acquires substantive content only when it is coupled with some concrete objective. The selection of the objective is the function of the self-defining subject whose main purpose in life happens to be the acquisition of wealth, power and prestige. What is thus distinctive about the modern age is the fusion of freedom and cupidity. What further adds to this is Lord Keynes' dictum, "economic development is the possibility of development." Thus, the securing of economic well-being is claimed to make self-formation of man possible by giving it a definite shape.

Pursuit of self-interest, however, fosters what Kant calls "social incompatibility." As he puts it:

> Nature should thus be thanked for fostering social incompatibility, enviously competitive vanity and insatiable desires for possession or even power. Without these desires, all man's excellent capacities would never be roused to develop. Man wishes concord, but nature knowing better what is good for his species, wishes discord. (1970: 45)

Thus, the pursuit of self-interest proves divisive; it divides man and man, separates man from society and alienates him from nature. It breaks social cohesion and harmony. It leads to "civil war carried out by other means" (MacIntyre 2008: 253). By the same token, the law of self-interest rules the moral universe and transforms morality into expediency. Elementary republics would not be exceptions to this.

The question of enlightened common reason emerging from the contention of interests, reason that can illumine public deliberation becomes quite doubtful given the predominance of self-interest in man's life. Consider the fact that free and full discussion does not automatically translate into impartial and objective public decisions. It needs the leaven of concern for others that alone can form the firm foundation for securing the good of others. However, opinions and views expressed during public deliberations would be laced with partisan considerations that are not conducive to public spirit. Thus, public deliberation would be characterized by partisan or personal idiosyncrasies; they would therefore prove a big hindrance to the emergence of enlightened common reason. What would prove decisive in this situation is the imposition of the will of the majority over minorities, signifying the use of brute force. Such a situation makes reconciliation between the good of one individual and the good of all individuals highly problematic.

It should be clear by now that the effectiveness of local community-level institutions of self-government depends on whether or not individuals are able to transcend self-interest; it is self-transcendence that makes reconciliation between the good of one individual and the good of all individuals possible. However, self-transcendence is not achieved by making changes in the external environment. These changes are aimed at reinvigorating society. However, these changes that are meant to be remedies to social ills that flow from the aggressive pursuit of self-interest, "cannot be simply institutional, social or political reforms" (Walsh 1997: 23). At the root of social ills is moral degeneration. The problem is, then spiritual or moral, not institutional.

The question, then, is: How is moral regeneration possible? Obviously, changes in the exterior of man are of no help here. What is required is internal change signifying self-transformation. Once internal change occurs, outward form would automatically change. Therefore, as Gandhi sees it, what everyone should be concerned with is "a radical change more in inward spirit than in the outward form. If the first is changed, the second will take care of itself. If the first remains unchanged, the second, no matter how radically changed, will be like a whited sepulchre" (1959: LV, 62).

To insist on inward change is to initiate the process of self-transformation. It signifies the overcoming of the beast situated in every man's breast. This can be accomplished only when man recognizes his true nature. By recognizing his true nature, man seeks to elevate himself from the brute state because "he is a special creation of God precisely to the extent that he is distinct from the rest of His creation" (Gandhi 1969: VI, 110). In this, he cannot rely on external freedom to protect internal freedom because relying on it, we often find that the laws made to secure freedom turn out to be shackles binding us (Gandhi 1959: XXXVIII, 18).

For Gandhi, then, swaraj or freedom means rule over one's self. It cannot come from any external circumstance or paying it lip service. "It is an inward change.... It is the transformation of the heart.... And that absolute transformation can only come by inward prayer and a definite and living recognition of the presence of the mighty spirit residing within" (Ibid.: XXXIV, 506). Internal transformation is possible only when man, as Plato suggests, takes recourse to *periagoge* or turning one's back on the concerns of the phenomenal world. This is possible only when man attunes his soul to the divine ground of reality. Alternatively, as *Chhandogya Upanishad* notes, man accepts the suzerainty of the mighty spirit that Gandhi talks about, that is, the indwelling *Purusha*. Man must accept this mighty spirit as his ruler if he wants to be at peace with himself and the world beyond (*Chhandogya Upanishad* 8.1.1).

Once he accepts the suzerainty of *Purusha*, he becomes *swarat*, self-sovereign. Thus, Gandhi's idea of freedom signifies inner freedom that can be attained only by attuning the soul to the divine ground of reality. It is this attuning that is the foundation of self-governing societies. "Unless humans are essentially self-governing beings, there can be no case for self-governing societies" (Walsh 1997: 17). Once it is recognized that there exists an essential linkage between self-governing persons and self-governing societies, it is not difficult to appreciate that the moral regeneration is facilitated by the extent to which human beings become self-governing entities.

By surrendering to God, man frees himself from moral conflicts. He comes to think that it is only by his effort to come in touch with the mighty spirit that the pettiness of his passions and unruly desires and preferences for self-interest can be transcended.

> For once man is in touch with his highest, he is in touch with God. He has then a broader and higher vision of man and his place in nature and so he identifies with God and finds that he has no special interest of his own to serve.... He perceives God in all things and all things in God. (Dasgupta 1965: II, 453)

To be in touch with God and serve Him, in this world of here and now, is to serve his creation. "Service of His creation is service of God" (Gandhi 1959: LXIII, 253). This service must, however, be self-less, without any desire of getting any return out of it. This constitutes *lokasamgraha* (sustenance of the lived world). The attitude of *lokasamgraha* prevents the split of the sensible world into subjective and objective and allows man to transcend his limitations; man then develops a sense of oneness of existence, which allows him to identify himself with the interests of all living beings. They become, in effect, an "extended self" of the individual. The larger vision promotes the sense of identity with all that exists and provides the basis for the individual to relate meaningfully with others. This, in turn, obliterates the separation between individual and society and establishes a relationship of drop and the ocean between them. "In this ocean of life we are little drops" and as such, we must "share the majesty of life in the presence of God" (Gandhi 1969: VI, 109).

Restating the relationship between individual and society, Gandhi notes:

> Individuality is and is not even as each drop in the ocean is and is not. It is not because apart from the ocean it has no existence. It is because the ocean has no existence if the drop has not, i.e., has no individuality. They are beautifully interdependent. And if this is true of the physical law, how much more so (it is) of the spiritual world" (Gandhi 1930).

As such, there cannot be any distinction between individual growth and "corporate growth," as Gandhi calls it. However, the focal point of this growth is the individual; the corporate growth is completely dependent upon individual growth (Gandhi 1959: XXXIV, 505).

It, then, follows that self-effort for self-development is as valuable as the sustenance that the individual can receive from his community. Sociability is necessary for self-development as individuality. The Enlightenment-view of man considers him to be the subject of egoistic desires; however, their satisfaction transforms both society and nature into merely means to help him realize his purposes. Such a view is, as Taylor suggests, "utilitarian in its ethical outlook, atomistic in its social philosophy, analytic in science of man" and looks to "a scientific social engineering to organize man and society and bring men happiness through perfect mutual adjustment" (1979: 1). Gandhi rejects this understanding of man and underlines the value of community for man's proper development and his relationship with the external world. He therefore stresses the need for reviving community living; this will allow man to enjoy more "affective ties, to experience some closer solidarity than the nature of urbanized and industrialized society seemed willing to grant" (Wolin 1960: 63–64).

The development of affective ties and the maintenance of closer solidarity are possible only in small, face-to-face communities. Unger therefore argues, "the development of the person has to be accomplished through the decentralization of society." Only such a society can "strive for natural harmony by giving freer play to instinctual needs within personality and by simplifying the conditions of social life, that man's life-giving relationship to nature can reassert itself" (1975: 251). It must, however, be made clear that the ability of a decentralized society comprising small communities to sustain affective relationship among the members of these communities and to enable them to become full participating members depend on two very important conditions.

One of these conditions is that the economy must be very simple, catering to minimum material needs of the people. This would allow greater dependence on locally available resources. This would check the invasion of larger market forces and safeguard social institutions and cultural ethos against pollution. Gandhi therefore insists on the minimization of wants as a means of promoting self-reliance and self-sufficiency. The second condition underlines the need for the full enjoyment of self-government. Gandhi is well aware of the fact that the tendency ingrained in representative democracy towards legal fictionalizing of representation increases the power of the state.

The government may be legitimate; it may also be garbed in appropriate constitutional form and have its sanction and be adorned with the rule of law. However, it would still be an institution that violates the moral principles that lend it authority. As such, democratic government, for Gandhi, is "a distant dream" (1959: LXXVI, 437). But the dream of democracy can be made real if true democracy can be established. True democracy represents a system in which decisions are made not based on the whims of rulers, nor based on the majority imposing its will on the weak minority, but on the basis of genuine public opinion that emerges out of free and fair exchange of views of those who have transcended their self-interest.

However, the formation and dissemination of genuine public opinion becomes difficult if there is a great distance between where public opinion is created and where the seat of authority is located. The larger the democratic polity, the more numerous would be intermediaries that exist to link public opinion at grass-roots communities with the distant seat of authority. Therefore, the danger would be ever present that the message would be misinterpreted and distorted and consequently, the possibility of inappropriate decisions would always vex the system. That is why Gandhi "does not believe in the accepted Western form of democracy with its universal voting for parliamentary representative" (Gandhi 1959: LXXVI, 437).

He therefore emphatically asserts that a dynamic democracy can grow only out of meaningful relationships and spontaneous organizations that spring among people, when they come together at the local level to solve their basic problems by cooperation among themselves. He further adds:

> In such a community, achievement of self-sufficiency and security by neighbourly cooperation engenders a strong sense of local strength and solidarity and the individuals' sense of responsibility to the community and concern for its welfare are at their highest. (Pyarelal 1958: II, 581)

The idea of democracy at the grassroots level translates, according to what Gandhi thinks about it, into village swaraj, that is, "a complete republic, independent of its neighbours for its vital wants and yet interdependent for many others in which dependence is necessary." This means, "every village's first concern will be to grow its food crops and cotton for its clothes..." (*Gandhi* 1942). Gandhi would like these village republics to conduct their activities on a cooperative basis and "non-violence with its technique of satyagraha and non-cooperation will be the sanction of the village community." There will, of course, be a village government conducted by a panchayat of five persons annually elected by adult villagers. In the village republic there would be perfect democracy based upon individual freedom. "The individual [will be] the architect of his Government. The law of non-violence [will rule] him and his Government. He and his village [will be] able to defy the might of the world" (Ibid.).

The village republics would constitute the basic building blocks of the larger political system. As Gandhi told Louis Fisher in 1942:

> There are seven hundred thousand villages in India. Each would be organized according to the will of its citizens, all of them voting. Then there would be seven hundred thousand votes and not four hundred millions. Each village, in other words, would have one vote. The villages would elect their district representatives and the district administrations would elect the provincial administration and these, in turn, would elect a president who would be the national chief executive. (Gandhi 1959: LXXVI, 437)

It is clear, then, that what Gandhi envisages is the reverse of the existing paradigm of government organization; it is, to say the least, a top-down approach, which Gandhi obviously rejects. What he proposes is a bottom-up approach to institutional arrangement in which the local community would be the locus of basic and primary authority and power; the upper echelons would have only residuary authority and power that are beyond the scope of village republics. It does not need to be pointed out that Gandhi's approach takes into account the micro-variability and micro-vitality of local communities. It is this approach of the constitution of village republics or Jefferson's elementary democracy that, according to Gandhi, would allow the creation of public spaces where true freedom could make its appearance.

V

The paradigm of political institutional arrangement that Gandhi proposes does not simply focus on political life and relations of the people residing in local communities; it also embraces the whole of the people's life activities at the local level. As such, it offers an appropriate corrective to Jefferson's proposal of elementary republics. Jefferson did seek to make the revolutionary spirit alive and durable. However, he failed to see that man in modern times is like the peasant who, in Lenin's view, possesses two souls: one covets gold, that is, affluence and the other dreams of the warmth of an intimate community—each pulling the individual in different directions. But as long as the goal of affluence untrammelled by moral values remains the pivot of human endeavour, neither the objective of gold for everybody nor that of strengthening community life as the ground for situating freedom as a fulcrum of real democracy seems to be achievable.

Note

1. This section relies heavily on Hannah Arendt's *On Revolution* (1950).

References

Arendt, Hannah. 1950. *The Human Condition*. New York: Anchor Books.
———. 1958. *The Human Condition*. Chicago: University of Chicago Press.
———. 1965. *On Revolution*. Hammondsworth: Pelican Books.
———. 1967. *Men in Dark Times*. New York: Houghton Mifflin Harcourt Publishing Company.
Boorstin, Daniel Joseph. 1981. *The Lost World of Thomas Jefferson*. Chicago: University of Chicago Press.
Dasgupta, S. 1965. *A History of Indian Philosophy*, 5 vols. Cambridge: Cambridge University Press.
Dickinson, John. 1765. Letter to William Pitt, 19 October.
Gandhi, M. K. 1942. *Harijan*. 26 July.
———. 1959. *Collected Works of Mahatma Gandhi*, 100 vols. New Delhi: The Publications Division, Ministry of Information and Broadcasting, Government of India.
———. 1969. *The Selected Works of Mahatma Gandhi*, Ed. Shriman Narayan, Ahmedabad: Navajivan Publishing House.
———. 1930. Letter to P. G. Mathew, 8 September.
Grey, Wood, and Richard Hofstadter. 1993. *An Outline of American History*. New Delhi: United State Information Agency.
Jefferson, Thomas. 1782. Letter to Colonel Edward Carrington. 16 January.
———. 1787a. Letter to Colonel William Stephen Smith, 13 November.
———. 1787b. Letter to James Madison, 20 December.
———. 1816. Letter to Samuel Kercheval, 12 July.
———. 1824. Letter to John Cartwright, 5 June.

Kant, Immanuel. 1970. *Kant's Political Writings*. Ed. Hans Reiss. Cambridge: Cambridge University Press.

Keane, John. 1984. *Public Life and Late Capitalism: Towards a Socialist Theory of Democracy*. Cambridge: Cambridge University Press.

MacIntyre, Alasdaire. 2008. *After Virtue: A Study in Moral Theory*. Notre Dame: University of Notre Dame Press.

Manicas, Peter T. 1988. "Foreclosure of Democracy in America," *History of Political Thought*, *IX*(1) (Spring).

Pyarelal. 1958. *Mahatma Gandhi: The Last Phase*. Ahmedabad: Navajivan Publishing House.

Rakove, Jack N. 1991. "Parchment Barriers and the Politics of Rights," in *A Culture of Rights: The Bill of Philosophy, Politics and Law 1779 and 1991*. Eds Michael J. Lacey and Knud Haakonssen. New York: Cambridge University Press.

Ronen, Dov. 1979. *The Quest for Self-determination*. New Haven: Yale University Press.

Roy, Ramashray. 2002. *Politics and Beyond*. Delhi: Shipra Publications.

Taylor, Charles. 1979. *Hegel and Modern Society*. Cambridge: Cambridge University Press.

———1955. *The Old Regime and The French revolution*. Trans. Stuart Gilbert. New York: Anchor Books.

Tocqueville, Alexis de. 1956. *Democracy in America*, 2 vols. New York: Vantage Books.

Unger, Roberto M. 1975. *Knowledge and Politics*. New York: The Free Press.

Walsh, David. 1997. *The Growth of the Liberal Soul*. Columbia: University of Missouri Press.

Wolin, Sheldon. 1960. *Politics and Vision: Continuity and Innovation in Western Thought*. Boston: Little, Brown and Co.

12

Sarvata: Modern Man in Search of Wholeness

The observation about "one became many and man tries to learn how the one can be made" in contemporary times reflects on a deep understanding of today's human condition. This observation represents a deep understanding of the human condition today. Man today is surely seeking to make the many into one. However, his attempt is bound to fail as long as modernity—the phenomenon that has enveloped man in the fog of materiality—continues to remain the main framework for him to work within. The reason for this is not far to seek. Human beings are endowed with what can be characterized as "dual nature." This means that man is bivalent; human being has dual nature in the sense that he is both physical or material and spiritual. It is as a being with a dual nature, that man confronts the world and seeks to make sense of it, for whatever ramifications it has for his own earthly existence. In confronting this world, the world that has been in existence even before man appeared on earth and set the physical conditions of his existence, man is both immersed in it and above and beyond it. It is as a spiritual being, that man is free from the environment and can objectify the world. A process necessary for comprehending what his environment holds for him. As Nagarjuna (Ramanan 1978) would say, man is a conditioned being, but his destiny is unconditioned.

Having discovered himself as a spiritual being, man can no longer pretend to be simply part of the world. This is precisely because, spiritual experience is accompanied by the insight and awareness that one's person transcends the forms of worldly being, namely space and time. Then he encounters the idea of an infinite absolute being beyond the world, the God. It is in view of this that man with his dual nature has to relate himself to an absolute Being, the God, if his spirituality is to play a significant role in the world of here and now. Moreover, what needs to be noted is that both matter and spirit that jointly constitute man as a spiritual being are interdependent and organically linked. It is this relationship between matter and spirit that provides the basis for man's understanding that leads to theophany. Once this fact is lost sight of and matter and spirit are treated as unlinked and independent phenomena, the way is paved for the eclipse of man as a spiritual being. When man's divine connection is cut off, man emerges simply as a narrow being, acquisitive and possessive. As a natural man, he simply lives his life without knowing how to lead it.

If he perchance lets his spiritual dimension dry up, he loses his *sarvata* (wholeness) and becomes what Iris Murdoch characterizes as "broken totality." As a broken totality, he becomes the creature of the world, the world with its snares of material attractions and narrowness of being. The narrowness of being leads to particularism. Long ago, Nagarjuna referred to the fact that the sense of "I" has a double significance; it has the tendencies of both particularizing and universalizing (Ramanan 1978: 100). If man chooses the former, he tends to cling to *samsara* (the world) and is immersed in materiality. This is the way of bondage, while the latter, the universalizing tendency, is liberating. Man in modern times has chosen the particularizing path and has come, as a result, to cling to *samsar*, a phenomenon known as appearance in perennial philosophy. The upsurge in the particularizing tendency is due principally to the rise in modern times of the self-defining subject.

The defining characteristic of the self-defining subject is not only that he gives himself up to the fulfilment of ordinary life-needs involved with the acquisition of wealth, power and prestige, but also that he treats the external world, both society and nature, as potential means for the realization of his purposes. Thus, man in modern times is not only immersed in subjectivity but he is also a disengaged person. As such, his life purposes can be collectively subsumed under the rubric of self-interest. Commitment to the pursuit of self-interest in a condition, where the fear of God has been lifted by the refusal to acknowledge the existence of any transcendental entity, the tendency to prefer one's own good against the good of all becomes a dominant tendency, which guides and controls the conduct of man in modern times. Even if a person is able to overcome this tendency, he is not able to do so for long, because he soon falls prey to cupidity. This is due, as Plato notes, to the fact that human nature will be always drawing him into avarice and selfishness, avoiding pain and pursuing pleasure without reason. It will bring these to the front, obscuring the more just and better and so working darkness in his soul. It will at last fill with evils, both him and the whole city (*Laws* 875b–c).

Given this strong tendency, man chooses to live in the shadowy world of appearance forsaking the world of truth and reality, even God. As a result, the individual whose soul is afflicted by the ill effects of appearance cannot see the whole for the parts. He is, therefore, prone to give preference to his own good. The result is the manipulation of the external world for realizing self-defined purposes. As Dobbs observes:

> Once freed from any mooring in reality, appearance no longer offers even as an oblique clue to what truly is. Appearance then exists as nothing more than a temptation to willful manipulation. As a result, of the soul's turn wholly towards appearance, reason becomes cramped and deformed. Reason ceases to search for the true and the good in considering the merit of justice and injustice; instead, it is wholly subsumed in "calculation," specifically the calculation which concludes that injustice is mightier than justice always and everywhere as long as one has the capacity to manipulate appearance. (1976: 1068)

Reason as a calculation, does not recognize any authority, sacred or otherwise, outside itself. Even the law, expected to regulate the wayward movement of reason as calculation or *banik buddhi* (the mind of the trader who always looks for profit), loses its educative value and degenerates into rational deliberation. The strategic use of *banik buddhi* is meant, not for seeking the welfare of the soul, but, for promoting bodily comfort, as Mahatma Gandhi used to underline. And a person, who makes the pleasure of the body the *summum bonum* of his life, may gain the whole world, but he certainly forfeits his soul. If the sacred is jettisoned, social life and relations degenerate into *matsya nyaya* (the justice of the strong gobbling up the weak). This underlines the fact that the conditioning of man today springs from an attitude that treats what is unreal as real and pushes the real to the backyard of consciousness.

As a consequence of the loss of the sacred, man today has lost his wholeness; he is simply a "broken totality." And when this broken totality finds only misery in his life, he seeks to regain wholeness. However, the trouble is that while man knows what the evil is, he does not know its cure. Moreover, he is also unable to overcome his hunger for worldly pleasure. As a disengaged subjectivity, man in modern times lacks the necessary knowledge to seek his redemption. In the lack of appropriate knowledge, he remains content with mere placebos. These placebos consist principally in changing the external world and its institutional format. In doing this, the fact is lost sight of that the problem that man faces today is neither social nor political; it is fundamentally moral and spiritual. As such, this problem cannot be dealt with effectively by relying solely on changing the external world. What is needed is to take proper action in the moral and spiritual fields of life. The problem can be dealt effectively only by spiritual self-transformation.

The fact, however, remains that man today resists spiritual self-transformation in the mistaken belief that the unbridled satisfaction of ordinary life-needs is the key to human well-being. And human well-being can, it is also believed, be best ensured by the exercise of freedom. The fact is, however, lost sight of that the freedom man relies upon today for securing his well-being is nothing more than negative freedom. Substantively, negative freedom does not mean anything more than the removal of constraints on action that the individual contemplates to engage in with a view to realizing his self-defined purposes. Insofar as freedom is negatively defined, it fails to achieve anything positive in improving man morally and spiritually. Yet, the belief is deeply ingrained in human psyche today that the exercise of negative freedom is the best way for guaranteeing human flourishing. But human flourishing remains undefined in the lack of a definite idea about "who man is." Unless we have an idea of man, we have no reference for the designation of human flourishing, in particular and human phenomenon as relevant or irrelevant, in general. Thus, if human flourishing has itself become an empty concept, of what value is freedom that is said to foster it? Note also the fact that the self-defining subject is a man alone, a man for himself. As Rousseau observes:

> A man for himself does not know what he wants. Forever in contradiction with himself, forever veering between his inclination and duty, he can never be either man or citizen. He can be no good to himself or to others. He will be man of our times: a Frenchman, a Bourgeois. He will be nothing. (Rousseau, quoted in Colletti 1972: 172)

Such a man, Heraclitus notes, is a sleeping person immersed in his own private world of dreams. Such a person, as Nietzsche points out, "has lost the faith in his own value when no infinitely valuable works through him."

He is isolated from his fellow-men because he has demolished the bridge of love, love that can be earned and sustained only if a person attunes his soul to the divine ground of being, the bridge that links one individual with another in an embrace of good will. This is symptomatic of the breakdown of community insofar as it underlines what Plato calls the breakdown of *philia politike* (friendship among the members of a community).

As a result, the loss of what Heraclitus calls *xynon* (loss of the sense of community) bespeaks of the lack of common sense. As long as man resists spiritual transformation, the loss of community persists. With this, there is less and less of common understanding of things with one another. With the loss of what is common, there is also the loss of community between human beings. The social situation that this state of affairs engenders resembles what Alasdair MacIntyre's describes as "civil war carried out by other means" (1984: 253).

Modern *problematique* is born out of this "civil war carried out by other means." Can this war be stopped and both man and society rescued from the prevailing rot? This problem, it is argued, can very well be tackled if self-government in the political sense is universally installed. However, unless humans are essentially self-governing beings, there can be no case for self-governing societies. The problem thus lies deeper in view of the fact that this proposal ignores the other side of the proposition, which underlines a dynamic relationship between auto-control and self-rule in the political sense. Thus, the tendency, as Mahatma Gandhi hinted long ago, to change the external dimension of man's existence to ensure his well-being is futile (1957: LV, 62).

But how does one become a self-governing being? Would it be the self as *ahamkar* of *Sankhya* or the self, touched by the hand of eternity that the Veda talks about? The Vedic word *swastha* is of great help here. "Swa" in the word *swastha* is not the *ahamkar,* the ego, but the soul attuned to the divine ground of being. But here we face three questions: What is that eternal divine ground of reality; how do we know it and how do we, when we know it, connect ourselves to it? It is quite clear that none of these three questions can be answered within the framework of the modern worldview. This is so for the reason that at the centre of the modern worldview stands man as a broken totality, and the very term "broken totality" underlines separation of man from the absolute. For answers to these questions, we have, then, to look elsewhere and most advisedly to our own ancient font of perennial serene knowledge. And this font is unquestionably the Veda, the nurturing source of our culture and tradition.

The trouble, however, is, as Renou points out, "Even in the most orthodox domain, the reverence to the Veda has come be a simple 'raising of the hat' in passing, to an idol which one no longer intends to be encumbered with" (quoted in Mehta 1990: 103). That the Veda has been misinterpreted, misconstrued and vilely condemned, Oldenberg notes (1988: 2), as the songs of the barbaric priests to please barbaric gods, is a truth well known in the interpretative literature focusing on the Vedic lore. And even more important, our own education in Western thought-ways has rendered us completely incapable of appreciating the philosophical thinking contained in the Veda; we are completely alienated from our cultural and traditional wealth that has boldly stood the test of time. As such, there may be, for the Veda, a token respect but no love. In the spreading darkness threatening to completely engulf the flickering flame of the Vedic *prajnana,* any discussion about the penetrative insight of the Veda is a welcome step, a step that may, we hope, turn us around towards the Vedic wisdom.

Why should we, one may ask, go back to the Veda for obtaining an insight in order to correct the errors of today? Is not the past dead and over? And is not our present entirely different from our past? But these are, to my mind, untenable questions. To say that the past is not present in our present is somewhat misleading. As T. S. Eliot says, "Every point of present is a point of intersection with the timeless." Moreover, the historical time is a series of present points in which none is ever past, but only in relation to their present, not really past. Moreover, as a Russian proverb puts it: "If you dwell on the past, you lose one of your eyes; if you forget the past, you lose your both eyes."

Also, the talk of going back to the past is not meant to revive into the institutional structure of the past; it is only to gain some insights in order to open new horizons of the future. Our past is defined by the insights taken from the Veda; it is, therefore, appropriate for us to have a close look at it for determining what it has for us. To begin with, the very term *veda* is pregnant with significations. The word *veda* is derived from the root *vid,* which, according to Bhattoji Dixit, is used to delineate four different meanings. As he says, the root *vid* signifies *sattanam vidyate,* that is, the absolute entity exists. Given the existence of the absolute, the Veda provides the knowledge, *par excellence,* of the absolute.

But then, as *Brihadaranyak Upanishad* IV.5.15 points out, *yeneti sarve vijanati ten ken vijanayat* (through what should one know that owing to which all this is known?) "To know the absolute, contemplation of the absolute becomes necessary. Only then there can be any achievement, that is, transformation of the self in the light of the knowledge?" If the absolute is unseen and cannot be directly apprehended, what does it mean to have its knowledge? The absolute is, to use a Vedic word, *apraket,* without any sign; it is only potency, full of infinite possibilities of *nama* (name) and *rupa* (form). As such, we cannot know it either intellectually or mystically, unless it becomes manifest. And the absolute manifests itself into *vishswa* through the process of creation. As Panikkar points out: "Creation is the act by which God or whatever name we may choose to express, the ultimate, affirms himself not only vis-à-vis the world, thus created, but vis-à-vis himself, for he certainly was neither creator before creation nor god for himself" (1983: 50).

Thus, it is through the act of creation that the un-manifest becomes manifest and the *apraket* exhibits its signs all over the world, both visible and invisible. But, then, we have to answer another question. What is *praket* is many and diverse. How is it possible to know the one and indivisible from that which is many and diverse? The one participates in the emergent many; without this participation, the existence of the many is inconceivable. However, does the One, in becoming many through participation, exhaust himself by being distributed over the many? As Coomaraswamy puts it:

> The notion of participation appears to be "irrational" and will be resisted only if we suppose that the product participates in its cause materially and not formally, or, in other words, if we suppose that the form participated in is divided up into parts and distributed in participants. On the contrary, that which participated in is always a total presence. (1972: 280, fn 25)

That the *vishwa* represents a multiplicity of *rupa* does not mean either that the creator has been partitioned in order to become many or that the *vishwa* has become something other than its maker as is the case with Platonic cosmogony or "likely story" of creation. As a matter of fact, the relationship between the One and the Many is understood in the Vedic perspective to be not One or Many but as the One and the Many (Shatpath Brahman X 5.2.16). Even while the One becomes Many, the *vishwa* remains one with its maker (*vishwam ekam*, Rigveda III.54.8) and therefore, it is also true (*vishwam satyam*, Rigveda II.24.12). That the *vishwa* is *ekam* as well as *satyam* is due to the fact that the absolute is the omphalos of the world (*vishwam garbham*, Rigveda 127.7). To emphasize the identity between the One and the Many, the Rigveda uses other metaphors. For example, in Rigveda VIII, 41.6, it is explicitly said that the One is that in which all created things (which can be likened to the rim of a wheel) are concentrated in Him (who is the omphalos of the world). Similarly, Rigveda X.82.6 speaks of the gods who are deposited in the navel of the unborn, in which all beings abide.

It is true that the One becomes Many and in so becoming the One abides in the Many without spending itself out, without being exhausted. The Vedic seer-poets saw this ultimate truth and gave it expression as the *Atharvaveda* X.6.29 testifies:

Purna purnamudachati purna purnena sischyate,

Uta tadadya vidyam yatastatparisichyate.

The full from the full he bends up; the full is pored with full; also we may know today whence that is poured out. The same sentiment is expressed in *Isopanishad* when it says:

Om, Purnamadah purnamidam purnatpurnamadachyate;

Purnasya purnamadaya purnamevavashishyatai.

That is full, this is full, from full proceeds the full. And when from the full, fullness is taken away, what remains is the full.

The complete identity between the One and the Many is the result of the procession of the One; it points to the fact of creation through which the *apraket* creates so many visible and invisible signs of his presence. However, the question "what that *apraket* is" still remains to be answered. It is true that the visible signs of the presence of the Absolute are symbolic indications. But symbols have the tendency to distort. It is this tendency towards distortion, intrinsic to symbols, that, as Hans Gadamar points out, prevents smooth and spontaneously enlightening transition from *praket* to *apraket*.

If the maker cannot be revealed by what he makes, the process of creation must be a mystery. As Rigveda X.129.7 puts it: "He from whom the creation arose, he may uphold it or he may not (no else can); he who is its superintendent in the highest heaven, (*parame vyoman*) he assuredly knows or if he knows not." In the lack of exact knowledge about the maker or about the process of the making of this universe, one can only speculate about both; one can only tell a likely story, as Plato points out (Timaenus 29c–1).

Given the inadequacy of discursive logic in explaining which is not directly perceptible, story-telling remains the only alternative for articulating what basically cannot be articulated. The Vedic seer-poets recognized this truth long ago and called the process of creation a *bhavavritta* or *srishtividya*, the knowledge pertaining to the process of creation. At the back of the Vedic likely story, is a great question, that is, *samprashna*. It is this *samprashna* that is the beginning of the process of knowing either mystically or intellectually. This *samprashna* has been asked and answered in numerous ways and couched in symbolic language. But behind the seemingly confusing, turbulent and conflicting tidal waves of symbolic articulation of the experience that is basically ineffable, flows the deep, serene and invigorating stream of grandiose vision of the world and its creator, the presence beyond the presence, that is, the *idam sarvam*. The likely story of creation has emerged out of this deeper experience. And since creation is a mystery, the Vedic Rishis, particularly Prajapati, must ask: "Who in this world verily knows the whole Truth? Divine beings were born long after the creation of this universe. From whom and by whom it came to be what it is—who then can have anything like direct knowledge thereof" (Rigveda X.129.16).

Vedic Rishis are clear about the fact that Swayambhu (the self-born) did not emerge from something that is subject to decay and death. Swayambhu, as *Taittiriya Brahman* II.8.9.6 puts it, is the Brahman who is the forest as well as the trees from which Heaven and Earth were fabricated. The term "Brahman" has been derived from the root *brih*, which, as Motilal Shastri notes (n.d.: 27–29), is a context-governed (*anugam bhaven*) term and means growth, expansion, development, swelling of the spirit, etc. (Monier-Williams 2011: 737). Brahma refers to an absolute power, a potency that, according to Gonda, demands expression (1950). And as Yask notes, Brahma signifies growing on all sides (Nirukta 1.8).

Thus, the term "Brahma" signifies potency referring to the inherent tendency to move, to be in motion, to change place, etc. This tendency has yet another property, that of causing something to move. Rigveda refers to Brahma not only in the sense of growth, as, for example, in I.117.11 and I.124.13, but also causing something to happen as in Rigveda V.40.8. In Rigveda VI.5.2 and VII.103.8 the term "Brahma" acquires another dimension, that of action when conjoined with the root *kri.* All this suggests that Brahma as a potency is not simply a dormant power; it can also be excited to action, to grow and undergo a process of change.

When this potency is dormant, it is called *anarambhan.* But when this *anarambhan* begins its journey of procession, it becomes *adhisthan* (support) of the universe constituting *arambhan,* the starting point of the process of creation. As is clear from the Nasadiya Sukta of the Rigveda (X.129), there was neither *asat* nor *sat,* nor yet anything else, before the world came into being. In the state of "thing-less-ness," there arose a desire on the part of Swayambhu (*kamastadagre*) to bring its state of loneliness to an end. The desire (*kama*) is the first occurrence at the beginning of the process of creation. It is this desire that, as Rigveda X.129.4 underlines, links together the existing and the non-existing.

The advent of desire splits the One into two opposite but complementary principles, Soma and Agni or Purush or Prakriti, whose syzygy begets the *vishwa.* When the creator is disturbed by desire, there occurs what is known as *dwedhapat* (*Bahadaranyak Upanishad 1.4.3*); when the Unborn is consumed by the desire to produce *praja,* he acts on himself, splits in two and becomes many through the act of syzygy. When it is overpowered by the desire to create, he splits into two and the two together beget the Many. This diremption would not have been possible, if the One were not the living conjoint (i.e., *ardhanareeshwar*), the unity of cohabitant parents (Rigveda 1.140.3 and III.7.1).

It is the *dwedhapat* that leads to the birth of the Son, that is, the Sun, the first material object to appear in the process of creation. "By the separation of the prior, the latter came forth" (Rigveda X.27.3). This *dwedhapat* is symptomatic of the conjunction of *manas* (intelligence) and *vak* (matter), which Meister Eckhart calls "the act of fecundation inherent in eternity." It is by virtue of this fecundation that *asat* is transformed into *sat*; that is to say, what was *ab initio* without a centre and formless now assumes concrete forms with individual centres. The process of transformation of *asat* into *sat,* undeniably a continuous process, is called *yajna,* a process in which different elements come together, intermingle and become something else by giving up their former form. That is why *yajna,* that is, the cosmic *yajna,* is characterized in Rigveda 1.164.35 as *bhuvanasya nabhih;* the omphalos of the *vishwa,* the universe (*Yajurveda* 23.62 and *Atharveda* IX.1.14). As Agrawala puts it, the *yajna* signifies a creative act at all levels. On the biological plane, it is the creation of new life in matter that is *yajna,* a union of Agni and Soma; whenever there is such a creative process, there is the centre of universe, the meaning being that the entire mystery or the potentiality of the cosmic process becomes inherent in the centre of that *yajna* (Agrawala 1963: 126).

The transformation of the One (*brahma*) into the Many (*vishwa*) through the ever-pervasive and ever-occurring process of *yajna* is what is recounted in the Vedic *Bhavavritta.* In this story, Brahma is the *tad ekam,* without form in his omnipresence, not yet "selfed" (*atmanvi*), as Coomaraswamy puts it (1985: 58 and R I.164.4); it is undifferentiated, yet un-manifest. Before the process of creation begins, before Brahman begins to grow, trans-mutate and take different shapes, it is neither the creator nor the God, the *vishwa* is aware of. It is only with the help of primordial self-sacrifice that the Absolute not only becomes aware of itself but also becomes the world; that is, it becomes a *creator.* In other words, the Absolute, according to the Vedic *srishtividya,* acts upon itself to create the world; it is quite unlike the Platonic Form who must install order on the materials produced by *Ananke* through the agency of Demiurgos.

The Vedic likely story recounts the process through which, to use another metaphor, Vaman becomes Virat through *vivarta* (transformation); this is again indicative of the fact that the universe is contained in him. It is the manifestation of this inherent tendency in Brahma that constitutes the process of *yajna* as a creative force. Thus, the *vishwa,* as we learn from the Vedic *Bhavavritta,* is the outcome of the *sarvahuta yajna,* as reflected in the *Purusha Sukta,* in which the *Purusha* offers himself as the sacrificial food (*medhya*) and it is from this primal sacrifice that the constitutive principles of the cosmos are engendered. It is these constitutive principles that are subsumed, in the Vedic perspective, under the rubric of *Rita.* It is this *Rita* that later came to be known as *dharma.*

Cosmos is not a thing among others, rather it is an embracing whole, the background of reality against which all existent things exist, including the quaternary structure of reality in the mode of existence articulated as *amartyas, martyas, Prithiwi and Dyau.* Cosmos, as Jonas points out, "is considered to be the perfect exemplar of order and at the same time, the cause of all order in particulars, which only in degrees can approximate the whole" (1963: 242).

It is true that particular components of the cosmos can approximate the whole only in degrees. However, it is also true that the totality has no being except through the expression of these particulars and the individual particulars have no "being" except by means of their mutual relation both with the totality and with other particulars (Collum 1995: 59–60) that constitute the whole. It is this fitting together of the different parts of the cosmos with each other as well as with the whole of the cosmos with its creator that is the basis of harmony in the world.

This harmony is symptomatic of the manifestation of the One through manifold *rupas* that make the *idam sarvam.* In this harmony, the responsible dignity of men's minds and will were felt to consist not specifically in their differences from one another but in the variety of their characteristic individuality, thrown into relief, precisely, by their mutual relation and their unity as component differentiated parts of one whole (Ibid.: 60). I have referred so far to two very important dimensions of the Vedic *srishtividya.* These two dimensions are: (a) an emphasis on and willing acceptance of the transcendental trans-individual entity, which ever-exists behind the ever-changing, impermanent world of phenomena, the *idam sarvam* and (b) the position of man in the cosmos.

As the preceding discussion makes it clear, the Veda treats the cosmos only as *praket,* that is, visible signs of the *apraket,* the invisible presence behind the visible presence that *Isopanishad* refers to as *isavasya idam sarvam yatkinchit jagatyamjagat* (in all the worlds, whatever there is spread before our eyes is the abode of the Absolute). The second dimension of the Vedic *srishtividya* is the story of creation, of the process through which the One becomes Many and in so becoming, he fashions the cosmos as the perfect exemplar of order. The third dimension concerns the question of man's role in maintaining the cosmic order by modelling his life pattern in conformity with the paradigmatic principles of the cosmic order.

We need to remind ourselves that, since the first two dimensions of the Vedic cosmogony have already been eclipsed by the rise of modern Gnosticism incarnate in the form of science and technology, the third dimension, too, has been thrown on the dung-heap of the modern commitment to the open-ended development of man today. It is this scientific "superstition" that reflects not only the abrogation of the graded system of knowledge construction, but also the notion of the self-making of man. It is this notion of the self-making of man that the Vedic cosmogony battles.

To come to the third dimension of the Vedic *srishtividya*, it posits the idea that this living, well-ordered, cosmos man is an integral part of and is related to God by virtue of his being the abode of the *Purusha*, the divine entity. This is well evidenced by what Dirghatamas says in Rigveda I.164.20: *Dwa suparna sayuja sakhaya....* This is reflected in *Chhandogya Upanishad* as well, which treats the body as *Brahmapur*, that is, the city in which Brahma resides. It is also confirmed by *Yajurveda* 31.19 when it says that *Prajapati* created the beings and then entered them. Thus, the Veda treats man as a part of the divine and man has to actively relate himself to the divine in him. To relate to the divine is to apprehend the order underlying the cosmos. The universe as cosmos must be distinguished from the lifeless world that is nothing more than a concourse of cause and effect, as modern physics understands it, while the cosmos is fully ordered and well regulated.

It is the understanding of the universe as cosmos that alone can restore the original unity between man and God. It is this understanding, again, that reminds man that he is not self-complete, nor he is autonomous, free of all restraints moral or social; he is a part of a larger order and has, therefore to conform to its constitutive principles. The original unity can be restored, if lost or activated, if dormant or passive, only when, as Cicero puts it, man "contemplates the cosmos and imitates it" (Cicero 1896). To understand the cosmos by contemplation in proper spirit, prompts man to realize order in his own life and through it, sustain the cosmic order.

Thus, the message the cosmos has for man is quite clear, even though it is seldom heeded in our own times: Man as a part of the cosmos must conform to the pattern it displays. Man must shape his existence in accordance with the principles that brace order and regularity in the cosmos. As such, order in the cosmos constitutes the paradigm of thought-ways and work-ways of man and establishes the "necessary connection between the apotheosis of the universe and the ideal of human perfection..." (Ibid.).

Contemplation of the cosmos presages the establishment of a proper relationship with the external world when man conforms to the constitutive principles of the cosmos. In Jonas' words:

> It is based in the interpretation of his existence in terms of larger whole, whose very perfection consists in the integration of all its parts. In this man's cosmic piety submits his being to the requirements of what is better than himself and the source of all that is good. (1963: 246–47)

To submit to the requirements of the whole, does not, by any means, signify the straightjacket-ing of man's freedom. As *Chhandogya Upanishad* underlines, man becomes *swarat* (self-sovereign) only when he submits to the in-dwelling *Purusha*. This submission does reveal the truth but not the whole truth. The truth to be delivered out of the meditative process is not the ultimate truth, the truth to end the search for all truth, a system to end all systems. Rather it is the illumination of the process of reality by bringing to bear the reflective consciousness of man in community with other men. It does not automatically liberate man from his bondage of the *samsar;* it only defines for him the parameters of conduct following which he can get liberated. This means that man can use his creative powers to establish right and proper relationships, not only with the in-dwelling *Purusha* but also with the external world, both society and nature. Also, it requires the realization that the creative power of each individual resides ultimately in his natural relations with others and with the whole of which every person is a reflecting facet. This natural relationship can become salubrious and benign only when man realizes that he is

> not just a part like other parts making up the universe, but through the possession of a mind, a part that enjoys *identity* with the ruling of the whole. Thus the other aspect of man's proper relationship with the universe is that *adequating* his own existence, confined as it is as a mere part, to the essence of the whole of reproducing the latter in his own being through understanding and action. (Ibid.)

Thus, the real significance of the cosmos, the universe reflecting order and regularity, is not only that it is a structure incorporating different parts of the cosmos, the cosmos itself and its creator but it also signifies certain intelligible principles. These principles, when realized in the life of the individual, become the instrument of not only the installation of order in man's interior, but also of safeguarding and preserving harmony in the lived world. It is in this sense that the Vedic *srishtividya* details the way cosmos has come into being and the principles of order that underlie it become relevant. Thus, *srishtividya* helps us to understand the world we are part of, how it has come into being and how we must shape our life as well as our surrounding socio-cultural system so that we can contribute to the preservation and sustenance of the cosmic order we are part of.

Thus, *srishtividya*, as a likely story of the transformation of the One into Many, offers not only the map, as it were, of the cosmos, it also constitutes the source for deriving the principles of harmony and regularity in the cosmos. The cosmic order, then, provides a paradigm, which can be used for ordering the interior world of the individual as well as the surrounding world, both social and natural. It is also the *srishtividya* that constitutes the fountainhead of culture in the sense of *samyaka kriti*. Culture in this sense signifies that it educates men in the ideal vision of the pattern of life, a vision that is salubrious not only for the individual but also for both society and nature.

Education in the ideal pattern of life is to create an awareness of a standard, grounded in a general consciousness of the values, which should govern human existence. In other words, education in this sense means to mould deliberately and consciously human character in accordance with an ideal. And it is this ideal that provides the standard for judging human motivation and action. A life rooted in such a culture is lived in the presence of the divine entity and is animated by the awareness of the ways and means through which the ideal vision of life can be actualized. Moreover, the life lived in the conscious awareness of man's linkage with a reality that is larger than his limited, contingent life, larger even than the society or nation he happens to be a member of, is to live according to a vision. In addition, William James reminds us of the ancient wisdom that, "Where there is no vision the people perish."

This is so for the reason that even the organization of society and its constitutive principles are themselves a conscious attempt to imitate in institutional form the ethos of the cosmic order. Social order, to borrow from Voegelin, "is an essay in world creation." Its significance lies in the fact that "out of the shapeless vastness of conflicting human desires rises a little world of order, a cosmion, leading a precarious life under the pressure of destructive forces within and without..." (Voegelin 1997).

And the function proper of order is the creation of a shelter in which man may give meaning to his life. Culture functions as a shelter, which serves as a shield for man against hazards that threaten to eclipse his well-being. Culture in this sense joins together two orders of being, the one relating to the finite existence of man and the other referring to the absolute source of truth, meaning and value. It is this linkage between the finite and the infinite through the medium of culture that functions as a shelter in which, to repeat, man may give his fragmentary existence a semblance of meaning.

The linkage between the finite and the infinite has, as indicated earlier, been forcefully snapped today. Man refuses to recognize the in-dwelling *Purusha* as the exemplar of order in the world, in society and in his own interior world. He has completely ignored the fact that it is the order or disorder of the soul that reflects man's harmony with or defection from the truth of being. Plato recognized the fundamental fact that the substance of society is psyche and society can destroy a man's soul because disorder of society is a disease of the psyche of its members. Forgetting the primal source of his being, man's soul becomes diseased. This, in turn, makes his life troubled and troubling for others. When he finds himself in difficulty, he runs to the nearest place of worship to seek protection and succour. The tremendous growth in religiosity and the multiplication of sects and proliferation of Gurus, both genuine and fake, testify to this. This, however, conceals the inner vacuum created by the indifference that we show to the divine ground of reality today. This vacuum torments man today insofar as uncertainties, frustrations and disillusionment that the failed promise of the creation of a terrestrial heaven prove too much to handle or endure. We live today in a de-divinized world and are reaping the bitter harvest that our own hubris has grown.

The de-divinization of the world in itself is the evidence of the disruption of its organic link and unity with the divine ground of reality. Drained of its divine essence, the world exists by itself and stands on its own. It has its own inherent order, but this order does not help in working for liberation, it only binds. Devoid of its divine presence, it is prone to corruption as well as to corrupting all that it contains. Cultivation of virtue in this corrupt and corrupting world becomes well nigh impossible. Yet, one cannot run away from this world and snap all worldly relations that involve man in *Karma*, action and thinking. For Jainism and Buddhism, *karma*, action, causes *dukha*. Man, therefore, must leave the world and seek his liberation, both Jainism and Buddhism prescribe.

This is not what the Veda teaches. It must be emphasized that this is the only world that we know and it happens not only to be our habitat but also the provider of our sustenance. As Mahatma Gandhi says, this world, even though it is unreal, does exist and therefore it is real. And since it is real, one has to bear the responsibilities that living in this world implies. This world is the arena of our *karma*, which can both liberate and bind, depending on what attitude we have towards our role in this world. Since the world cannot be denied, our attitude towards it must change and change in a way that prevents the disintegration of the quaternarian primal community of *amartyas, martyas, Prithiwi and Dyau*.

Thus, any reconstructive thinking about the proper relationship propitious for this primal community must make this world the point of departure as well as that of eventual return. The Vedic philosophy does exactly this. The point of departure for the Vedic thinking is the question of how harmony in the quaternarian community can be established and maintained. The central factor that can sustain this harmony is the recognition that there is an identity between *martya* and *amartya*. According to *Brihadaranyak Upanishad* II.1.20, man is the spark of the divine fire: *yathagne kshudra visphullinga vyucharanti*. Also, *Taittiriya Upanishad* notes that *sa yashchayam purushe yashchaditya sa ekam* (He that is here in the human form and He that is there in the Sun are one).

Refusal to recognize this identity and make this identity the guiding principle of life is the root cause of the loss of harmony in the primal community; the loss of harmony, in turn, affects the psyche of man himself. This loss is due, in the Vedic perspective, to *avidya*, nescience. Nescience, as Abhinavagupta points out, is twofold: *paurusha* and *buddhigata*. The former signifies auto-limitation of God in the process of creation and the latter is caused by *pramad*, that is, uncertain and erroneous judgement (*Tantrasara*, 3). *Pramada* signifies a particular representation of reality; this representation is not merely a theoretical fallacy, it also carries a self-defeating factor by forcing thought and action along perversely mistaken lines with disastrous consequences for man, society and nature.

The Vedic philosophy concerns itself with *buddhigata avidya,* which can be conquered through the restoration of man's link with the divine ground of reality. This divine ground is no other than what *Brihadaranyak Upanishad* calls *satasyasatyam,* the truth of truth. One has to return to the *satasyasatyam* by removing the grievance articulated in Rigveda VII.86.6: the elder brother (*parmatma, asti jyayana kanisya upare*) stays with the younger brother (*Jivatma*); however, the younger brother seldom acknowledges the existence of the elder brother. To remove this grievance, one has to avoid becoming what *Chhandogya Upanishad* calls *kamachar* (a person moved by his desires); as a *kamachar,* he becomes *arthasamagrahi* (one who goes on acquiring the means of satisfying his desires, that is, wealth and power). And God does not become a friend of those who become acquisitive and possessive (*naki revantam sakhyaya vindase*) because "those who are puffed with wine offend you" (*piyante te surashwah,* Rigveda VIII.21.14; cf. Plato, Gorgias 5e7e).

It is no wonder, then, that, as Coomaraswamy underlines, "natural man is spiritually blind."[35] That is why he cannot make a distinction between the Sun whom everybody sees and the Sun whom not all know with the mind (*pashyante sarve chakshusha na sarve manasa vida,* Atharvaveda X.8.14). Although it is necessary to see the Sun, the other Sun than the one visible to the bare eyes, "it cannot be comprehended through the eye, nor can it be comprehended through speech, nor through other senses" (*Mundaka Upanishad* III.I.8). Similarly, it cannot be attained through study or the intellect or hearing (*Mundaka Upanishad* III.II.3). It is so for the simple reason that the senses, when not associated with the in-dwelling *Purusha,* becomes attached to external objects.

A person, who is attached to external objects, becomes an externalized creature as Wood notes (1972: 11). In effect, interest replaces man's inner being; man becomes, in essence, a receptacle of interest. When so attached, man becomes covetous. And a covetous life becomes what Cooper calls "open-ended." An open-ended life bids us

> To maximize in our lives as a whole the amount of a certain good but without specifying what this maximum may be. It leaves it entirely to us, in principle at any rate, to alter our mode of life in adjustment to changing circumstances and altered capacities for enjoyment as our lives themselves develop" (1975: 83).

Such a life is governed by rules of thumb and not fixed principles.

The consequence is that an open-ended life paves the way for the rise of what Sennet calls a narcissistic person. As he puts it, the person becomes narcissistic, where he originally was not. For such a person, the world becomes the mirror of the self. The world exists only to fulfil the self. There are no "human objects" or object relations with a reality of their own. The peculiarity and the destructiveness of the narcissistic vision is that, the more the environment of the human being is judged in terms of its congruence with or subservience to self-needs, the less fulfilling it becomes. For the very reason that expectation or fulfilment becomes at once so vast and amorphous, the possibilities of fulfilment are diminished (1977: 117).

And "he, who covets things, while brooding on their virtue, is born amidst those surroundings along with the desires" (*Mundak Upanishad* III. iii.2). He becomes, as Plato says, "the slave of many mad masters." As a slave of many mad masters, he cannot rise above the conflict of multitudinous desires, although it is necessary to do so in order to be liberated from the allurements of *samsara*. The mind engrossed in the pragmatic affairs of existence has to be weaned away from the attractions of the phenomenal world. And it is possible only when, as Rigveda VIII.67.17 underlines, the mind turns back from the world: *shashwantam hi prachetasah pratiyantam chidenasah Devah Krinutha jiwase*, may Aditya turn all those back who live in sin so that they can live. It is the art of living that man in the modern times has completely forgotten

It is, therefore, not surprising that what in the Vedic parlance is known as *Nirriti* (living in contravention of *Rita*) is that which causes terror in man; he is gripped with *amhas,* the sense of being hemmed in and trapped. It is, again, the infringement of *Rita* that violates the principles of right living. Vedic Rishis identify *pramada* as the root cause of this non-conformity to *Rita.* It is the disjunction of man from the light, when this light alone can illumine his interior. It is only on the basis of this illumination that the specification of the pattern of man's relationship with the well-structured world, as an aspect of his mode of being, his being-in-the-world, as the unified play of *Prithiwi, Dyau, Amartyas and Martyas* can be made.

To turn back from the allurements of the lived world, that is, the factual order, man needs to have *avritta chakshuh*, the turning back of the mortal eye to the immortal eye, which is the Sun, because it is the Sun that, as the *Gayatri mantra* testifies, sharpens *dhi* (intellect): *Bhargo devasya dhi mahi dhiyoyona prachodayat.* It is with the help of the inner light that, as *Atharvaveda* IX.51 underlines, man attains *sarvata* (wholeness). To Vedic seer-poets, man is the son of light; he must, therefore, pursue light to become what Rigveda VII.5.6 calls a true Arya; and as Rigveda I.195.9 notes, man also claims an ancestral relationship with the seven rays of the Sun. When dirempted from the source of light, man gets enclosed in darkness (nescience) and then must yearn to find his way back to the light.

It is in this context that we can appreciate why Rigveda I.109.3 prays that the line of progeny relating man with his primordial source must not be broken. However, the danger of the severance of this link is forever present and therefore the possibility of the closure of the sacred space, as symbolized by *jyotir abhayam,* as the result of the invasion of *tamas* ever exists. That is why there is reflected in the Veda a strong longing to cleave through the mental darkness or the limitation that prevents man from seeing further, from seeing the light and penetrating into the beyond.

In order to be able to see the light, man has to become sun-eyed, *sura-chakshuh;* this alone makes a person capable of seeing by the light of the heaven (*swaradrishah*). This, in turn, depends on *dhi* or *dhih,* a visionary thought, which sharpens a far-reaching insight, *suchetas,* as Rigveda VII.3.10 calls it; it yields a flawless understanding, *medham arishtam* (Rigveda II.34.7). To achieve *medham arishtam,* it is necessary to go through the process of self-transformation. As Heinrich Zimmer informs us, the Indian tradition of thinking does not seek information but transformation of man. What the Veda insists on is "a radical changing of man's nature and therewith, a renovation of understanding both of the outer world and of his existence; a transformation as complete as possible, such as will amount when successful to a total conversion or rebirth." (Zimmer 1952: 4) Such a transformation signifies the emergence of a *dwija* (the twice-born).

And the process of self-transformation is *Yajna,* a *yajna* specifically as the means of self-transformation. According to an *akhyan* in *Taittiriya Brahman,* gods performed *yajna,* which immensely pleased Brahma. He gave them a ladder by climbing which they reached heaven. However, before reaching heaven, the gods reversed the ladder so that man could not get to the heaven without performing *yajna.* It is, therefore, necessary for man to perform *yajna* if he desires happiness by winning *sarvata.* But this *yajna* is an *antaram agnihotra* (interior sacrifice) in which external *havya* (offering) is not used; this *yajna* is *vihavy*. What counts in this *yajna* is not what is enacted inwardly, but what is accomplished internally. In this *anataram agnihotra* the one who sacrifices, Rigveda V.46.1 declares, yokes himself like an understanding horse.

To yoke oneself like an understanding horse is to achieve what Rigveda VI.18.6 speaks of *kamyam sanim,* that longed for gift, that is, the heavenly light the Vedic Rishis yearn to obtain: "Would that we might reach the spacious mansion of ye (Mitravarunau)." But since the gift eludes him, he must surrender to the God and declare that "well knowing I have bound me horse-like to the pole.... I seek for no release, no turning back there from. May he who knows the way, the leader, guide me straight" (Rigveda V.46.1). Once this *kamyam sanim* is obtained, man becomes capable of seeing the inner light. "Who sees, he becomes and is that Being" (*tad pashyat tad bhavattadasit, Yajurveda* XXXII.12 and *Atharvaveda* X.7.24). "When he sees, he makes gods residing in his body active and then his body becomes pure; no body becomes pure without the gods" (*yebhyo na rite pavate dham kinchan, Yajurveda* XVII.14).

Thus, the Vedic perspective on man redefines human condition in a way that encourages man to transcend sorrow by "rolling up the skies," (Miller 1985: 132) or by going to the other shore of sorrow (*Chhandogya Upnishad* VII.1.3). It underlines the fact that to be fully aware of the human condition is to pave the way to transcend it. The Vedic vision does not deny life; it only aims at enriching it, at making it benign and blissful by linking man with the primordial source of his existence. And it is through the quest for liberation that man can strengthen the ties of the quaternarian community of *martyas, amrtyas, Prithiwi* and *Dyau.* In the words of J. L. Mehta:

> (M)an dwells on earth in his home, under the heavens, in friendly commerce with the gods, with his fellow men and with things, building and making, ultimately with thoughts and words and things keenly aware of his finitude, man in this text (that is, the *Rigveda*) is always "the mortal" (*martah*), exigent, desirous of earthly goods, needing help in the conduct of his life, unable to see clearly through the perils of living to know the truth of what is within him or things beyond. (Mehta 1990: 278–79)

It is against this background that we can appreciate why the Vedic man seeks the help of the God to find his way out of the darkness that threatens to engulf his existence and get joined again with the effulgent light. The Vedic man is not a selfish person; he does not seek the light for himself alone. He prays: Let all be granted the boon of light (*jiva jyoti rashimahi, Samaveda* 259, Rigveda II.27.1). We also must join our voice with Rigveda X.191.2:

> *Samani va akutih; samani hridayani vah;*
>
> *Samanmastu vo manovah susahasati.*

May the inmost aspiration of us all be perfectly harmonious; May our hearts be in unison; may absolute concord reign in our minds, so that we may be welded into strong fellowship and unity.

References

Agrawala, Vasudeva Sharan Nanaras. 1963. *The Thousand Syllabled Speech: Being a Study in Cosmic Symbolism in the Vedic Version.* Banaras: Author

Cicero, Marcus Tullius. 1896. *De Natura Deorum (On the Nature of the Gods).* Trans. Francis Brooks. London: Methuen.

Colleti, L. 1972. *From Rousseau to Lenin: Studies in Ideology and Society.* New York: The Monthly Review Press.

Collum. 1995. *Manifest Unity: The Ancient World's Perception of the Divine Pattern of Harmony.* Calcutta: Rupa & Co.

Cooper, John M. 1975. *Reason and Human Good in Aristotle.* Cambridge, MA: Harvard University Press.

Coomaraswamy, A. K. 1972. *Selected Papers: Traditional Art and Symbolism.* Ed. Robert E. Lipsey. Princeton: Princeton University Press.

———. 1985. *A New Approach to the Vedas.* Delhi: Aparna Publication.

Dobbs, D. 1976. "Choosing Justice: Socrates' Morality and the Practice of Dialectics," *American Political Science Review,* 70(3) (September).

Gadamar, H. 2004. *Truth and Method.* 2nd revised edition. Trans. J. Weinsheimer and D. G. Marshall. New York: Crossroad. For details, also see Grondin, J. 2002. *The Philosophy of Gadamer.* Trans. Kathryn Plant. New York: McGill-Queens University Press.

Gandhi, M. K. 1957. *Collected Works of Mahatma Gandhi.* Delhi: Publication Division, Government of India.

Gonda, Jan. 1950. *Notes on Brahman.* Utrecht: J. L. Beyers. For further details, see Gonda, Jan. 1975–91. Selected Studies, 6 vols. Leiden: E. J. Brill.

Jonas, Hans. 1963. *The Gnostic Religion: The Message of the Alien God and the Beginnings of Christianity.* Boston: Beacon Press.

Macintyre, A. 1984. *After Virtue,* 3rd edition. Notre Dame: Notre Dame University Press.

Miller, J. 1985. *The Vision of the Cosmic Order in the Veda*. London: Routeledge & Kegan Paul.

Oldenberg, H. 1988. *The Religion of the Veda*. Delhi: Motilal Banarsidas.

Panikkar, R. 1983. *The Vedic Experience: Mantramañjari*. Pondicherry: All India Books.

Plato. *Laws* 875 b–c. For details, see Jaeger, W. 1986. *Paideia: The Ideals of Greek Culture*, Vol. 1–2, second edition. Oxford: Oxford University Press.

Plato. *Timaenus* 29c-1. For details, see Jaeger, W. 1986. *Paideia: The Ideals of Greek Culture*, Vol. 1–2, second edition. Oxford: Oxford University Press.

Rajavade, V. K. 1993. *Yāska's Nirukta*. Government Oriental Series Class A, no.7. Pune: Bhandarkar Oriental Research Institute.

Ramanan, V. 1978. *Nagarjuna's Philosophy*. Delhi: Motilal Banarsidas.

Renou, L. 1990. "Destiny? of the Veda in India," in *Philosophy and Religion: Essays in interpretation*. Ed. J. L. Mehta. New Delhi: Indian Council of Philosophical Research and Munshiram Manoharlal Publishers.

Shastri, M. n.d. *Bhartiya Dristikon Se Vigyana Shabada Ka Samnvaya*. Jaipur: Rajasthan Patrika.

Voegelin, E. 1997. *Collected Works of Eric Voegelin*. Vol. 19, *History of Political Ideas, Vol. I: Hellenism, Rome, and Early Christianity*. Ed. Athanasios Moulakis. Columbia: University of Missouri Press.

Williams, M. 2011. *A Sanskrit English Dictionary*. Delhi: Motilal Banarsidas Publishers.

Wood, E. M. 1972. *Mind and Politics: An Approach to the Meaning of Liberal and Socialist Individualism*. Berkeley: University of California Press.

Zimmer, Heinrich. 1952. *Philosophies of India*. Ed. Joseph Campbell. London: Routeledge & Kegan Paul.

Index

About the Authors

Ramashray Roy, an eminent political scientist, earned his PhD in Political Science from the University of California, Berkeley, in 1965. One of the founding members of the Centre for the Study of Developing Societies, New Delhi, he functioned as its Director from 1976 to 1982. Professor Roy was also associated with the Indian Council of Social Science Research, New Delhi, as its Director. Among many academic achievements credited to his name, some include National Fellow of the Indian Council of Social Science Research, 1993–96, Senior Fellow of the Indian Council of Historical Research, New Delhi, as well as Fellow at the Indian Institute of Advanced Study, Shimla. He taught at the University of Delhi, University of Texas at Austin and University of California, Los Angeles. He was a Visiting Fellow at the Survey Research Centre, University of California, Berkeley and Columbia. An academic expert on diverse themes ranging from political philosophy to development studies, party system, Gandhian studies, Vedic philosophy, Indian tradition and culture, he has authored more than 40 books. Few of his important books include *Relation between Politicians and Administrators at the District Level; Uncertain Verdict: 1969 Elections in Four States; Dialogues on Development; Self and Society: A Study in Gandhian Thought; Gandhi: Soundings in Political Philosophy; Understanding Gandhi; Democracy in India: Form and Substance; Economy, Democracy and the State: The Indian Experience; Beyond Ego's Domain: Being and Order in the Veda; Samsakaras in Indian Tradition and Culture; Perspective on Political Order: East and West; India's 2009 Elections* (co-edited with Paul Wallace), etc. He has also contributed papers and articles to numerous seminars, conferences and journals.

Ravi Ranjan is a Political Science faculty at Zakir Husain Delhi College, University of Delhi. Till very recent, as a Fellow at Developing Countries Research Centre, University of Delhi, he has coordinated many research projects, supported by UGC, London School of Economics and Institute of Development Studies (IDS), University of Sussex, Brighton, UK. He is also a Member of the Advisory Committee for the Indian Council of Social Science (ICSSR, New Delhi), Commissioned State Level Studies on "Educational Status of Schedule Castes: Attainments & Challenges in Delhi." He is an executive member of the Indian Association for Asian & Pacific Studies and was an IUC-IIAS Associate at the Indian Institute of Advance Study, Shimla. He is a regular contributor to various Hindi and English newspapers that include *Dainik Jagran, Amar Ujjala and the Hindustan Times*. He recently published chapters in the book edited by Paul Wallace titled *India's 2014 Elections*. He has also contributed research papers to peer-reviewed, referred academic and research journals like *Gandhi Marg and Social Action*. He has also presented papers at national and international seminars in India and abroad.